SPITFIRE

SPIT

ICON OF A NATION IVAN RENDALL

FIRE

WEIDENFELD & NICOLSON

NATIONAL ICON (*page 1*): Spitfires at dawn in October 2005 ready for a flying display — 65 years after the fighter played its key role in victory in the Battle of Britain and ensured its place in history.

DESIGN CLASSIC (*previous page*): the Spitfire was developed for specialist fighting tasks throughout the Second World War; the Mk XIX photo-reconnaissance version was among the most advanced, and was still operational in 1954, eighteen years after the prototype flew — yet the Spitfire's distinctive profile remains clear.

INTRODUCTION

THE SPITFIRE has the radiance and simplicity of a true icon: the striking image that conveys shared values and shared history; the quiet presence that unlocks the national imagination. Britain's favourite aeroplane is neither modern nor antique, it just is. Like the White Cliffs of Dover and immemorial country lanes, the Spitfire is both mysterious and familiar, an inspirational fusion of form and function beyond the simple appeal of classic design.

And yet, the Spitfire is a triumph of design. In original concept it was the work of one man, Reginald J. Mitchell, in his quest to give the RAF the best fighting aeroplane in the world. What came off his drawing board was a superb fighter, but the Spitfire transcends the definable needs of military science and technology. Its clean lines eloquently and loudly proclaim the stylistic

DESIGN GENIUS: R.J. Mitchell on his investiture with the CBE in 1932 (*right*) awarded following Britain's outright victory in the Schneider Trophy in 1931. Mitchell's broad insight into aircraft design could create a winning racer or an effective fighter with the same result — the beauty that comes from purity of purpose, as with the Spitfire (*opposite*).

revolution of the inter-war years; it revels in the curves and geometric shapes of the Art Deco world that swept away Edwardian decorative clutter.

The Spitfire is the ultimate paradox: a beautiful weapon. Flying low and fast, the effortless urgency of its Merlin engine announcing its arrival, it stirs contradictory emotions: awe at its sheer elegance in flight, and a troubling admiration for its obvious and deadly purpose — to destroy and to kill. On the ground, the detail emphasizes the Spitfire's perfection: the flush rivets and smooth skin that give it its slipperiness in the air, the parallel banks of stubby exhaust pipes that hint at the horse power under the long nose, the exquisitely thin but broad, elliptical wings, the gun ports and the protruding cannon. To the expert eye, the Spitfire's synthesis of engineering and fighting potential is clear, unconstrained by cost-effectiveness or compromise. To the untutored eye too, the balance between its elements, like the composition of a painting or a piece of music, give it a visual perfection, a mystical quality suggesting timeless energy, a sharpness ready to be unleashed in defence of ancient, national freedoms. It is a modern Excalibur.

The Spitfire's ambiguous place between ancient mythology and 20th-century functionality reflects the complex genius of the man who created it. R.J. Mitchell's life and character embraced conflicting impulses. He was a trained engineer, a gifted mathematician, an amateur artist; instinctively practical, his skills extended to tooling up and operating a lathe. He was born in the last years of the Victorian age; his father was a teacher and printer, and he grew up in the potteries of Newcastle-under-Lyme, the cradle of

FILM DEBUT: The American poster for the 1942 British film telling the story of R. J. Mitchell and the birth of the Spitfire. The film was released under the title *The First of the Few*, but its American distributors preferred the directness of a wartime name with real meaning.

the Industrial Revolution, where innovative technology, the decorative arts, and industry had been stable-mates for over a century.

Mitchell was stubborn, blunt and impatient, all in pursuit of uncompromising perfectionism. He had the individualism of pioneering engineers of the 18th and 19th centuries, men such as Matthew Boulton and Isambard Kingdom Brunel, but he was also shy in temperament and artistic in talent; a skilled, freehand illustrator of ideas rather than a great speaker. Mitchell was never a dominant personality, nor a celebrity: he worked hard, but within a team, providing supportive leadership of a kind that was repaid quietly and with complete loyalty. In an age of individual heroes, a culture of personal endeavour that encompassed war, business, science, exploration and the arts, in which men like Gordon, Rhodes, Lister, Stanley and Lutyens left huge imprints on history, Mitchell was never more than a first among equals. His informal team had its own unspoken micro-culture of excellence, based

on people who recognized and valued each other's contribution. Some of them came from the same kind of humble origins as Mitchell, like his dedicated assistant at Supermarine, Joe Smith, Sir Henry Royce and Ernest Hives, who provided the Merlin engine. Others, RAF pilots such as George Stainforth and John Boothman, test pilots Joseph 'Mutt' Summers and Jeffrey Quill, came from different social strata, and still others came from right inside the establishment – figures such as Air Marshal Sir Hugh Dowding, Sir Wilfrid Freeman, Neville Chamberlain and Lord Beaverbrook, all of whom had backed the Spitfire and supported Mitchell's vision of excellence, challenging reactionaries who would gladly have seen the Spitfire strangled at birth.

Through his talent and his efforts, Mitchell became a modestly wealthy man with a country house and a Rolls-Royce car of which he was extremely proud. But ultimately he was a tragic figure. In 1933, aged thirty-eight, he was diagnosed with bowel cancer. After major surgery he was advised to rest, but he went back to work, where, paradoxically, his creativity and drive reached a peak during the last years of his life. Perhaps because his mind was concentrated by the closeness of death, he discovered a fresh original-ity and, more importantly, new reserves of boldness and persistence, which resulted in the RAF effectively abandoning its official specification for a new fighter and writing a new one to fit his streamlined, powerful and highly manoeuvrable alternative. Mitchell lived to see the prototype Spitfire fly, and to contribute to its early develop-ment, and towards the end of his life, he would drive in his Rolls to the edge of Eastleigh airfield to watch its test flights. Before it entered RAF service, however, he was dead. Mitchell was determined, moody, hopelessly disorganized, studiously self-effacing and inspired by an inner energy. His ultimate talent—designing beautiful, functional aircraft—has never been seriously disputed, but, because of the man he was, the legacy of true celebrity which might have accrued to him personally has accrued instead to his most inspirational creation: the Spitfire.

This creation radiates Mitchell's values of decency, integrity and love: qualities that have evolved in the seventy years since he died. His life and genius is celebrated quietly, in a very British idiom, by a bust in the Science Museum's Spitfire exhibition and a blue plaque on the house where he lived while he was designing it. More vividly, his name is evoked by air show commentators whenever one of the fifty Spitfires flying today displays its unique blend of aggression and humanity, whenever its troublesome appeal as

an aesthetic weapon becomes an art form that directly communicates our shared sense of history and pride.

The Spitfire's special reputation with the British people was made in the Battle of Britain, in 1940: as long as Spitfires were overhead, the country seemed safe. Its presence in wartime Britain was an elixir, a tonic, that lifted the spirits of an extraordinary range of people, from RAF pilots who experienced its utter dependability and placed in it that rarest and most precious of things, trust, to factory workers, many of them women, for whom building Spitfires was a personal contribution, a way of participating daily in winning the war. It had the power to inspire on a wide scale: the population at large, who saw the dogfights, the vapour trails and the crumpled wreckage of German aircraft in the fields of Kent, gave generously to the Spitfire Fund to build more of them; foreign ambassadors presented finished Spitfires to the RAF as gifts from their own countries; war artists painted them. People wanted to be part of the Spitfire story. One factory worker, Frank Edwards, wrote in his Mass Observation diary that he spent a day off in London going to see a Spitfire that went through the Battle of Britain: 'I joined a long queue to gain admission to the hall, which I estimate has been visited by some thousands of people today'.

Three quarters of a century after the Spitfire was born in R. J. Mitchell's mind, third and fourth generations still come to see the Spitfire, on the ground and in the air. The Battle of Britain Memorial Flight has five of them which are as much an attraction as the Red Arrows. The Flight makes 700 appearances annually, from national

10 Enduring symbol: more
than seventy years after
its first flight, English football
fans in Germany for the
FIFA World Cup in June
2006 adopted the Spitfire
as a national symbol (*right*),
evidence of the enduring
connection between
Britain's favourite aircraft
and the idea of victory.

Iconic moment: two
Spitfires (*opposite*) provide
a redolent moment for the
crowd at an air show with
a high-speed, low-level
formation run and break.
The lead aircraft is flown
by Squadron Leader Ray
Hannah, a great British
display pilot and one-time
leader of the Red Arrows.

celebrations, such as the Queen's Birthday, to village fêtes, keeping the RAF in the public mind. They still appeal across social and cultural boundaries, with admirers as likely to be young people wearing Spitfire baseball caps as silver-haired ex-serviceman with RAF ties and Spitfire pins. Man-size, inflatable model Spitfires have become the symbol of choice for English football fans to wave at their German counterparts as they gyrate in the stands; the most powerful representation of victory they know.

There are many reasons for the Spitfire's enduring appeal, and one is the way it has always had a very public face — one which has adapted to changes in popular culture and new forms of media. Its first live public appearance was at an air show in 1936, and it is still gigging. Its weekly appearances in newsreels before, during and after the war were clear propaganda, but people didn't care because it made them feel good; its role in several feature films made it a cinema star; it has been a television news and documentary staple, and the Spitfire is of course widely accessible on the world wide web.

From Leslie Howard and David Niven in *The First of the Few* in 1942, and William Walton's orchestral piece, *Spitfire Prelude,* to 'The Godiva Affair', a 1974 episode of *Dad's Army* based on Captain Mainwaring and his men Morris dancing to raise money for the Spitfire Fund, to the tribute in the stained glass windows of St George's Chapel at Biggin Hill, the Spitfire has entered the national consciousness as the most powerful expression of the martial, social and cultural fabric of Britain as it was during in the Second World War, the positive and understated focal point of millions of people, their icon.

Its power to attract love and attention was there from the start. In 1942, when the wartime documentary maker, Humphrey Jennings, produced *Listen to Britain* to stir hearts in wartime, in the opening commentary he picked out the Spitfire as the only weapon in a lyrical film: 'Blended together in one great symphony is the music of Britain at war: the evening hymn of the lark, the roar of Spitfires, the dances in the great ballroom at Blackpool, the clank of machinery and shunting trains, the BBC, sending truth on its journey around the world, the trumpet call of freedom …' This book sets out to record how and why the Spitfire became an icon.

Speed is an aircraft's lifeblood. Movement through the air is what keeps it aloft; speed can be converted into height and height can be re-converted into speed. Fuel efficiency, range, payload, stealth technology and on-board systems and sensors define aircraft today, but in the first half of the 20th century the Holy Grail was speed, an ever-present theme in the story of the Spitfire.

SPEED

14

THE QUEST FOR SPEED (*previous page*): in 1936, the level speed of the first Spitfire was 349 mph. In 1944, a Spitfire Mk XI, chosen for speed trials and flown by Squadron Leader John Martindale, reached 606 mph (Mach 0.89) in a 45-degree dive.

ULTIMATE SPITFIRE (*opposite*): unarmed and relying on speed to evade the enemy, the last of the photo-reconnaissance Spitfires had a cruising speed of 445 mph; one flown by Flight Lieutenant Ted Powles set an unofficial record for propeller-driven aircraft of Mach 0.94 in 1952, which still stands—huge testimony to the integrity of R.J. Mitchell's basic design.

AIRCRAFT BELONG IN FAMILIES. The Dakota, the Comet, the Jumbo Jet and the Concorde all have a common lineage: although they are from different generations, they are alike in that each has put its stamp on a particular period of history — and not just aviation history — by reaching out and connecting with the popular imagination. Millions of people have seen them, marvelled at them, and flown in them. They are individuals, immediately recognizable, symbolic for having stretched the human experience in some way, by carrying ever more passengers, in greater comfort, to ever more destinations, and by being built in great numbers. Collectively, they have shaped the modern world by challenging old ideas with new technologies, performing the seemingly impossible in their day through a mixture of innovation and long service. And, more than that, they all express something about the ever-changing human condition which is positive and liberating.

A second, and very different, family comprises landmark aircraft that are virtually unknown beyond the realm of aviation history, a family whose contribution was made through brief moments of glory. These aircraft are identified by manufacturer: the Deperdussin Monocoque, Supermarine S.6B, the Bell X-1, the Fairey Delta 2, the Douglas D-558-II, and the North American X-15A-2. They were built in very small numbers and flown by a tiny number of pilots in short flights, but however brief their flying lives, they pushed back the boundaries of aeronautical science, testing the materials, the theories and the limits of contemporary knowledge to become the

fastest machines on Earth in their day. These are the aircraft that pushed manned flight from under 100 mph to over 4,500 mph in what was a continuous theme in the history of aviation for a century: the quest for ever greater speed.

Rarely do aircraft belong to both families, but the Spitfire is one of the few that does — sitting as comfortably with the household names as with the record-breakers and pioneers. Not only did it play a central role in shaping the modern world, by contributing to victory in the Second World War, it was also among the fastest aircraft in the world at different times in the 1930s and 1940s as part of one of the most distinctive families of aircraft ever: the all-metal, highly streamlined, propeller-driven fighters of that war. The Spitfire was born out of an urgent need for speed in the 1930s; what we see today, after a flying life that spans more than two thirds of the whole history of aviation, is the same pencil-thin shape, exotic wings, huge engine and robust delicacy — all qualities rooted in that original quest for speed.

The Spitfire is a thoroughbred, its pedigree traceable all the way back to the very first aircraft. The ideas, the seeds that would grow into this magnificent aeroplane, making it a national icon and worldwide celebrity as well as a fast and manoeuvrable fighter — its aerodynamics, its ancestry — were sown a quarter of a century before it flew. In the decade before the Great War, aviation was in its infancy, steam trains and steam cars were faster than aircraft, and it was not yet clear that aircraft would have any practical value except to provide novelty and public spectacle.

CHANGING THE WORLD: Wilbur Wright filming his brother Orville, who is demonstrating the Flyer to the US Army at Fort Myer, Virginia, in September 1908 (*above*) and again in July 1909 when the US government bought it as the world's first military aircraft (*left*).

SHRINKING THE WORLD: on 25 July 1909, Louis Bleriot crossed the White Cliffs of Dover (*right top*), demonstrating the military and commercial potential of aircraft. In the process, he became a media celebrity (*right bottom*) — aviation's first true hero.

In August 1908, *Le Petit Journal*, a mass-circulation French magazine, dedicated its cover story to one man and one aircraft: Wilbur Wright and the Flyer. Fed up with Europeans not believing that he and his brother Orville had built and flown a powered aircraft under full control, and had done so nearly five years previously at Kittyhawk, North Carolina, Wilbur had brought his machine to a large field near Paris to demonstrate it. He instantly silenced his doubters. His technological innovation and mastery as a pilot impressed the small group of experts from the French Aero Club who had gathered to watch. In fact, his flights caused such excitement that the next day, thousands of people turned up in the expectation that they would see another spectacular flying display. They were disappointed: it was a Sunday, and Wilbur, the son of a Protestant bishop, would not fly. On the Monday, an even bigger crowd turned up. By the end of the week he had set European media alight, and even featured in a short film which was shown in film theatres all over the world. Flying displays and the media, especially film, have had a close relationship ever since.

That autumn and winter, the Wright Brothers gave dozens of demonstration flights and made many friends in Europe. However, the Wrights were taciturn, unbending, reserved and impecunious men whose primary aim was to profit from their invention by licensing the use of their patents to European business, and they saw no reason to capitalize on their popularity. They did not understand that *The Flyer* was not just a collection of patents, they had not just invented a machine, they had fulfilled one of the oldest human dreams, to fly like a bird. When Lord Northcliffe, owner of

The Daily Mail, offered a prize of $2,500 for a cross-Channel flight, privately assuring Wilbur Wright of a further $7,500 if he achieved it, Wilbur turned him down, considering it no more than a stunt, and went back to America. A year later, in July 1909, Louis Bleriot claimed the prize, making the crossing in a tiny monoplane in just

POPULAR CULTURE: Louis Bleriot is greeted by an ecstatic London crowd at Victoria Station; he is seated next to Lord Northcliffe, who had sponsored the cross-Channel flight through his mass-circulation newspaper, *The Daily Mail*.

forty minutes. The world was changing: the fact, no longer simply the idea, that an aircraft could fly over the sea from France to England, and in less than an hour, caused huge popular excitement. This time there was media coverage on a scale even greater than Wilbur Wright had generated two years previously — so much so that Harry Selfridge paid handsomely for the Bleriot monoplane to be displayed in his Oxford Street store, where thousands flocked to see it.

Bleriot's flight was a gift to the popular imagination, a technical achievement which defied comprehension. But the implication was clear: Britain's island status had been challenged by the aeroplane's potential to transport people faster than steam packets and to be forged into a new weapon of war. Science fiction was turning into science fact on the front pages of the mass-circulation newspapers, bringing the themes of H.G. Wells' novels to life: the gloomy prediction of the bomber in *The War in the Air* published in 1908,

The Time Machine, in 1905, and *The First Men on the Moon* in 1901.

The fantasies and the facts mingled easily. In August 1909, a month after Bleriot's flight, crowds of enthusiasts migrated to Rheims for a completely new form of entertainment, the first ever organized air display. The show lasted a whole week, and was a highly choreographed showcase for French aviation sponsored by the great Champagne houses of the region and attended by President Fallieres of France and David Lloyd George, Britain's Chancellor of the Exchequer, as well as journalists and opinion formers from Europe and the United States. The great and the good adorned specially built pavilions and restaurants overlooking the airfield in an almost gladiatorial setting, while round the perimeter and in the roads and fields beyond, thousands of normal people who just wanted to witness for themselves the spectacle of flight picnicked and watched at a distance. The few

THE WORLD'S FIRST AIR SHOW: August 1909 saw European society flock to Rheims, led by President Fallieres of France and his wife (*bottom right*), to be entertained and to witness the birth of the air age (*top right*) while basking in romantic perceptions of aircraft (*below*).

dozen pilots were there to compete for hundreds of thousands of francs in prizes; the most sought-after prize was the Gordon Bennett Cup for speed, presented by the American publisher and racing enthusiast in person.

Britain's Hubert Latham won the endurance prize, covering 100 kilometres at an average speed of 42 mph, and in doing so set the world's first speed record for an aeroplane. Then an American, Glenn Curtiss, flew three laps of the airfield and raised Latham's record to 46.6 mph to become

the official winner. With French honour at stake, France's local hero, Louis Bleriot, chopped several feet off the trailing edges of his monoplane's wings to coax more speed out of it and over a single lap raised the record again, to 47.8 mph. The actual speed was not the real attraction in 1910 — after all, it was still slower than the first ever speed record of 56 mph set by the steam locomotive *Lucifer,* in 1839, and well below the then official land speed record held by an American steam car, the *Stanley Rocket,* at 121 mph. The popular

THE FIRST AIRCRAFT FACTORY: art, science and technology came together under the supervision of Gabriel and Charles Voisin in their assembly hall at Billancourt in Paris. Alongside their own designs, they accepted plans from clients, who paid handsomely to have them built.

attraction was the close-up spectacle of seeing aeroplanes fly competitively. However, the Gordon Bennett Cup linked the idea of speed and aeroplanes in the popular imagination and helped to establish air racing as part of the charisma of the aeroplane, as well as playing a role in its technical development.

The infant aviation industry received a huge boost from the Rheims air show. Similar events followed quickly in Italy, Germany, Britain and the United States. But the home of the aviation industry in 1909 was France. A month after Rheims, Paris was the setting for the International Exposition of Aerial Locomotion in the Grand Palais, at which over 300 exhibitors, nearly all French, exhibited their machines. They looked more like works of art than industrial products: the first aircraft factory had been opened in Britain in 1909 to build Wright *Flyers* under licence, but aircraft manufacture in France at the time was done in surroundings more like artists' studios or salons, and rather than pieces of advanced technology they were seen as objects

of desire, elegance, character and beauty, produced by artisanal skill rather than industrial efficiency. The idea that aircraft were beautiful as well as functional was captured in the stylized and romanticized aircraft depicted in the posters of the day. Even though there were more biplanes than monoplanes flying at the time, it was noticeable that it was the less cluttered, sleeker, faster-looking monoplanes that caught the artists' imagination.

Speed, spectacle and beauty, brought together by a new and exciting technology, made the aeroplane one of the sensations of the Edwardian age. Having a Flying Certificate conveyed huge social status, and flying schools sprang up to meet the demand from rich socialites, men and some women, who wanted to learn to fly. Once they could fly, a small number bought aircraft for the purpose of winning one of the prizes offered by newspapers, for example Claude Graham White, who flew Britain's first home-built aircraft, a Bristol Boxkite, from the Hurlingham Club to Manchester for a prize of £10,000 along a route

BRITAIN CATCHES UP: the publicity for Britain's first air show concentrated on the monoplane. The high point of the meeting was Samuel Cody, an American showman and the first person to fly in Britain, signing his naturalization papers on the Mayor of Doncaster's back so that he could take part in races restricted to British subjects.

lined by thousands of sightseers, many of whom stayed up all night to see him pass.

Aeroplanes were not just public spectacles: national governments recognized both the commercial and security implications of aircraft, and took an immediate interest in the science of aviation. In 1910, aeronautical research establishments were founded in France, Germany, and Russia as well as in Britain, at HM Balloon Factory at Farnborough—which became the Royal Aircraft Factory in 1912 when the military potential in aircraft was beginning to become evident. As the first fledgling air forces, such as the Air

Battalion of the Royal Engineers in Britain, were formed, aircraft began to have secret, as well as public, lives. The first machine gun had been fired from a Wright Type B, the first bombs and torpedoes had been dropped, aircraft had landed and taken off from warships and made observation flights during military manoeuvres. In North Africa, the Italian Air Flotilla used aircraft in anger for the first time in their war with Turkey, carrying out reconnaissance and dropping small bombs. While military aviation went through its experimental stage, and while many soldiers believed that aeroplanes had little military value, the idea of the fighter, an aircraft designed for combat with other fighters for control of the skies, was barely considered. However, air-minded soldiers and racing enthusiasts alike continued to take a keen interest in the effect the basic configuration of aircraft, whether biplane or monoplane, would have on the quest for speed.

The forum for what became an unofficial contest to build the fastest aircraft was a mixture of racing and the setting of the world's speed record for

THE GLITTERING PRIZE: the bronze statuette of a winged nymph kissing the sea earned the Schneider Trophy the nickname 'Flying Flirt'. It cost £1,000 in 1913, but over the course of twelve races, several million pounds were spent, and a number of pilots' lives lost, in pursuit of it.

aircraft—and in its early stages, it was conducted largely between French manufacturers seeking to promote their machines. Between 1910 and 1914, that record increased dramatically and the fastest aircraft were all monoplanes: on 21 June 1911 Edouard Nieuport raised it to 82 mph in his Nieuport IVG, which had a fully enclosed fuselage and a much more streamlined appearance than its predecessors; in January 1912, Jules Vedrines raised it to 90 mph in the most advanced racing aircraft to date, the Deperdussin Monococque. The Deperdussin had started life as a thoroughbred racing aircraft, a beautiful, futuristic, sleek monoplane with a fully enclosed monocoque fuselage skinned with wood veneer that tapered uniformly to a swept-back tail plane; it had an aluminium cowl to enclose the Gnome rotary engine, a coned propeller boss, and the single wing was braced with wire—the only break in the

streamlined effect. In 1913, Marcel Prevost flew an improved Deperdussin to 126.66 mph, a new record, and established the monoplane as embodying all the right characteristics for speed and hence influential in the shape of things to come.

Following the success of air races at Rheims, James Gordon Bennett had decided to introduce an annual race that combined speed, nationalism, individualism, technology and the large sums of hard cash which were almost guaranteed to capture public imagination. In September 1912, the race had been held in Chicago, and Jules Vedrines had won in a Deperdussin Monococque at 108.16 mph, a world record speed at the time. At the victory banquet afterwards, the French Under-Secretary for Air, Jacques Schneider, a balloon and aircraft pilot himself and the son of a wealthy arms manufacturer, announced a new race, the Schneider Cup. Schneider believed the future of commercial aviation lay with fast seaplanes, which might one day take over from passenger-carrying ocean liners. He argued that landplanes of a size to carry large numbers of passengers would require long and expensive runways, while the sea had limitless space to take off. He also pointed out that seventy per cent of the world's surface is covered in water, and that a large proportion of the world's population lived near the coasts of the great continents. The main hubs of international trade and travel were already established in ports such as Southampton, Le Havre and New York, where all the necessary infrastructure existed and commerce thrived. Great flying boats could therefore service the existing great cities of the world, moving people between them in hours rather than days or weeks. Schneider was aiming

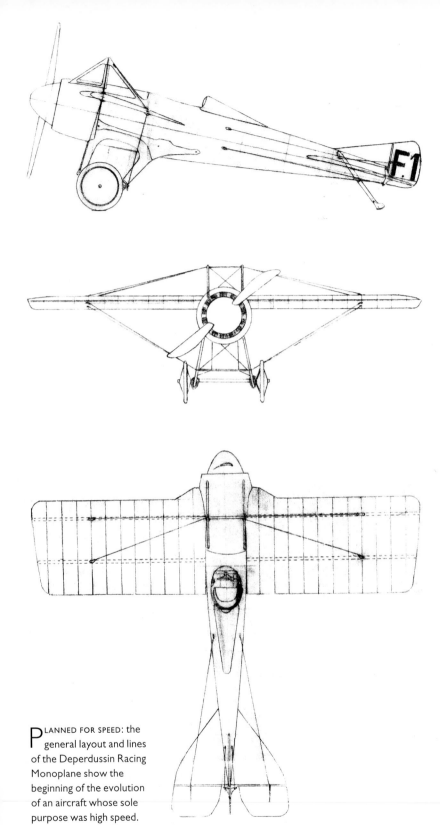

PLANNED FOR SPEED: the general layout and lines of the Deperdussin Racing Monoplane show the beginning of the evolution of an aircraft whose sole purpose was high speed. Its strength came from the monocoque fuselage and the wire bracing; its speed, from the clean profile and from streamlining.

at the rich, for there was no vision of mass air travel; it would be government and business only. The Schneider Cup had one objective: to encourage the development of seaplane technology. To that end, the rules enshrined seaworthiness and sea navigability trials, and landings on water were mandatory.

Schneider's ideas for the future turned out to be visionary: in the late 1930s, Britain and America in particular operated global scheduled services in luxury, trans-oceanic flying boats, using seaports as hubs. However, the more immediate effect of the Schneider Cup was to foster international rivalry that would surpass any other prize in aviation, before or since. It would have the unintended consequence of creating a series of racing monoplanes that would lead, more than twenty years later, to the most advanced, fastest and most beautiful fighter in the world —the Spitfire.

Growing up in those heady years, when technical progress in aviation was almost a daily event and media attention was rife, was a young man whose destiny was to design the Spitfire: Reginald J. Mitchell. In 1911, aged sixteen, he was taking his first steps into the world of work. He had been a bright scholar, was fascinated by aircraft and would build models of his own design with his brother, but he started work as an engineering apprentice at Kerr Stuart & Co, a firm of railway engineers in Stoke-on-Trent. After serving his time on the shop floor, Mitchell moved to the drawing office, which was his natural environment: he had been exposed in his formative years to technical drawing and engineering, while spending his waking hours outside work studying mathematics. Mitchell's enquiring mind was

always looking for new stimulation, be it making a billiard table for the family, reading the entire works of Sir Walter Scott, building a dynamo by making all the parts himself, playing chess with his father or keeping racing pigeons. Whatever he turned his hand or brain to he did thoroughly, and saw through to the end. At the same time, he was absorbing the progress of aeronautics as it evolved from a sport and a circus act into a new science with sound engineering at its heart, especially when it came to building ever faster aircraft.

While Mitchell was learning his trade as an engineer, two businessmen, Hubert Scott-Paine and Noel Pemberton Billing, formed a company in Southampton: Pemberton-Billing Ltd, with the purpose of building seaplanes. Pemberton Billing was a serial entrepreneur, writer, soldier of the

Boer War, reserve naval officer, and property developer who had learned to fly in twenty-four hours; Scott-Paine had worked as his assistant selling yachts. Both men had an interest in the sea. Perhaps impressed by Jacques Schneider's arguments about the future of passenger flying boats, they established the company in 1913, the year of the first Schneider Cup race. The company's telegraphic address was 'Supermarine', a name that was to become inseparable from the Spitfire.

The entrants for the first Schneider Cup race at Monaco were all French, all monoplanes, and all seaworthy versions of racing landplanes that had been adapted for the race: two Nieuports, a Morane-Saulnier and a Deperdussin Mono-cocque. The race was run in bright sunshine on a closed circuit over the calm waters of Monaco harbour; it was won, to great local acclaim, by

Marcel Prevost in the Deperdussin, at an average speed of 45 mph.

The following year, in 1914, Prevost was eliminated in the early trials and did not join the six starters, but there was a privately entered Deperdussin, flown by Lord Carberry, along with two Nieuports, a German Aviatik, a Swiss FBA flying boat and a British biplane, the Sopwith Tabloid. Flown by an Australian, Howard Pixton, the semi-military Tabloid won the 1914 Schneider Trophy at an average speed of 86 mph, and then by flying a further two laps Pixton raised the speed record for seaplanes to 86.6 mph. The needs of

air racing and the needs of war overlapped in the Tabloid. Fast, manoeuvrable and powered by a 160 hp, Le Rhone Monosoupape rotary engine, it was the floatplane version of a landplane which, with war clouds gathering in Europe, had recently been ordered in large numbers by the British Government as a scout for the Royal Flying Corps (RFC) and the Royal Naval Air Service (RNAS).

In preparing for war, European governments had concentrated on harnessing the fruits of the chemical, electrical and heavy industrial revolutions of the 19th century to develop long-range artillery, high explosives, machine guns, big-gun

25

MORANE-SAULNIER: Roland Garros over Monaco harbour (*below*) after coming second in the 1913 Schneider race. His aircraft was powered by the same 160 hp engine as the Deperdussin, but its conventional wood-and-fabric construction weighed twice as much.

PRE-WAR SUCCESS: a post-card celebrating the victory of Britain's Sopwith Tabloid in the 1914 Schneider Trophy race. The aircraft started life as a military scout, an early example of the common need for speed shared by racing and military aircraft.

dreadnaughts and submarines. Few military and naval experts had anticipated the way the aeroplane would develop as a weapon, and those that did saw it almost exclusively as an observation platform, a way of spotting for artillery and gathering intelligence, rather than as a weapon that would revolutionize warfare. No one envisaged at that time that the sky would become a battlefield in its own right and that aircraft would engage in combat for control of air space just as armies controlled the ground and ships controlled the sea.

In truth, not only did aircraft revolutionize warfare, the Great War also revolutionized aircraft production — as the appetite for more and more sophisticated aeroplanes turned it from an artisanal craft into an industrialized process. Design and production were intertwined and homogenized, simply to cope with the scale and complexity of the task. Between them, the combatant nations built over 200,000 aircraft in the four years of the Great War. In 1914, the RFC had sixty-three assorted machines, none of them armed; by 1918, as the newly independent air arm of the British armed forces, the Royal Air Force, it had 22,500 specialized fighters, bombers, reconnaissance and training aircraft and 300,000 men. In the push to meet the demands of military necessity, the designers' scope for flair and imagination had been narrowed, and what had been solely a source of entertainment and spectacle was transformed into an airborne arsenal. The catalyst was money. The combatant nations' governments distributed almost limitless resources to national aircraft manufacturers and in Britain, companies such as Vickers, Sopwith and the engine maker Rolls-Royce grew into very

substantial and profitable businesses.

The needs of war had also turned the aeroplane from a delicate, hand-crafted machine into a more technically robust piece of military equipment capable of far greater performance. In 1914, the distance record for aircraft stood at 634 miles; in June 1919, the RAF's Captain John Alcock and Lieutenant Arthur Whitten Brown trebled it, flying 1,900 miles non-stop across the Atlantic in a converted bomber. In 1914, the altitude record stood at 20,079 feet; in 1918, fighters such as Britain's Se.5a routinely flew to that height and in February 1920, the US Army's Major R.W. Schroeder set a new record of 33,113 feet. In 1914, the speed record was 126.66 mph, held by the Deperdussin Monocoque; in 1918, the fastest aircraft was the Nieuport-Delage 29, a single-seat fighter with a top speed of 143 mph.

Such increases in aircraft performance were achieved largely through huge improvements in the power and reliability of aero engines during the war. However, much of the increased power had been used to overcome increases in weight and drag, not towards increasing speed. In a dogfight, agility was more valuable than outright speed. The most successful fighter, the highly manoeuvrable Sopwith Camel, with 1,294 aerial victories, had a top speed of just 115 mph.

The Nieuport and the Camel both conformed to what was almost the universal design in 1918: a biplane braced with struts and wires, with a heavy, fixed undercarriage and an open cockpit — design features that all increased weight and drag and resisted speed. Pre-war racing aircraft, especially the speed record holders, had largely been monoplanes, like the Deperdussin, and

CHALLENGER: Fairey III, which was converted for the 1919 Schneider Cup race from a 1917 prototype Royal Navy carrier-borne floatplane. It was the forerunner of the fast, light biplane bombers that dominated the RAF inventory in the 1920s.

though German manufacturers were experimenting with high-wing monoplane fighters in the last months of the Great War, they were rare in 1918.

If the aeroplane itself had been transformed by war, what had not changed since 1914 was its ability to entertain. Not long after the armistice, and before the Versailles Treaty had even been ratified, the first post-war air show in Britain was held at Hendon, in June 1919. War had changed the focus of the air show and this display was an aerial victory parade, designed to present the Royal Air Force to the public. It was what the RAF called a Pageant, a show of massed biplanes flying in formation with great precision and timing before thousands of spectators anxious for entertainment after four years of war. The show was organized by a former soldier turned fighter pilot, Colonel Hugh Dowding, a taciturn but gifted, precise, and determined administrator who would later play a central role in the birth of the Spitfire.

That first RAF Pageant acknowledged the attraction of speed, and included a short local

race. There were plans to revive the great, pre-war, international air races, with their cash prizes —the Gordon Bennett Cup, the Coupe Deutsch de la Muerthe—and to organize a new addition, the Pulitzer Trophy. However, the first major post-war race was not for cash, it was for prestige, for national pride. By winning the Schneider Trophy in 1914, Howard Pixton had given Britain the right to stage the next race and in 1919 the Royal Aero Club lost no time planning the race off Bournemouth beach for 10 September.

As an air race, the first post-war Schneider Cup race was a disaster. Race day was shrouded in thick fog and the French team withdrew having failed the navigability tests, leaving four British and one Italian aircraft, all of which were flying boats rather than floatplanes, and all of which were biplanes of a distinctively military appearance. Of the British aircraft, the Avro 539 floatplane failed the preliminary trials, while the Sopwith Schneider and Fairey III both withdrew on the first lap. The Supermarine Sea Lion, flown by Basil Hobbs,

28 Post-war failure: specially-built for the 1919 race, the Sopwith Schneider, with its 450 hp Jupiter radial engine, was one of Sopwith's last aircraft before the company collapsed financially. Revived as Hawker, it went on to produce many British fighters, including the Fury, the Hurricane, the Tempest, the Hunter and the Harrier, which is still flying today.

a decorated ex-RAF pilot, took off through the fog, but fearful of flying into the cliffs Hobbs landed on the water again, where he damaged the hull on some floating wreckage. He re-started, but when he alighted on the water on lap one, as required by the rules, the hull filled with water and the Sea Lion sank. The Italian pilot, Guido Jannello, finished the course in his Savoia S.13, but the race committee disqualified him for mistaking a buoy for one of the turning points. After a brief debate, by way of a consolation prize, Italy was awarded the right to stage the 1920 race.

If the 1919 Schneider Cup race had been a disaster, it was also a landmark in the development of high-speed aircraft in Britain. Preparation of the Supermarine Sea Lion had been delegated to a twenty-four-year-old designer whose name would eventually be forever linked to the Schneider Cup and through that to the Spitfire: R.J. Mitchell. He had been turned down for military service in the Great War on the grounds that his technical

qualifications were of greater value to industry, so when he finished his apprenticeship in 1917 he had written to Hubert Scott-Paine seeking a job with Supermarine. His application arrived after there had been huge changes at the company, most significantly the departure of Noel Pemberton Billing, who had become a Member of Parliament the year before. Pemberton Billing had served in the RNAS early in the war, planning the bombing of the German Zeppelin sheds on Lake Constance, but he stood for Parliament in order to argue for greater emphasis on bombing and he sold his share of the company to Scott-Paine so that he could not be accused of acting out of self interest. Once Scott-Paine had control of the company, he concentrated on building flying boats for the Admiralty, among them the Sea Lion. He was so struck with Mitchell that he offered him a job as his personal assistant on the spot, and Mitchell started work at the Woolston works on Southampton Water without even returning to Stoke-on-Trent for his belongings. His rise at Supermarine was by any standards meteoric: by 1918 he was assistant manager of the whole company and by 1920 he was chief designer, responsible for a whole range of military and civilian flying boats which were the backbone of the business. Among the projects on his drawing board in 1920 was a future entry in the Schneider Cup.

The 1920 Schneider race was held at the San Andrea naval base at Venice. The only entrants were Italian, largely because it was a long way for the British and French industries to travel, and Luigi Bologna won in a Savoia S.12 at an average speed of 107 mph. Meanwhile, the French industry concentrated on winning the Gordon Bennett

S AVOIA S.13: converted
from a light bomber and
reconnaissance flying boat,
Italy's 1919 Schneider entry
was, like the Supermarine
Sea Lion, closer to what
Jacques Schneider was
seeking to promote – but
flying boats were slower
than the floatplanes.

Cup and securing the world speed record instead.
Nieuport-Delage stripped their NiD 29 fighter of
all its armament and excess weight, unleashing as
much of the increased engine power as possible
to be turned into speed. It was designated the
NiD 29a, and in it Sadi Lecointe set the record at
171 mph, and just before the end of the year he
raised it again, to 194 mph. Shorn of military
needs, the quest for speed had achieved a greater

increase in speed in two post-war years than in
the whole of the war.

The 1921 Schneider Cup race was also held at
Venice. There were sixteen Italian flying boats,
all pusher biplanes, and one seaplane version of
the Nieuport-Delage 29a from France, flown by
Sadi Lecointe. The day before the race, one
of Lecointe's floats failed, leaving Giovanni de
Briganti of the Italian team of three Macchis to win

Winning team (*left*): Hubert Scott-Paine, Henri Biard, R.J. Mitchell and Victor Scott-Paine in discussion prior to the 1922 race; the aircraft cost around £6,000, all of which was either committed by Supermarine or borrowed in kind from suppliers.

at an average speed of 117 mph and take the trophy for Italy a second time.

Under the rules, if the Italians also won the 1922 race at Naples they would win the Schneider Cup outright. In an expression of nationalism, and to show the superiority of his fascist ideology, Benito Mussolini, the Italian dictator who had came to power in Italy the same year, provided funds to back the attempt and exerted huge pressure on the Italian aircraft industry to produce a winning aeroplane. There were four Italian entries, two Macchis and two Savoias, including the aesthetically pleasing S.51, a sleek, post-war design. The French government did the same, entering two flying boats backed with government finance. The single British entry was the Sea Lion Mk II, but there was no British government money. With the support of the engine manufacturer, Napier, and free fuel and oil from Shell, Hubert Scott-Paine gave Mitchell the go-ahead to modify the Mk I, which had itself been an adaptation of a wartime design: he shortened the wooden hull, covered it in fabric, doped it, gave it a longer, narrower wing with a smaller wing area, and, most importantly, installed a 450 hp engine, an increase of fifty per cent over the Mk I. In tests on the Solent, at full throttle, the fearless Henri Biard reached 150 mph, something the team kept a closely guarded secret.

Biard never showed the full capability of the Sea Lion until the race. The weather was perfect in the Bay of Naples, and the beaches crowded with spectators there to see Italy win the trophy outright. The French entries were withdrawn after capsizing during the seaworthiness trials, leaving the S.51 as the most serious opposition to Biard. In the event, the combination of Mitchell's detailed

and single-minded concentration on maximizing speed and skilful handling by Biard snatched the Schneider Trophy from the Italians in their own back yard by just 2 mph over the S.51. The close result and the failure on the part of the Italians to win the trophy outright only served to spice up the national rivalry, making the result headline news across Europe. This not only kept the race alive, it increased its status as the world's premier air race.

The popularity of air races and the competition to break the world speed record became increasingly nationalistic. They represented a forum, other than war, for the development of aircraft through the expression of national rivalry. But the development of high-speed aircraft could also have long-term military importance to the major powers. On 13 October 1922, Brigadier 'Billy' Mitchell raised the world speed record to 222 mph in a US Army Curtiss R-6 biplane powered by a Curtiss D-12 engine specially prepared for the attempt by a military team. The Curtiss R-6 was a post-war design with just one strut between the wings, sleeker and more streamlined even with the addition of floats than wartime machines, and it had achieved over 200 mph in trials. When the R-6's record was trumped in 1923 with a run of 232.98 mph by the ageing Nieuport 29a, within weeks Lieutenant Russell Maughan snatched it back for the US Army with 236.59 mph in the R-6. The military involvement in setting records and winning races received official backing and the US Army continued to tackle the speed record while the US Navy prepared to enter the 1923 Schneider Cup with a team of specially prepared Curtiss CR-3 floatplanes with four US Navy test pilots to fly them.

WINNING AIRCRAFT: the Supermarine Sea Lion II being prepared for the 1922 race. When the Italian pilots realized that it was faster than their machines, they tried to block Henri Biard at the turns — so he flew slightly higher, then dived over them to the next pylon. It worked, and he returned to Britain a national hero.

32

AMERICAN INTERLUDE: the elegant Curtiss CR-3 (*above*), which Rutledge Irvine flew into second place at Cowes in 1923. The founder of the company, Glenn Curtiss, had won the first Gordon Bennett race at Rheims in 1909 in an aircraft of his own design.

A MITCHELL MASTERPIECE (*opposite*): the beautiful Supermarine Southampton maritime reconnaissance flying boat brought Supermarine financial stability. Knowing Mitchell's reputation, the RAF ordered six off the drawing board and following its first flight in March 1925, a total of eighty-three were built, the later models with duralumin rather than wooden hulls.

The 1923 race was held at Cowes on the Isle of Wight. The French challenge collapsed again, with engine malfunctions and a collision. To defend the trophy, R.J. Mitchell built the Sea Lion Mk III, squeezing every last drop of performance out of the same airframe by installing a new 525 hp Lion engine. Once again, the sole British entry was not backed by government money or military resources and expertise, and it quickly became evident that the Navy-backed, streamlined CR-3 floatplanes were in a class of their own: Lieutenant David Rittenhouse won with a final lap at 181 mph and an average speed of 177 mph, an increase of 32 mph over Biard's winning speed the previous year; his team mate, Lieutenant Rutledge Irvine, was second at 173 mph; Biard was third at 157 mph.

Supermarine and Mitchell had lost, but they had achieved the almost impossible by producing a 12 mph increase in the average speed of the Sea Lion. However, the margin by which they had lost was nearly three times that amount: the reliability of the Curtiss CR-3s and their D-12 engines had given the Americans first and second places by a wide margin in their first Schneider Cup challenge. As if to emphasize the point, in November 1923, Lieutenant A. Brown of the US Army raised the world speed record to 255 mph in a landplane Curtiss and a month later, Lieutenant Alford Williams of the US Marine Corps (USMC) raised it to 267 mph. The reasons were clear: streamlined design, engine power, the resources that only governments could command — and military planning down to the last detail.

The Curtiss family of racing and record-breaking biplanes marked the high point of one era in high-speed design and the beginning of another.

Building superfast biplanes had won America some glittering prizes, but even with its much sleeker form, the biplane configuration had limited scope for development beyond simply adding more and more powerful engines. To beat the American racers would take a fundamental shift in design, away from the tried-and-tested biplane configuration and towards more demanding but inherently faster monoplanes — such as the winner of the first ever Schneider Trophy race, the Deperdussin Monocoque of 1913, and the Bernard Ferbois V-2 monoplane in which Florentin Bonnet had taken the world speed record from the Americans in 1924 with a run of 278 mph.

R. J. Mitchell and Supermarine were at the forefront of that revolution. Following the 1922 success, Scott-Paine had sold the company to Commander Bird who had joined as works manager in 1919; Bird realized that the company's reputation rested on Mitchell's inspired designs, not only in racing aircraft but also in its elegant family of military and civil flying boats. In a small company that still relied on the quality of its aircraft for its business, rather than volume, Mitchell was effectively the design department, and in early 1924 the directors recognized his talent and position by giving him a ten-year contract and two new projects: masterminding the Supermarine Southampton, the next generation of anti-submarine and reconnaissance flying boats for the Royal Navy, and delivering the first of a new family of monoplane racers aimed solely at the Schneider Trophy, the radical S.4.

There was no Schneider race in 1924. The US National Aeronautic Association sportingly cancelled it because the European countries were not ready. Seeing what had been achieved

Back to the future: the Supermarine S.4 (*above* and *below*) was the first Schneider Trophy racer to return to the monoplane configuration and wooden, monococque construction pioneered by the winning Deperdussin of 1913. In September 1925, Henri Biard (pictured *above* with R.J. Mitchell) broke the world speed record for floatplanes of 226.75 mph before going to America where it crashed, nearly killing him.

by US military involvement, the Air Ministry now stepped in with funds and resources for research, spreading their risk by backing two entries for the 1925 race: the Supermarine S.4 monoplane and the Gloster III biplane. Mitchell decided on the most streamlined configuration possible, which meant using a cantilever wing rigid enough to support the aircraft without the wire bracing that had given the Deperdussin Monococque its inherent strength. Doing without any bracing wires made streamlining the fuselage easier too, but the penalty for the reduced wind resistance was a loss of strength, which became more and more important as the aerodynamic stresses induced by the higher speeds had to be borne by the structure without adding too much extra weight. Mitchell was not alone in going for the cantilever monoplane design for 1925: Mario Castoldi, the designer at Italy's Macchi, used the same approach in the M.33, but it was a flying boat — an inherently stronger design — rather than a floatplane.

The more delicate, but faster, floatplane configuration of the S.4 encased a 680 hp Lion engine in elegantly sculptured fairings — and it looked superb, catching the fashionable wave of uncluttered modernity and clean lines that characterized the art and design

of the mid 1920s. However, the race at Baltimore was a disaster for Britain, for Supermarine and for Mitchell: the S.4 crashed into the sea in the preliminary trials and Henri Biard narrowly escaped with his life. The cause of the crash was never fully established, but Biard believed it was wing flutter, or possibly aileron flutter — in other words, that the high speeds had set off a flexing of the wing which rapidly weakened the whole structure and effectively tore the wing off. Mitchell believed he might have come close to killing his friend Biard and it had a profound effect on him. He was acutely aware how narrow the margins of safety were in competitive racing aircraft flying at the frontiers of technology, but now he had experienced the consequences at first hand.

That race was the last triumph of the biplane over the monoplane. The winner was Lieutenant James Doolittle of the US Army in the latest Curtiss biplane, which was powered by a new V-1,400, 4,655 hp engine, at 232.562 mph; in second place was Britain's Hubert Broad in the Gloster III, at 199 mph. In third place, and a long way behind at 168 mph, was the Italian Giovanni de Briganti in the Macchi M.33 — the first cantilever monoplane to compete in the race for the Schneider Trophy.

THE SHAPE OF THINGS TO COME: built largely out of wood, with steel A-frames for strength and a duralumin engine cover, the sheer sculpted beauty of Mitchell's design left no doubt that speed was its only purpose.

In the unstable economic climate of the mid 1920s, funding for one-off racing aircraft in pursuit of national glory was too costly to be commercially sensible for the manufacturers, particularly as there was no obvious profit to be gained from the aeronautical advances made. The races could have withered away, but they were such a popular spectacle, and they commanded such strong national sentiment, that governments continued to support the manufacturers and engine builders on the basis that the knowledge and technology might be of benefit in the future — and it was better to stay in than leave the field to international competitors.

In 1926, once again, it came down to a race between biplanes and monoplanes and between the United States and Italy. If America could win a third time, they would keep the trophy forever. Britain did not enter what turned out to be the watershed year for the Schneider Trophy at Hampton Roads. Mussolini once again made winning the Schneider Trophy a political imperative, more or less ordering the Italian military

pilots assigned to the job to win and providing the funds for them to do so. America continued to rely on its Curtiss biplanes, Mario Castoldi continued down the monoplane route with the M.39, using wire bracing for the single wing, which was highly reminiscent of the Deperdussin Monocoque. A significant difference, however, was that sixty per cent of the M.39's wing was covered in a brass radiator for the monster, 800 hp, water-cooled Fiat AS.2 engine. Mussolini's backing provided enough capital to build three racing M.39s, two more for training and practice, and a sixth for structural tests, plus models for wind-tunnel testing. It was a highly organized and professional team, but nevertheless, the narrow margins of safety were evident again when the team captain, Commandante Vittorio Centurione, crashed while practising a steep turn and was instantly killed. His replacement, Major Mario di Barnardi, carried out Mussolini's order and won the Trophy in the M.39, at an average speed of 246 mph. US Navy Lieutenant Christian Schilt's R3C-2 could only average 231 mph.

36

Macchi m.39 (*above*): Italy's Mario Castoldi embodied the lessons of the 1925 Schneider Trophy race in his 1926 winning entry—most obviously, a return to a monoplane configuration, but also incorporating wire bracing rather than relying on cantilever wings.

Gloster iv (*right*): while Mitchell and Supermarine focused on monoplanes, the RAF kept the biplane alive through Gloster and its Chief Designer, Henry P. Folland. In the 1927 race in Venice it was lapping just below the winning speed of the S.5 when a propeller shaft broke and it retired.

It was the first victory by a monoplane since 1913 and a sure sign that monoplanes were the way to higher speeds in the future. To emphasize this change, four days after the race di Barnardi raised the speed record for seaplanes to 258 mph in the M.39, just 20 mph slower than the official absolute speed record of 278 mph. His achievement was once again made possible by the financial support of the Italian government. Mussolini was delighted: Italy had the Schneider Trophy; its team had prevented the Americans from winning it outright; the development of high-speed aircraft in Italy had made a significant advance based on a professional, military approach to winning; and the next race would be controlled by Italy in Venice.

Also in 1926, Jacques Schneider, the founder of the races, died. The seaplanes which had evolved from the nine races that had borne his name— aircraft like the S.4 and the M.39— were a long way from what he had envisaged in 1912. They were one-off

machines, barely safe to fly, made difficult to design because of the huge floats that had no particular purpose other than to meet the regulations. They were optimized for speed in a form of gladiatorial competition that happened to take place over water, but had not been developed for any other use. Commercial air travel, even for the very rich, was not yet on the horizon.

Following the S.4 crash, the Air Ministry asked Mitchell for three models of different designs for its successor, the S.5, to be tested in wind tunnels at The Royal Aircraft Establishment at Farnborough and at the National Physical Laboratory. The results showed that the best was a low-wing monoplane configuration with wire bracing, a small frontal area, and powered by the 900 hp Napier Lion engine. This aircraft should be capable of 300 mph, a 70 mph improvement on the S.4. The Ministry's determination to win the next race was demonstrated by its decision to order three aircraft: the Supermarine S.5, the Gloster IV, a wonderfully streamlined biplane

The Gloster IV machine flown by Flight-Lieutenant S. M. Kinkead in the race for the Schneider Trophy

SUPERMARINE S.5: R.J. Mitchell and Flight Lieutenant S.N. Webster of the RAF High Speed Flight with he Supermarine team, in Venice to challenge the Italians' attempt for outright possession of the Schneider Trophy. The wire-braced S.5 was the last Supermarine racer to use the Napier Lion engine, which produced 900 hp in 1927.

also powered by the Napier engine, and the Short Crusader, which was powered by a Bristol Mercury 960 hp radial engine. In October 1926, the Air Ministry also sanctioned a well-organized military team, the RAF High Speed Flight, commanded by an Air Vice Marshal and comprising an elite group of RAF pilots dedicated to winning the Schneider Cup as a national enterprise.

Unable to secure further government support, the Americans did not enter the 1927 Schneider Cup. Mussolini continued to support the Italian team with money to develop a new aircraft, the Macchi M.52. It had slightly smaller wings compared with the M.39, making it faster, but otherwise it looked similar; the main difference was in the new Fiat engine, which used very high compression to produce 1,000 hp. The prospect

of new aircraft flown by military teams from Britain and Italy ensured the bathing beaches along the Venice Lido were packed to capacity with spectators, and they had an excellent view of the fifty-kilometre course from one end to the other, including the two virtual U-turns at either end where the strain on aircraft and pilots would be at its most demanding.

The race lived up to expectations. Three M.52s, two S.5s and the Gloster IV crossed the start line; on the first lap, one of the M.52s had a spectacular engine fire and retired; a lap later di Barnardi's also caught fire when a con rod broke. The third Italian pilot, Captain Frederico Guazetti, continued, but lost speed in the turns because when banking steeply he climbed slightly, while the British pilots, Flight Lieutenants S.N. Webster and O.E. Worsley,

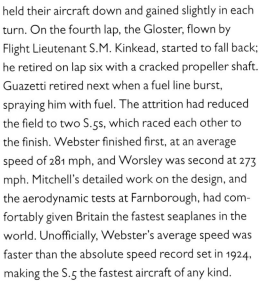

held their aircraft down and gained slightly in each turn. On the fourth lap, the Gloster, flown by Flight Lieutenant S.M. Kinkead, started to fall back; he retired on lap six with a cracked propeller shaft. Guazetti retired next when a fuel line burst, spraying him with fuel. The attrition had reduced the field to two S.5s, which raced each other to the finish. Webster finished first, at an average speed of 281 mph, and Worsley was second at 273 mph. Mitchell's detailed work on the design, and the aerodynamic tests at Farnborough, had comfortably given Britain the fastest seaplanes in the world. Unofficially, Webster's average speed was faster than the absolute speed record set in 1924, making the S.5 the fastest aircraft of any kind.

Reclaiming the Schneider Trophy was a huge national achievement for Britain, an expression of engineering excellence but also of the way that, with the right backing, relationships could be forged between committed people and institutions to a achieve a national goal. By the same token, the British victory was a huge national humiliation for Italy and for Fiat, whose engines

had simply not managed to keep going under the pressure of racing speeds. To claw back some national prestige, and recover a dividend for all the expenditure, a month after the race, di Barnardi flew an M.52 to 297 mph. In response, on 12 March 1928, the RAF High Speed Flight sent Flight Lieutenant Kinkead out in an S.5 to break the Italian record. Sadly, in a shallow dive leading to the high-speed run, he misjudged his height in fading light and hit the water at around 300 mph. He was killed instantly. Two weeks later, di Barnardi put the world record beyond any doubt with a run of 318.57 mph.

The superiority of the quirky racing floatplanes that had been developed for the Schneider Trophy was now beyond doubt. Between them, Italian and British racing aircraft were to hold the official absolute speed record until 1939. However, developing new aircraft each year for the race had become both expensive and time consuming, and in 1928, the Federation Aeronautique Internationale (FAI) agreed that the race should be held every two years rather than every year. This spurred

39

NATIONAL PRIDE: 250,000 Italians were in Venice (*left*) to support Captain Frederico Guazetti, who completed six laps in his Macchi M.52 before retiring with a broken fuel pipe.

NATIONAL TRIUMPH: Flight Lieutenant Worsley taxiing (*right*) and above a sullen Italian crowd (*overleaf*) on his way to second place behind RAF colleague Flight Lieutenant Webster.

NATIONAL DUEL: by the late 1920s, Britain and Italy were the prime contestants for the Schneider Cup. The British artist Coombe Richards captured the unique combination of nationalism, technology, and romance evoked by the shapes the races produced.

activity in the United States and France as well as Italy and Britain — such was the national prestige that went with winning the Schneider Trophy. The extra time gave everybody the opportunity to develop new technologies and apply aeronautical science more effectively, and as a result there was a flowering of new ideas and national variations on the basic design that had been pioneered in the S.5 and the M.52.

In America, just as the government and armed forces withdrew their financial support, two wealthy businessmen pledged the finance to build two wire-braced monoplanes: the Kirkham-Williams, built around a monster 24-cylinder Packard engine, which unofficially reached 322 mph, and the Williams-Mercury. The French government in turn financed two monoplanes: the Haute Vitesse 40/42, built by Bernard Ferbois, and the Nieuport-Delage ND450.

Italy's air minister, General Balbo, decided to spread state largesse even more thinly. In addition to Macchi, he brought three new contenders. The first was a low-wing monoplane developed by Fiat around its 1,000 hp engine; the second, the Piaggio-Pegna Pc.7, a pencil-shaped monoplane in which the pilot sat just in front of the tail fin, with stubby wings, and two hydrofoils instead of floats; and the even more futuristic monoplane Savoia-Marchetti S.65, in which the pilot sat between two engines, one pusher and one puller. Even Germany, whose aircraft industry was not permitted to build military aircraft under the terms of the Versailles Treaty, entered the international fray, backing a Dornier pusher/puller design — although it never flew.

The designers all realized that while refined aerodynamics were the key to racing success, the quest for speed also required ever-greater engine power. How to achieve that extra power divided designers: some, like Savoia and Dornier, incorporated two separate smaller engines; others preferred to increase the size of the engine to raise horsepower. The 1,250 hp Packard was effectively two Curtiss V-1,500s back-to-back. Ferbois used an 18-cylinder, 1,680 hp Hispano-Suiza in the H.V.42; Mario Castoldi used a heavy and complicated 1,800 hp, 18-cylinder Isotta-Franchini in the Macchi M.67.

R. J. Mitchell chose a different route to greater engine power. The Napier Lion had done sterling work, but just as the other designers were looking for a quantum leap in engine power, it was reaching the point where it could not be developed further. The idea of doubling the size of the engine did not appeal to Mitchell: he wanted to take a

Revolution: for the 1929 race, Italian designers explored revolutionary technologies to find more speed, but this occasionally led to problems. The Savoia-Marchetti S.65 (*above left*), with its forward- and backward-facing engines, had heat dissipation problems, and the hydrofoil-based Piaggio-Pegna Pc.7 (*above right*) never managed to transfer power successfully between its two propulsion systems.

Evolution (*right*): Mitchell sought new technology to increase engine power for minimum extra weight, and in doing so formed a relationship of mutual regard with one of Britain's greatest engineers, Sir Henry Royce, far right.

more scientific approach to greater speed, one that would lead to a technological solution rather than the simple application of brute force. To find it, the Assistant Director of Research and Development at the Air Ministry, Major Bulman, steered Mitchell towards Rolls-Royce's experimental division at Derby.

Rolls-Royce had built aero engines during the Great War, when its main competitor had been Napier, but since then it had concentrated on its motor car business while Napier, Bristol and Siddeley supplied most of the RAF's engine needs.

The Air Ministry had approached Rolls-Royce in 1926 to build an engine for a new, high-speed bomber, the Fairey Fox. They wanted a British engine to replace the Fox's American D-12 — which Fairey had been building under a licence from Curtiss since seeing its performance in the 1923 Schneider Trophy. The Ministry sent Rolls a D-12 engine to look at, and though little or nothing was learned from it, they improved on it to produce the Kestrel, which powered later models of the Fairey Fox.

Mitchell followed up Major Bulman's suggestion by going to see Sir Henry Royce, who was an old man in 1928. Royce immediately found a rapport with the much younger Mitchell. Both men had started life in humble circumstances and came from railway engineering backgrounds, but more importantly they shared a determination to solve problems by finding the best possible technological solution — a shared philosophy of perfection based on creative thinking, improved technology and precision engineering rather than slavish adherence to industrial efficiency or any interest in quick fixes.

Royce no longer managed the business he had founded, but he was widely respected as one of its foremost inspirational engineers. Mitchell wanted an engine with more power but as little extra weight as possible. Following their conversation, Sir Henry invited the Rolls-Royce experimental team from Derby to his seafront home at West Wittering, Sussex. They walked along the beach together while he briefed them on his ideas for a lightweight racing engine, sketching some of his thoughts in the sand with a stick and inviting anybody to change it. The result was the R (for racing) engine, and at its heart was a simple,

RARE BREED: the Rolls-Royce R engine introduced new standards of power output and reliability. Following its triumph in the Schneider races, it went on to power the fastest aircraft, boats and cars in the world, while its derivative, the Merlin, became the most successful military aircraft engine of all time.

radical step for an engine that would only be used at low altitudes: supercharging. It was the first stage in the development of an aero engine that would dominate the British engine industry during the Second World War, and the beginning of a relationship between Rolls-Royce and the Spitfire which has lasted to the present day.

Supercharging is a system for forcing air and fuel into the engine under pressure in greater volume than it could suck in on its own. It was not, in itself, new. The Kestrel had started out as a normally aspirated engine before having a supercharger added as a way of restoring power in thin air at high altitude. The R's lightweight, innovative supercharger was designed from scratch to give extra performance literally at sea level. To make it as light and narrow as possible a double-sided impeller was used to feed air into

ducting of decreasing cross section, so that the air pressure rose as its speed dropped. To add further pressure, a forward-facing air intake was added to scoop up high-speed air and feed that into the engine as well. The first R engine was ready in May 1929: it produced 1,545 hp at 2,750 rpm, but it only lasted about fifteen minutes. However, by the end of the month, the Derby team had increased the power to 1,850 hp and the engine could survive for an hour and a half on a special, high-octane fuel.

R.J. Mitchell designed a new airframe, the S.6, with bigger floats to hold the extra fuel consumed by supercharging and a longer engine compartment than the S.5, giving it an even more streamlined and modern look. The S.6 airframe and engine were finally brought together for the first time in August 1929 for testing, barely a month

THE ULTIMATE TEAM: the quest for technical excellence combined with popular enthusiasm for the Schneider Trophy created a common goal and encouraged teamwork between the RAF High Speed Flight pilots and Rolls-Royce (*above*). The subtle mind of R.J. Mitchell helped to draw together the range of talent, including the technical staff at Supermarine, to produce the S.6 (*below*).

before the race. When Squadron Leader A.H. Orlebar tried to take off for the first time, the extra power produced such strong torque that it swung the aircraft to the left, pushing the left float under the water before it could get airborne. Mitchell solved the problem by putting more fuel into the right float to compensate. Orlebar took off and reported that the aircraft handled well and only minor problems needed to be solved, a great testimony to Mitchell and his team. They had built a new aeroplane, ready to race, at close to the highest low-level speeds ever achieved by a man-made machine without a hitch after nearly two years of preparation. It could not have been done without the informal network that Mitchell had developed among the RAF High Speed Flight, Supermarine and Rolls-Royce, and the sense of

common purpose that the challenge fostered. There was certainly a strong sense of teamwork and common purpose. The night before the race, a Rolls-Royce mechanic found a flake of white metal on a spark plug he was changing. Rather than take any chances, he called together a team of his colleagues who were down from Derby for the race and having a good time at their hotel; between them, they managed a full engine change before dawn.

The 1929 Schneider Trophy was billed as The World's Fastest Air Race. A huge crowd packed the Calshot beaches, stretching from the water's edge to the roofs of waterfront houses; even the Prince of Wales came to Calshot to support the High Speed Flight. Sadly, the promise of several nations competing had disappeared:

46 RECORD BREAKER: the emphatic win of the Schneider Trophy in 1929, and the successful attempt on the world speed record, provided an image of Supermarine as masters of high-speed flight, which the company sought to translate into tangible public support.

the Americans never made it because the money ran out and the French were not ready and withdrew just before the race. The Italians, too, knew that the M.67 was not ready. One of its pilots, Motta, had been killed when his aircraft dived into Lake Garda on a test flight, having been overcome by fumes from the engine. Instead, two Macchis were at the start line. First away was Flight Lieutenant H.R.D. Waghorn in an S.6, posting lap speeds of 324 mph, 329 mph and 331 mph. Warrant Officer Dal Molin of Italy, flying a 1927 vintage Macchi M.52R — prepared in case the M.67s were not ready — was next, clocking

SUPERMARINE

WINNER OF THE 1922
INTERNATIONAL 1927
SCHNEIDER
TROPHY 1929

Supermarine Rolls-Royce "S.6"

HOLDER OF THE
WORLD'S
SPEED
RECORD
357·7 M.P.H.

DESIGNED AND CONSTRUCTED TO THE
ORDER OF THE BRITISH AIR MINISTRY BY

THE SUPERMARINE AVIATION WORKS
(VICKERS) LIMITED   PHONE: VICTORIA 6900
SOUTHAMPTON, ENGLAND.
LONDON OFFICE: VICKERS HOUSE, BROADWAY, WESTMINSTER, S.W.I.

286 mph. Third was Flight Lieutenant D'Arcy Greig in the S.5, which was a bit slower than the Macchi. The first M.67, flown by Lieutenant Remo Cadringher, quickly retired when the cockpit filled with fumes from its lethal Isotta-Franchini engine, and an engine fault also brought the hopes of Lieutenant Giovanni Monti to an end when part of the cooling system failed, spraying the inside of his cockpit with boiling water and badly scalding him. Finally, the second S.6, flown by Flying Officer Richard Atcherley, was disqualified for missing a pylon, leaving Waghorn to win at an average of 328 mph, a 43 mph margin over Dal Molin.

Once again, it had been a race of attrition: the advantage of reliable technology over sheer power had never been more vividly demonstrated. Shortly after the race Squadron Leader Orlebar set a new, but unofficial, world speed record of 357 mph in an S.6, reinforcing the Schneider Trophy's reputation as the world's fastest air race and enhancing Britain's reputation for managing the whole enterprise — proof, if it was needed, that the pursuit of speed through imagination and perfectionist engineering was the key to success. The public applause in the aftermath of the race was unprecedented. Everything seemed just right: the brave pilots, the clean lines of the S.6, the distinctive sound of the supercharged R engine, the involvement of great names like Rolls-Royce, all rolled up into the prospect that with one more victory Britain could keep the Schneider Trophy forever. As a symbol of national success in tune with the spirit of the times, and with the aircraft's appeal across social and cultural boundaries, the victory inevitably became political. The Prime Minister, Ramsay MacDonald, who had

CROWD PULLER: the British crowd that gathered at Cowes for the 1931 Schneider Trophy race was estimated at half a million people, stretching along the beaches and spilling out onto rooftops to secure the best view.

been leading a minority Labour government since the general election four months earlier, saw the political value in supporting a British success, making a sort of promise with the words: 'We're going to do our level best to win again.'

Winning was also good for business. The R engine had put Rolls-Royce back in the public eye as the supreme aero engine builder. Supermarine was no longer a small, independent company: Commander Bird had sold it to the Vickers industrial conglomerate in 1928 on the condition that Mitchell stayed under a new, highly remunerative, ten-year contract. And the victory benefited Mitchell personally; his genius was recognized by Rolls-Royce in the gift of one of their best cars. But above all it was Mitchell's reputation that had been enhanced by the victories in Venice and Calshot: he had been shown to be not just a man of high

intellect, but one with the determination to keep the ideas flowing even when disaster intervened. It was a rare gift: Mitchell made things happen, he was a winner, and while he never promoted himself as the man behind the success, those on the inside track of aviation's official and commercial networks knew exactly how important he was.

The sense of triumph was short-lived. In October 1929, barely a month after the glow of success in the Schneider Cup had warmed the nation, the Wall Street Crash brought an abrupt end to the carefree mood of the 1920s, shocking the whole world and ushering in a darker, more complex period. Ramsay MacDonald's Cabinet had been elected on a commitment to ease unemployment and increase social benefits. Instead, in the new economic climate, they had to cut budgets — which reduced industrial activity and increased unemployment,

48

THE FRUITS OF VICTORY: the winning S.6 displayed in the foyer of Vickers' head-quarters (*above*); the win was a great bonus for the engineering and armaments conglomerate, which had acquired Supermarine in 1927. A knowledgeable crowd gathered on 11 August 1931 for the first public appearance of the S.6B, to witness what most knew would be the last race of one of the marvels of the age (*opposite*).

causing bitter splits in the Labour Party. Inevitably, military spending was cut too, and the Air Ministry could no longer afford to fritter away its reduced research and development funds building one-off, exotic racing aircraft, however popular that might be with national sentiment. The cost of continuing was put at £100,000. Having welcomed the success in 1929, the government later announced that the RAF would not take part in the 1931 Schneider Trophy race. The official money that had funded the development of the S.6, and kept the contest alive, had dried up.

What had been a national enterprise became a national political debate, not just about money, but about whether it was appropriate for Britain to compete in seaplane racing against other national governments. The discussion moved to the press and then to Parliament, where Marshal of the Royal Air Force Sir Hugh Trenchard, who had recently retired from the RAF after more than a decade at its helm, protested to the Secretary of State for Air that all that could be learned about high-speed flight had been learned, and that British participation should get no further state support. On the other side, a deputation of MPs led by the Chairman of the Royal Aero Club, Sir Philip Sassoon, went to No.10 Downing Street, but failed to convince MacDonald to part with any cash. As a compro-

mise, the Prime Minister did agree that RAF pilots would be released to fly the aircraft provided private funds were used to build them. The private funds came from an unexpected, but highly political, quarter. A right-wing socialite, patriot, philanthropist, one-time suffragette and former chorus girl, Lady Lucy Houston, whose super-rich husband had died four years previously leaving her a large fortune, and who was notorious for her view that 'one Englishman was worth any three foreigners,' sent Supermarine a cheque for £100,000 in a calculated snub to MacDonald and socialism in general. Rolls-Royce funded further development of the R engine and Mitchell improved the S.6 rather than embark on a new design.

The High Speed Flight reassembled in August to carry out technical and handling trials with the S.6B, which was now christened 'the flying radiator' by those who built it because almost its entire skin was used to cool the latest, 2,350 hp, R engine. Two aircraft were lost in accidents, one of them fatal when Lieutenant G.L. Brinton, RN bounced thirty feet on take-off, failed to recover, and hit the water nose first, breaking his neck—a reminder of the demands on the pilot of flying finely tuned racers close to the limits of safety. By early September, the British team was ready, but once again, the French and the Italians were not,

50   THE FASTEST MAN AND MACHINE ON EARTH: RAF airmen launch Flight Lieutenant George Stainforth in his S.6B during preparations for an attempt on the world speed record. On 29 September 1931 he succeeded with an average speed of 407.5 mph over two four-mile runs, for which he was awarded the Air Force Cross.

52

and death struck in both teams in the last frantic weeks before race day. On 2 August, Lieutenant Giovanni Monti died when the contra rotating propellers on his giant Macchi MC.72, driven by the 24-cylider Fiat AS.6 engine, touched, sending him into the water. Then Lieutenant Bougalt crashed in the Bernard H.V.120 and was also killed. Two days before the race, a second Italian pilot, Bellini, was killed when he hit low ground on the edge of Lake Garda while making an attempt on the world speed record in an MC.72. The French and Italian aero clubs asked for a postponement of six months, but the Royal Aero Club refused and both teams withdrew.

The four deaths cast something of a shadow over the Schneider Trophy. The S.6B had no

competition, depriving the race of the excitement generated in previous years, but in an extraordinary testimony to it, and more importantly to British participation in it, an estimated half a million spectators turned up to find standing room only along miles of beaches at Cowes. In just forty-seven minutes, Flight Lieutenant John Boothman circulated the course like clockwork, completing seven laps at an average speed of 340.08 mph. The beaches erupted in spontaneous applause and the assembled yachts and warships sounded their hooters and foghorns in unison: the Schneider Cup was Britain's forever. But the day was not quite over: that afternoon, in a calculated attempt to reward the general public for their enthusiasm and support, Flight Lieutenant Stainforth established a new world speed record of 379.05 mph.

Two weeks later, while the team was still together and the aircraft still in racing trim, they came back with an R engine boosted to 2,600 hp with a specially-prepared and potent fuel cocktail to attempt the landmark of 400 mph. In what was described by one of the pilots as 'an imitation of lightning' Stainforth gave Britain the official fastest aeroplane in the world title with a run of 407 mph.

The fading note of the R engine as Stainforth throttled back and landed truly did mark the end of an era. The 1920s had been a decade of speed in aircraft development. There had been twelve Schneider races in all, with just six aircraft in each race. Britain won five, all of them in Supermarine aircraft designed by Mitchell; Italy won four; the US two; and France one. Producing the fastest aircraft in the world — aircraft whose useful life was measured in hours and which carried just one very brave and skilled pilot round in circles, was

END OF AN ERA:
a peaceful image
of the S.6B adorns
the souvenir programme
for the last Schneider
Trophy race.

CLASS OF 1931: Lady Lucy Houston entertains the winning team on her yacht *Liberty*: Flight Lieutenant George Stainforth is to her left, and Flight Lieutenant John Boothman, who won the Schneider Trophy outright for Britain, to her right. R.J. Mitchell is standing on the far right of the shot.

not what Jacques Schneider had had in mind when he had established the race. But Supermarine's achievement cannot be measured in race wins or speed alone: its contribution was to increase understanding of the problems of high-speed flight, raising it from 126 mph to over 400 mph. The strange lure of the Schneider Trophy produced a breed of aircraft that grasped the absolute world speed record in 1928 and held it for over a decade: Stainforth's record lasted until April 1934, when Warrant Officer Francesco Agnello of the Italian Air Force flew an MC.72 to 423 mph. In October he raised it again to 440 mph, and that record stood until March 1939 and the brink of war.

The Schneider Trophy's legacy was immense. Internationally, it paved the way for the huge increases in aircraft performance that were to come in the 1930s by testing new materials and developing new engines. In Britain, the achievement of winning the trophy outright had a particular effect on national morale. Part of the mystique of the S.4, S.5, S.6 and S.6B family was that they were all prototypes, built and flown by people who knew they were stepping into the unknown with each flight. The aircraft were symbolic of the age, their sleek beauty somewhere between a work of art

and a work of nature, brought together by imagination and technology. In 1931, they were a much-needed symbol of success in the middle of the worst economic crisis the world had known. The sense of occasion transcended social, cultural and political divisions, bringing people together around a potent and beautiful symbol of common purpose, and newspapers and newsreels reflected that emotional mood, basking in the aircraft and its victory as a great national achievement.

The truth was slightly more prosaic, but the triumph for the network of talent that had made it possible was unique. The loosely based but tightly knit group of professional engineers, designers, aerodynamicists, pilots, RAF officers, businessmen, fitters and mechanics, who understood each other, how to pool their resources, how to operate with no margin for error in a scientific endeavour beyond contemporary knowledge, in the context of politics, nationalism and funding crises, while maintaining their taste for victory, put down roots far deeper than winning the trophy. Shortly after their victory, that sense of purpose was rekindled when the same people turned their attention to the context of war, and the challenge that led to producing the Spitfire.

Air Power is the use of armed
force from the air in pursuit
of a military objective. More
narrowly, it has been defined
as a means of waging war
independently of armies and
navies by the offensive use of
bombers against an enemy's
national territory, industry and
population. In the 1930s, air
power had a dark and troubling
meaning; it was considered by
many a force that could not be
countered. But in the search for
just such a defence a truly great
British fighter was developed:
the Spitfire.

AIR
POWER

56 Twentieth century icon (*previous page*): a full-scale replica of the prototype Spitfire, built over half a century after the first flight, can still be seen as a static exhibit at air shows. The original prototype was written off in a crash on 4 September 1939 and the replica was airworthy until a crash in 1994.

One month after Britain won the Schneider Trophy outright, in October 1931, the Air Ministry issued an official RAF Specification for a new fighter: F7/30. It had been drawn up in 1930 and called for a single-seat fighter with a minimum top speed of 195 mph in level flight at 15,000 feet, a ceiling of 28,000 feet, armed with four .303 machine guns mounted outside the propeller disc. The Ministry then invited seven aircraft manufac-turers to submit designs to meet it: Bristol, Hawker, Westland, Blackburn, Gloster, Vickers and Supermarine.

The Specification was unusual. It challenged established RAF policies and technical theories about what was desirable in a fighter and its importance relative to the bomber. As F7/30 was being drawn up, the RAF was introducing its latest bomber, the biplane Hawker Hart powered by the Rolls-Royce Kestrel engine, the fastest RAF aircraft at the time with a top speed of 184 mph. It was faster than the fastest contemporary fighter, the 178 mph Bristol Bulldog, also a biplane. Bombers were the RAF's priority, reflecting its doctrine of the offensive use of air power, and the Hart's introduction in 1930 had been celebrated as a great British achievement in newsreels that showed formations of Harts flying towards an imaginary target above fluffy white clouds, unimpeded by fighters. The RAF's post-war fighter designs owed everything to the

RAF AIR POWER: the Hawker Hart light bomber (*opposite, left*) was the backbone of Britain's offensive air power in the early 1930s; many were adapted for an imperial policing role on British India's North-West Frontier. The Hawker Demon two-seater fighter (*opposite, right*), a derivative of the Hart, was intended as an interceptor, but lacked any real performance advantage over the bombers of the day.

RAF AIR DEFENCE: the Hawker Fury single-seat fighter (*right*) was the first to exceed 200 mph, giving it a speed advantage over contemporary bombers, but it was produced only in small numbers initially. Designed by Sydney Camm, it handled superbly, making it ideal for the close-formation flying required by the tactics of the day, and at RAF summer flying displays (*below right*).

aircraft of the Great War and were not much faster. The Hawker Fury had appeared in 1931, but only three squadrons were equipped with them initially on grounds of cost. The Fury was another biplane powered by the Kestrel engine, with a top speed of 223 mph, a little over half the speed of the S.6B. It was almost as though the revolution in aircraft design heralded by the streamlined Schneider Trophy monoplanes had gone unnoticed by the RAF in its search for new fighters and bombers. The future, it seemed, was to reflect a selective view of the past: that biplanes would last forever and the bomber would reign supreme.

Specification F7/30 challenged that view, albeit rather vaguely. It specified a minimum, but not a target or maximum speed, and it was silent on whether the fighter should be a biplane or monoplane. However, five years later, after a tortuous and bureaucratic debate, a much-

ROYAL AIR FORCE DISPLAY

HENDON. SAT. 24TH JUNE

BOXES FOR SIX £7·£5·& £4·ENCLOSURES 10'·5'·& 2'·
CARS 10'·& 5'·
TICKETS FOR ENCLOSURES AND RESERVED SEATS CAN BE
OBTAINED FROM THE DISPLAY SECRETARY R·A·F STATION
HENDON N·W·9. OR FROM THE USUAL AGENCIES
THE DISPLAY IS IN AID OF R·A·F CHARITIES

58

modified specification that had originated in F7/30 led to the first flight of the most recognizable and celebrated fighter in the world: the Supermarine Spitfire, which some RAF officers would have been happy to see strangled at birth.

The gainsayers based their theories on the bomber's ability to overfly national borders and destroy a country's homeland and industry, threatening the traditional certainties of land and sea warfare by putting air power at the centre of future wars. They believed that one day, even armies and navies would be redundant. Those in this camp included a number of high-ranking air force officers influenced by their own experience

in the Great War and by a book published in 1921 and updated in 1927 by an Italian General, Giulio Douhet: *The Command of the Air*. It argued that warfare would, in future, become a matter of targeting a nation's cities, industry and population, effectively terrorizing the enemy into submission. It gave primacy to what Douhet called the 'battle-plane', a large, armed and armoured machine capable of protecting itself against fighters, which he referred to rather disparagingly as 'auxiliary aviation'. Taken to its extreme, this argument suggested that since bombers could be used pre-emptively, first against the enemy's air forces on the ground, then against its industry and

PROPONENT OF AIR POWER: Marshal of the RAF Sir Hugh Trenchard, the so-called 'Father of the RAF', centre, built his air force on the principle that air power depended on offensive operations and would ultimately be independent of armies and navies; analysis of RAF bombing of Germany in 1918 had shown its effect on the German people had been to weaken national morale.

OPPONENTS OF AIR POWER: the Women's International League for Peace and Freedom presented a petition with six million signatures to the delegates to the first Disarmament Conference in Geneva in 1932; it was aimed particularly at the submarine and the bomber, both of which were seen as highly immoral weapons following their use against civilian targets in the Great War.

59

ultimately against its population, it followed that defensive fighters were marginal.

The RAF had been founded on that broad principle and there were politicians and senior RAF officers who believed fervently in the independent use of air power. Among them was Marshal of the Royal Air Force Sir Hugh Trenchard, the so-called 'father' of the RAF who retired in 1929 after more than a decade in the top job. To demonstrate the cost-effectiveness of independent air power, he had subdued an Islamist insurgency in British Somaliland in 1919 at a cost far below that needed to deploy troops on the ground; he had repeated the process in the later 1920s in Iraq, where the RAF took charge and tribal villages that resisted British control were bombed. In 1926, during the General Strike, in an almost obsessive concern to see air power as new and independent, he had even suggested to Winston Churchill that aircraft could be used to control strikers. Not a squeamish man, even Churchill had been horrified at that suggestion.

By the early 1930s, the idea that fleets of bombers could flatten towns and threaten annihilation of an entire nation had become part of a much wider political debate about the development of air power and the threat it posed to civilization. In January 1932, the same newsreels that had celebrated the introduction of the Hawker Hart bomber showed British protesters

delivering a petition with 2,071,000 signatures to the Foreign Office in Whitehall ahead of the World Disarmament Conference at Geneva later that year, pressing the British government to limit not only the advance of air power, but of tanks, big guns, giant warships and submarines as well. However, the Geneva Conference failed to ban or limit the size of bomber fleets, and on 10 November 1932, the day before Armistice Day, the House of Commons held a poignant debate on disarmament. Stanley Baldwin, the Conservative leader and Lord President of the Council in Ramsay MacDonald's government, made a long and moving speech on the theme that air power had changed warfare fundamentally. He clearly found the whole business deeply troubling, but the only policy he seemed to offer was a mixture of despair and procrastination, effectively leaving the following generation to find a solution. He warned that the deterrent value of bombing, far from preventing war, which some advocates of air power believed it would, could in fact provoke it because the natural instinct to protect one's own nation in the face of a real or perceived threat was so great:

I think it is well for the man in the street to realize that there is no power on Earth that can protect him from being bombed, whatever people may tell him; the bomber will always get through… the only defence is offence which means you have to kill more women and children more quickly than the enemy if you want to save yourself.

He went on to argue against disarmament and banning bombers by international agreement:

… will any form of prohibition of bombing by convention, treaty, or agreement … be effective in war? … I doubt it … the stern test of war will break down all conventions.

Baldwin's speech is best remembered for six words: 'the bomber will always get through'. This simple phrase articulated an idea that had informed many, although not all, senior RAF officers. With Trenchard's retirement in 1929, there was more debate about the future of air power within the Air Ministry. His successor, Air Chief Marshal Sir John Salmond, a former army officer who had commanded the Royal Flying Corps (RFC) on the Western Front in the Great War, while generally supportive of independent air power, was also identified with innovation, as was his Deputy, Air Chief Marshal Sir Charles Burnett. Both men wanted to at least question the almost religious faith in bombers and the biplane tradition, and it was under their regime that the tentative Specification F7/30 had been drawn up.

In the forefront of those who really challenged the orthodoxy of the previous decade was the Air Council Member for Supply and Research: Air Marshal Sir Hugh Dowding. He was another ex-soldier who had been an RFC pilot and field commander in France in the early years of the

Great War, but whom Trenchard had kept on the sidelines after 1916. Dowding did not accept theories: he believed in technological innovation, but above all he wanted evidence based on practical experiments before accepting new ideas. In the debate over money in the run up to the 1931 Schneider Cup, there had been a proposal that, should Britain win it outright, the RAF would institute a new competition to encourage the development of aircraft capable of greater speed. Dowding argued against it, preferring to use the sparse funds available to contract aircraft manu-facturers to build prototypes of innovative fighters that could be tested rather than produce another line of brutish racing aircraft that won prizes. He was a thinker, and he was forming a heretical view, namely that there was a defence against the bomber. He later encapsulated the idea as the opposite of 'fear of the bomber':

The best defence of the country is fear of the fighter. If we are strong in fighters we should probably never be attacked in force. If we are moderately strong we shall probably be attacked and the attack will probably be brought to a standstill. If we are weak in fighter strength the attacks will not be brought to a standstill, and the productive capacity of the country will be virtually destroyed.

The debate about air power was, like a set of Russian dolls, three debates, one inside the other. At the political level it was between the popularity of disarmament and the realities of an unstable, nationalistic world; within that debate was the question whether air power could be effective

ARCHITECT OF AIR DEFENCE: Air Marshal Sir Hugh Dowding (*below*) believed in practical experiment rather than theoretical dogma. His title on appointment to the Air Council was Air Member for Supply and Research, but it was changed to Air Member for Research and Development as he increasingly demonstrated his grasp of issues such as the need to replace biplane fighters with monoplanes.

61

using bombers alone, or whether fast, well-armed fighters could be an effective defence against them, and concealed in that debate was the question whether aerial warfare was distinct from land and sea warfare or an extension of them. That last debate was fundamental to the existence of the RAF: if aircraft were re-integrated into military and naval operations, as some Generals and Admirals believed they should be, rather than free to act independently, then it followed that an independent RAF was unnecessary. In arguing to preserve an independent RAF, the Air Marshals had concentrated on a doctrine based on the primacy of the bomber. To admit that fighters could be an adequate defence against the bomber would undermine their argument and hence their very existence.

However, this theory was contrary to the broad experience of the Great War and the idea of air superiority. When Europe had gone to war in 1914, many senior officers had been sceptical of the military value of aircraft in general, largely because of their limited operational capacity and fragility; the idea that aviation might one day dominate the conduct of war had been little more than the distant dream of a few visionaries. However, in the first year of the war, the value of tactical intelligence gathered by aircraft was such that both sides had scrambled to fly over the battlefield to gather information while simultaneously seeking to deny that opportunity to the enemy. By early 1915, each side's aircraft had been armed to shoot down the other's reconnaissance machines. The fighter had been born — out of necessity in the heat of battle. The next step was simple: opposing fighters began attacking each other, engaging with

A GREAT BRITISH FIGHTER: the Sopwith Camel was not an easy aircraft to fly, but it was highly manoeuvrable in a dogfight. It was also effective against the German Gotha bombers that attacked mainland Britain, demonstrating that a fighter with the right characteristics, and in the right hands, could defend cities against the bomber.

enemy fighters to control the air space over the front line. Aerial combat had been born. By 1918 the majority of aircraft produced by all combatants were fighters: machines optimized to fight for air superiority. Other aircraft, whose role was to carry out visual and photographic reconnaissance, spot for artillery, strafe and bomb enemy troops, supply lines and communications, and generally dislocate the enemy's rear areas, both physically and psychologically, did so under the protection of the fighters.

The general rules of aerial combat, or 'scientific murder' as it was described by some, were learned during the Great War by bloody experience. Foremost amongst those rules was the importance of any advantage over the enemy: surprise, shoot your opponent in the back, use decoys, come out of the sun, get close, use the best possible armament, use manoeuvre and speed differentials to catch the enemy and to escape. It had been a gruesome business: some fighter pilots had landed with their aircraft covered in a film of their opponents' blood, which had been sprayed evenly over their aircraft by the propeller. The reality of aerial combat had been nothing like the chivalrous business depicted in the imagery of the time, of heroic pilots locked in individual combat in a war where countless thousands of men had died unimaginable and anonymous deaths on the ground. Nevertheless, the fighter had become the quintessential military aircraft in the popular imagination and the fighter pilot had become a symbol of national martial prowess. Pilots' skills had even been measured in terms of the numbers of enemy they had killed: once a pilot had downed five enemy aircraft, he

was described as an 'ace'. In Germany and France, the most successful aces were accorded celebrity status, their tally of enemy shot down recorded daily in the national press, like grisly football scores. The RFC, on the other hand, had shunned the cult of the individual warrior hero and stressed the collec-tive effort of its pilots — even though its ranks produced 784 aces, more than double the German count.

Bombers had lacked the glamour of the fighter, at least early on in the war. They had developed later, in two quite distinctive roles: tactical bombing, attacking enemy positions on or near the front in support of troops on the ground, and strategic bombing, attacking the enemy's home territory. The Germans had used airships to bomb Britain in the early years of the war, but the damage had been small and the huge, hydrogen-filled airships had been very vulnerable to defensive fighters. Then, in 1916, the German army had formed a special squadron of two-engined, long-range Gotha biplane bombers to attack London. In May 1917, making use of surprise tactics and unhampered by fighters except one armed but elderly BE2c reconnaissance aircraft, the bombers had struck, killing 162 people, thirty of them school children, and injuring 432. All the Gothas had returned safely to their base. Strategic bombing had been born. The British public, outraged rather than terrorized by the raid, had demanded retaliation, and the immediate response had been to withdraw several squadrons of Britain's most advanced fighter at the time, the Sopwith Camel, from France to defend London. The generals in France had been dismayed, but the Camels had been effective, first

FIREPOWER VERSUS FLEXIBILITY: in a classic air battle towards the end of the Great War, DH9 light bombers of the RAF Independent Force heading for German targets come under attack from German fighters. Their gunners are unable to counter a concerted attack.

forcing the Gothas to bomb at night, making them less effective, and in March 1918 shooting down six out of thirty-eight in one night. Such losses were unsustainable, and the German campaign had stopped.

The longer-term British response was to retaliate. In October 1917, the government authorized an 'Independent Force' of bombers, outside the control of the generals in France, to carry out strategic raids on German industrial, communications and civilian targets. Its commander was Hugh Trenchard. Operating from bases in France, the Independent Force made a total of fifty-seven raids on German cities, mainly in the Ruhr area, using a mixture of aircraft that ranged from fighters carrying individual bombs to a specialized bomber, the Handley Page 0/100. The Germans had also withdrawn fighters from France to protect their homeland and they had proved as effective as the Camels had been

over England: on one raid against Saarbrücken on 31 July 1918 by twelve De Havilland bombers, German fighters had shot down ten—again, an unsustainable rate of attrition.

The success of the British fighters against the German bombers, and vice versa, had failed to deter the bomber enthusiasts. At the end of the war in November 1918, Britain had two new bombers nearing completion: the Handley Page 1/1500 and the Vickers Vimy, both of which had been designed with enough range to reach Berlin. The idea that independent air power had become 'the principal operation of war to which the older forms of military and naval operations may become secondary and subordinate,' as a report to the Cabinet put it, was embedded in official thinking, and embodied in the establishment of the Royal Air Force. On 1 April 1918 when all military and naval aircraft were pooled to form the RAF, the world's first independent

64

SUPERMARINE: the company's factory was on a human scale, tailor-made to produce seaplanes on the banks of the Solent. Mitchell was deeply protective of its isolation from the influence of the big company culture of the Vickers conglomerate, and insisted on preserving his tightly knit team.

air force, its first Commander in Chief was Sir Hugh Trenchard.

That same spring, a British general closely associated with the development of the tank and arguably one of the most significant military thinkers in modern warfare, Major General John F.C. Fuller, wrote a paper called 'Plan 19'. He presented a very different, evolutionary vision of the future: mechanized warfare. His idea was to breach the static trench lines using tanks and aircraft then create havoc in the enemy's rear areas by destroying reserves and supplies and disrupting headquarters and communications, destabilizing the enemy physically and psychologically. The war ended before Plan 19 could be tested, but it was developed further by Fuller and described by Captain Basil Liddell-Hart, a military historian and journalist, as what he called the 'indirect approach' in the 1930s. Unfortunately, he influenced German rather

than British military thinking and unwittingly contributed to the integrated form of warfare using tanks and aircraft which, by 1940, became known as blitzkrieg.

In Britain, the hard lessons of the first three years of the Great War, that you had to fight for control of the air just as you had to fight to hold ground or control the sea, had been all but discarded in the search for a completely new method in warfare based on the experience of the last year and a half of the war and the decade of peace that followed. Unlike the conventional criticism levelled at conservative generals, that they equip and train their armies for the last war, Trenchard, Douhet, and General William Mitchell, the US advocate of air power, were doing the reverse: equipping and training their armies for the next war on the basis of largely untried theories.

That was the complex debate that military planners were faced with in the 1930s, and RAF Specification F7/30 was part of trying to resolve it. In 1932, the climate of cautious change at the Air Ministry that had produced that specification was rewarded when all seven British companies approached responded, giving the assessors five biplane and three monoplane designs to consider. The variety of submissions reflected the continuing search for an innovative compromise between the competing criteria of manoeuvrability and speed. Any aircraft manufacturer who could combine these two parameters successfully would reap significant commercial rewards.

For Supermarine, success would mean a quantum leap in its size as a business, for despite

FALSE START: the Super-marine Type 224 outside the main hangar at Eastleigh airfield, where it had to be moved for test flights. It was an ungainly machine, with its cranked wing and faired, fixed undercarriage all designed to accommodate the cooling system for the 600 hp Rolls-Royce Goshawk engine.

being part of the Vickers conglomerate, it remained a relatively small concern, producing specialized aircraft rather than being geared up for volume. Mitchell had never designed a fighter, but the network of people, businesses and institutions behind the Schneider Cup success, which had included the Air Ministry, remained intact and had not gone unnoticed. Mitchell's proposal was based on what he knew best, and even though it meant almost re-inventing the fighter as an all-metal, cantilever monoplane, that was the route he took. He understood that there were formidable technical obstacles to over-come, but for once it seems he may have com-promised the customary boldness of his imagination with too much caution.

Rather than starting from scratch, as he had with the S.4 in 1925, or drawing in Sir Henry Royce to produce the R engine as he had in 1927, Mitchell's proposal, the Supermarine Type 224,

was built to accommodate the latest Rolls-Royce engine, the Goshawk, a derivative of the Kestrel. It was an ungainly-looking aircraft with none of the inspired elegance of the Schneider family of racers. The primary reason for that was that large parts of its basic design were determined by the need to accommodate the Goshawk's complex evaporative cooling system. A mixture of coolant and water were pumped round the engine block under pressure. The coolant had a higher boiling point than water, preventing the mixture from turning into steam in the block, but when it had been through the engine and depressurized, it boiled and formed steam, which then ran through pipes to the leading edge of the wing where it was re-condensed into water, collected in a tank and pumped up to the engine block again. The leading edges of the wings were made into a corrugated radiator to assist the condensation process — to the detriment of its aerodynamic slipperiness and ultimately to its speed; the needs of the engine were driving the design rather than the other way round.

Despite some official misgivings at the time, Mitchell's reputation as a designer, and his experience with monoplanes, helped to ensure that the Air Ministry included the Type 224 as the sole monoplane to go forward to the prototype stage, alongside two biplane proposals. There was little overt enthusiasm for it: where the Schneider racers had expressed a single, coherent vision of purpose, the Type 224 reeked of compromise: its fixed undercarriage faired in as part of the cooling system; its long, thick, cranked, cantilever wing, also part of the cooling system, probably thicker than necessary because Mitchell wanted to make sure that it would be strong enough to avoid the flutter that he believed had afflicted the S.4 and nearly killed his friend Henri Biard in 1926. The pessimism turned out to be justified: when the Type 224 made its maiden flight on 20 February 1934, the compromises made to accommodate the Goshawk proved pointless: there were persistent overheating problems with the engine but the effort to use it gave the Type 224 a poor rate of climb and its top speed in level flight was only 238 mph. The Gloster biplane design for F7/30, also powered by the Goshawk engine, had a top speed of 242 mph and a much better rate of climb, and it was clear that the evaporative cooling system was much more suited to biplanes, where the cooled water could be collected in the upper wing and fed back to the engine via gravity. The Gloster biplane design was chosen, and it would eventually become the last RAF front-line biplane fighter,

the Gladiator, seeing service during the early years of the Second World War.

Specification F7/30 had produced the next generation of biplane fighters, but it had failed to produce the innovation which its authors had hoped for. The Type 224 was a disaster for Supermarine and Mitchell, the first time they had got something very wrong. Mitchell knew it, and even before it had flown, he had returned to his own first principles and a new design began to take shape in his mind and in his soft pencil drawings: the Type 300. This aircraft was still powered by the Goshawk engine, but it was a radical departure from the Type 224: the cockpit was enclosed, the undercarriage was retractable, the wing was no longer cranked, and it was six feet shorter.

However, even while Mitchell was redeeming the disappointment of the Type 224 with the Type 300, he was coping with a personal tragedy: in the summer of 1933 he had been diagnosed with rectal cancer and had to have major surgery. He was away for the rest of 1933 while his team continued to do the detailed work on the Type 300, responding to the quiet form of leadership which Mitchell exerted and the dynamics of the small group which he had brought together to win the Schneider Cup. Lesser men would have given up work after the surgery and facing the probability that the cancer would return, but for reasons known only to him — but undoubtedly including loyalty and personal stubbornness — he was back at his drawing board in early 1934. Mitchell not only returned to work, he learnt to fly at Eastleigh and made his first solo flight in a Gypsy Moth on 1 July 1934. At the same time,

A MAN FOR ALL SEASONS:
R.J. Mitchell's integrity and disarming modesty shine through the difficulties in his life. As the Spitfire was taking shape in his mind following the failure of the Type 224, he also had to come to terms with the news that he was suffering from cancer.

he breathed new life into the Type 300, re-committed to the idea that Supermarine could build a radical new fighter for the RAF at a time when pressure was mounting on the Air Ministry planners to order new fighters.

Whether Mitchell had been inspired by that pressure, by learning to fly, or by facing the probability that he did not have long to live, it was during the summer and autumn of 1934 that the singular vision that was his hallmark returned. The Type 300, or simply 'The Fighter' as it was known at Supermarine, had taken on its final shape and character. There were two key components that defined it: the wing and the engine.

By late summer Mitchell was considering abandoning the Goshawk in favour of a new Rolls-Royce engine known at the time as the Private Venture XII, or the P.V.12. It had been initiated by Sir Henry Royce as a private venture before he died in 1933, and was designed to produce 1,000 hp from twenty-seven litres. It was not airworthy in 1934, but that hardly mattered, because its basic features were already familiar to Mitchell and his team: it was derived from the Schneider Trophy racing engine, the R.

The wing was Mitchell's masterpiece. Its elliptical plan form will always be the external defining characteristic of what became the Spitfire, making it immediately recognizable, and it remains to this day part of the aircraft's iconic image. That shape allowed the wing to taper gradually towards the tip, making it thicker at the root, where it could contain the retracted undercarriage. Further along, it was still thick enough to contain the four guns. Less visible was the wing's 'washout': the way it twisted along its length so that it would stall at the root first, letting the pilot know of the impending stall while the wing tips were still above stalling speed, and while he still had control through the ailerons. It was a characteristic straight out of air-combat experience: in a tight turn, the tighter the pilot makes it, the closer his aircraft gets to the stall (when the aircraft would suddenly fall and slow down, making it highly vulnerable to attack).

Completely invisible, inside the wing, was the true engineering breakthrough that gave the wing its strength, the complex main spar that took all the wing loads. The spar was made up of a pair of booms, each constructed out of five different

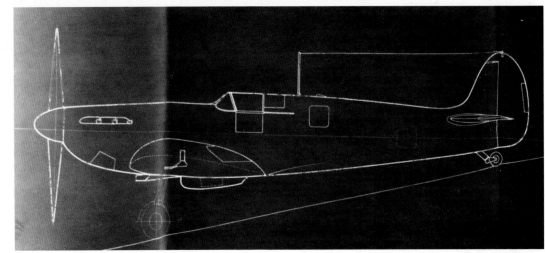

PROFOUNDLY SIMPLE: early drawings of the Spitfire show the leap of imagination R. J. Mitchell made from the Type 224 to the Spitfire. The defining elliptical wings (*left*), the slim fuselage with its disappearing wheels (*above*) and the streamlined profile (*right*), could only be the product of a single, inspired and gifted mind.

sized tubes that fitted inside each other, and held together by a spar web which, with the skin that formed the leading edge of the wing, formed a D-shaped box of great strength and lightness that also had the space inside to double up to act as a radiator.

While Mitchell was refining the design in the second half of 1934, the pace of events in Whitehall increased and a new urgency permeated the Ministry's relationship with Supermarine. In August, Air Commodore Cave-Brown-Cave, the RAF's Director of Technical Development, went to Southampton to see Mitchell and check on progress. He was pleased with what he saw, and wrote to Dowding the next day suggesting the Air Ministry purchase a prototype of the Type 300. Within a month, Supermarine had been

asked to quote for building a prototype. In early November, Sir Robert McLean, the Managing Director of Vickers, authorized commitment to detailed design work on the Type 300 as a private venture based on Mitchell's new ideas. On 8 November, Dowding visited Mitchell, and the next day authorized a contract for £10,000 to build a prototype. Dowding did not specify an engine because he wanted to give Mitchell and his creative team its head. Mitchell was already convinced that the P.V.12 was the answer and when Rolls-Royce added a further £7,500 towards Supermarine's development costs, the team dynamics that had produced the Schneider victory re-emerged. A month later, there was a design conference between Supermarine and the RAF that agreed on the details of the Type 300 design and at which all agreed to use the P.V.12 engine.

The new speed of decision making reflected a new urgency to modernize the RAF, which in turn reflected political events far away in Berlin. In January 1933, Adolf Hitler had promised to overthrow the constraints of the Versailles Treaty which prevented Germany, amongst other things, from having an air force; when he and his National Socialist Party were elected later that year, Britain was forced to think more urgently about re-armament, about the RAF's priorities and even about its organization. In November 1933, just two weeks after Hitler had been elected Chan-cellor of Germany, the politics of rearmament were reignited in Britain with the announcement that the RAF would be increased in size. At the time, the RAF was about half the size of the French *Armée de l'Air,* and while theoretically there was no German air force, a former RFC pilot, Frederick Winterbotham, who started working for MI6 in 1929, had established through agents in Germany that there was a secret programme to train pilots and build aircraft which on the face of it were civil airliners, but which in fact could easily be converted into bombers and fighters.

In July 1934, the Cabinet had agreed on the expansion of the RAF Metropolitan Force with an emphasis on building 1,250 fighters, a decision that acknowledged the possibility of a viable defence against the bomber. It was a policy based on important political support from the Chancellor of the Exchequer, Neville Chamberlain, but it was not a policy that had universal support: Lord Londonderry, the Secretary of State for Air, and Sir Edward Ellington, the RAF Chief of the

Air Staff, were both indecisive and ineffective and they vacillated. Ellington believed that the single-seater fighter with fixed guns was obsol-escent and favoured a two-seater fighter with a rearward-facing turret as a bomber destroyer based on the expectation that bombers would not be escorted by fighters. It was Sir Hugh Dowding who provided the far-sighted leadership needed on the Air Council: he would not accept compromise and continued to argue for the most advanced fighters possible, based on proven technological solutions. He believed that a defensive screen based on fast, manoeuvrable fighters could counter the threat of the bomber, and he worked with quiet determination, pushing for single-seat fighters to be given priority. In an age in which rank and formality was more impor-tant than it is today, Dowding was able to fit into the informal network of relationships around the Spitfire, and he steadily became a pivotal figure within it, although he retained his rather aloof, even distant, manner.

That network of dogged perfectionists had changed with the death of Sir Henry Royce in 1933. However, his successor, Ernest Hives, took over the development of the P.V.12 and would see it become the Merlin, the most successful piston aero engine of all time. The decision to move to the P.V.12, and the contract from the Air Ministry to produce a prototype of the Type 300 meant the Spitfire was in business. But it was not alone. Dowding had hedged his bets, and while he had been pressing Supermarine he had also been courting Hawker and Sir Sydney Camm, its chief designer, since 1925. Camm was the complete opposite of Mitchell: he had been the architect of

a long line of biplane fighters and bombers such as the Fury and the Hart, but he worked in an industrial rather than artisanal system, designing aircraft that could be produced on a large scale and at a competitive price. As Hawker's contender for a new fighter he came up with a monoplane version of the Fury known as 'The Interceptor'. Camm had played to Hawker's strength by designing an aircraft that was not only a development of one that had gone before, but also one that could be produced in quantity and quickly.

At the end of 1934, Dowding therefore had two designs for a modern, monoplane, single-seat fighter on his desk: Supermarine's Type 300 and Hawker's 'Interceptor' monoplane. In early 1935, Camm presented a mock-up to the Air Ministry experts and followed it up with performance estimates of 330 mph using the Rolls-Royce P.V.12 engine, well above expectations. The Type 300 was built around the same engine but other than

that, it came from a completely different stable: Supermarine had no history of fighter production; Mitchell had designed the Type 300 as an exercise in perfection, finding the best design before considering cost; it was fashioned from the best engineering solutions rather than for industrial expediency. That approach put the Type 300 out on its own, but also made it vulnerable to the cost-conscious Air Ministry, where some experts saw the extra expense as having no purpose. It took 13,800 man hours to build the Type 300, compared with 5,000 for the Interceptor. Much of the extra effort and cost went into building the Type 300's thin, elliptical wing—not just its defining component, but the root of its success as a fighter, and the feature that would endear it to fighter pilots.

The momentum created by Dowding culminated in January 1935 in a complete reversal of the normal bureaucratic process: the RAF issued two new Specifications, F37/34 and F36/34, the first to meet the characteristics of the Type 300, which became the Spitfire, the second to meet the characteristics of the Interceptor, which became the Hurricane; the Specifications had been determined by the characteristics of the air-craft rather than the other way round.

The decisions to move ahead with the two monoplane fighters came just before political announcements in Berlin put them in context. In March 1935, Hitler renounced the Versailles Treaty and announced a huge rearmament programme on the basis that Germany needed

parity with Britain. As part of that rearmament, he declared openly what Britain had known secretly for some time, that Germany had an air force, the *Luftwaffe*, built in secret. The *Luftwaffe's* Commander in Chief was Hermann Goering, a Great War fighter pilot who had commanded the celebrated Richthofen Flying Circus in the last months of that war. Since 1933, he had been ordering dual-purpose aircraft: the first Heinkel 111s were built as airliners, although they were monoplanes capable of 224 mph, about the same speed as Britain's fastest fighters; the Dornier 17, another monoplane, was built to carry mail and six people at 214 mph when it was introduced as an airliner in 1934, and even the Bf 109 fighter, which made its first flight in October 1935, using a Rolls-Royce Kestrel engine, incorporated many design features of Messer-schmitt's earlier four-seater, monoplane touring aircraft, the Bf 108 Taifun, which had a maximum speed of 188 mph.

The *Luftwaffe* was a tactical rather than a strategic air force, intended to work with armour and troops on the ground rather than be deployed as a bomber force against an enemy nation's industry and population. More import-antly, it was designed from the outset as a political weapon as well as a war-making weapon; Dornier and Heinkel both had designs for long-range, fast, strategic bombers, but Hitler wanted large numbers of aircraft to intimidate his enemies and get what he wanted without having to fight for it. When he announced the *Luftwaffe's* existence, he proclaimed that it already had parity with the RAF, and when Goering announced more details to the press at his headquarters in Berlin, some

Messerschmitt bf 108 Taifun (*top*): designed by Willi Messerschmitt, the Bf 108 was a four-seat civilian monoplane with advanced characteristics such as all-metal stressed skin, low wing, enclosed cockpit and retractable undercarriage; it flew for the first time in early 1934 and its performance influenced Messerschmitt's next design, the Bf 109 fighter (*bottom*).

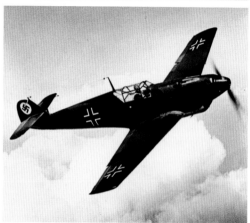

Aviation Militaire du Reich

GERMAN AIR POWER: the *Luftwaffe* had been developed in secret for many years before Hitler presented it to the world in March 1935; he used it as a propaganda tool, to intimidate other European nations, but in Britain particularly the reaction was to redouble efforts to get the Hurricane and Spitfire into service as quickly as possible.

four hundred aircraft flew overhead, some of them several times. Politically, the German policy of overstating its capability as a way of intimidating potential enemies backfired, working in favour of those who advocated rearmament. In Britain it also had a direct effect on the development of the two monoplane fighters: a month after Hitler's announcement, in April 1935, the RAF issued Specification 10/35, which called for a fighter with 'a speed 40 mph in excess of the contemporary bomber at 15,000 feet' — which in practical terms meant around 310 mph; the same specification demanded increased hitting power from six or eight .303 machine guns with 300 rounds of ammunition each. The thinking behind the increase in firepower was that speeds had increased so much that there would only be time for one attack, so the ability of a single-seat fighter to deliver a lethal dose of fire in a two-second burst would be crucial. In fact it was also a statement of faith in the ability of fighters to tackle high-speed bombers, challenging the

school of thought that put its faith in the primacy of the bomber.

In late April 1935, Squadron Leader Ralph Sorley, who looked after the RAF operational requirements, visited both Supermarine and Hawker to inspect mock-ups of the two mono-plane fighters and discussed building them to the new 10/35 Specification; both agreed it could be done. On his return to Whitehall, Sorley recom-mended that both fighters should be ordered at that point and that it would be worth the Air Ministry meeting the cost of preparing the jigs and tooling for both, to save time when it came to re-equipping fighter squadrons. Dowding responded that he wanted to wait until they had flown.

In June, four decisions were taken that would determine the fighters the RAF would have in the Second World War, bringing the indecision of the previous five years to a conclusion, albeit one based on compromise: the Gladiator, the RAF's last biplane fighter, which had flown as a proto-type on 12 September 1934, was ordered into

74

STOP GAP: in June 1935, the Gloster Gladiator (*below*) became the RAF's last biplane fighter, adopted to meet the Specification F7/30; it had flown in 1934, but it was 1937 before they reached RAF fighter squadrons, replacing Furies and Bulldogs until the mono-planes became operational.

YEAR OF REVOLUTION (*opposite*): 1935 was the year of the cantilever mono-plane fighter. The Soviet Union's Polikarpov Il-16 (*top right*) entered service that year; the US' Seversky P-35 (*centre right*), Japan's Mitsubishi A5M (*bottom right*) and Germany's Messerschmitt Bf 109

(*bottom centre*) all flew in 1935 and entered service in 1937; the Morane-Saulnier MS 405 (*top left*) also flew in 1935 but did not enter service until 1939, and Italy's Macchi C200 Saetta (*bottom left*), designed by Mario Castoldi of Schneider fame, flew in 1937 and entered service in 1939.

production, finally meeting Specification F7/30; Boulton Paul were contracted to start work on a prototype of the Defiant, powered by the P.V.12, to meet Specification F9/35 and Ellington's wish for a two-seater monoplane fighter with a rear-facing gun turret; Hawker was contracted to produce a prototype Hurricane to Specification 10/35, and Supermarine was contracted to do the same with the Type 300. The Spitfire, as some people were already calling Britain's most advanced fighter, was step closer to reality.

None of the monoplane fighters had flown and the evidence of British backwardness in thinking was on show when King George V reviewed the RAF on 6 July 1935: it had thirty-seven squadrons and a total of 356 operational aircraft of all kinds, all of them biplanes, the fastest being the Hawker Fury and the Gloster Gauntlet fighters. It was the last time the public face of the RAF would be all biplane: in private, the speed of the monoplane had been acknowledged and in addition to the two fighters, a prototype of the RAF's first monoplane bomber, the Wellington, designed by Barnes Wallis, was under construction to Specifi-cation B9/32 by Supermarine's sister company, Vickers Armstrongs (Aircraft). On paper it had a top speed over 230 mph, but like the Hurricane and Spitfire it still had not flown. The monoplane air force was developing behind the scenes, but the new fighters were still seen mainly as bomber destroyers, not as a means of fighting for air superiority in aerial combat; one argument was that fighter pilots would only be able to keep the enemy in his sights for such a short time that the whole idea of aerial combat was obsolete, precisely because of the fighter's speed.

MORANE-SAULNIER

The need for a fast monoplane fighter, made of metal, with an enclosed cockpit and retractable undercarriage, had been recognized internationally. By 1935 all the major powers' air forces would have flying prototypes. Russia had been first, with the Poliarkov Il-16, which was in squadron service but had a top speed of only 224 mph; in August 1935 the United States was evaluating the Seversky P-35, which had a top speed of 281 mph, and in the same month the French Morane MS 405 made its maiden flight with a top speed of 298 mph. In September the Messerschmitt Bf 109 made its maiden flight with an initial top speed of 292 mph. By comparison, the Gloster Gladiator, Britain's biplane fighter which had just

been put into production, lagged behind with a top speed of 257 mph.

All these fighters remained much slower than pure racers and the fastest aircraft in the world was still a relic of the Schneider Trophy races, the MC.72. Warrant Officer Francesco Agnello used this aircraft to set a new absolute record of 440.6 mph over Lake Garda on 24 October 1934. On 13 September 1935, Howard Hughes then raised the record for a landplane to 352.39 mph in his all-metal H-2 racer, which had an enclosed cockpit and a retractable undercarriage; Hughes had offered the design to the US as the basis of a fighter, but was turned down. To put these aircraft records in perspective, ten days before Hughes

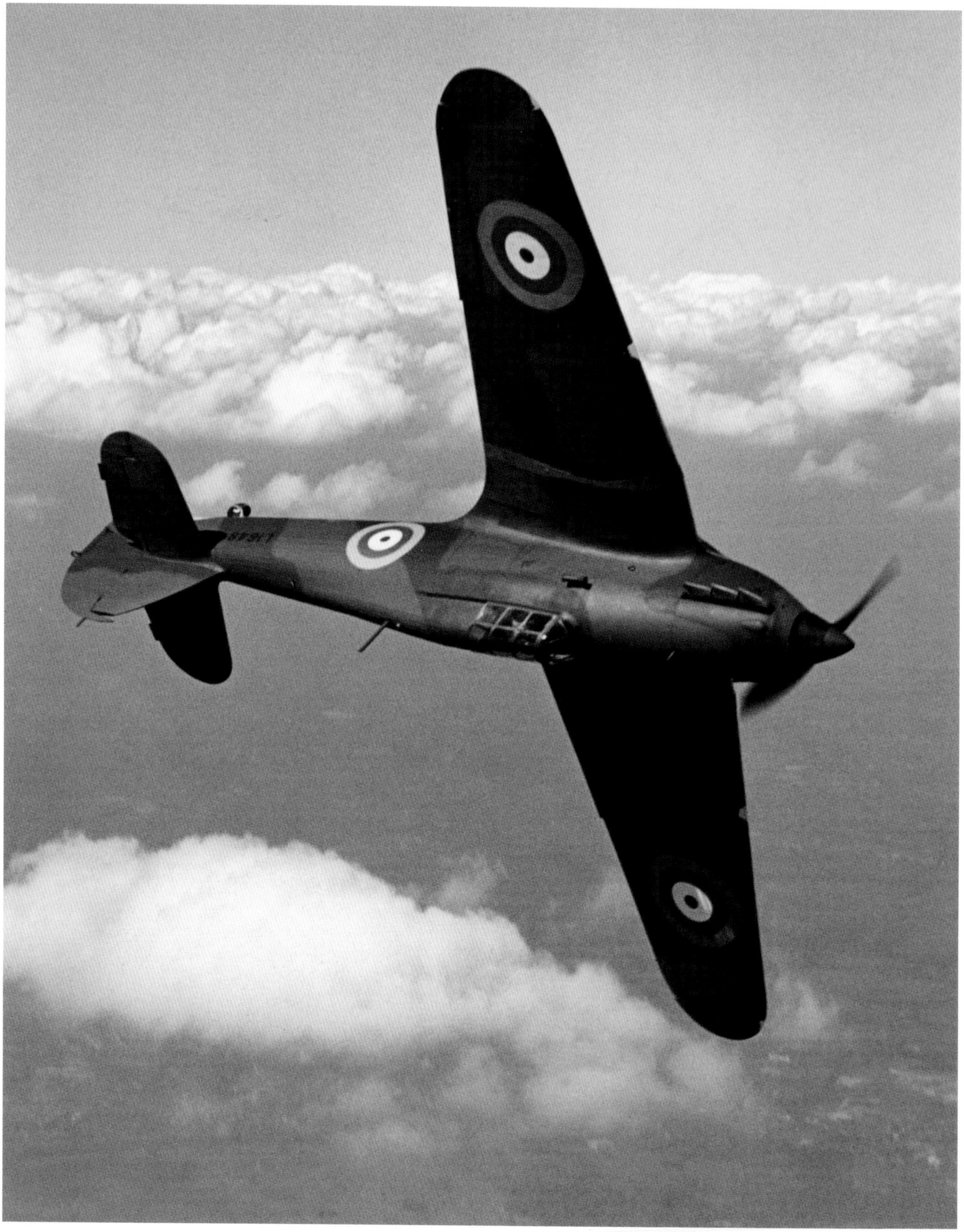

HAWKER HURRICANE: the RAF's first monoplane fighter. Early models had a two-blade propeller and fabric-covered wings. The propeller was soon replaced by a three bladed, constant-speed version, though later models retained a fabric-covered rear fuselage; pilots found its aerobatic qualities superb.

set his record, on 3 September 1935, Donald Campbell had set a new land speed record of 301.92 mph in a beautiful, streamlined car called the Bluebird, which was, somewhat ironically, powered by two Rolls-Royce R engines.

On 6 November 1935 the Hurricane became the first aircraft to fly with the Merlin engine, achieving 322 mph, very close to predictions and faster than any other country's fighters at the time. At least in prototype form, the RAF was moving towards the forefront in the international competition. However, while it was faster than the Bluebird, the Hurricane was still slower than Howard Hughes' H-2 racer.

The pace of change in decision making to re-equip the RAF with monoplanes had run in parallel with the pace of political change in Britain. On 7 June 1935 Stanley Baldwin had replaced Ramsay MacDonald as Prime Minister in what continued to be nominally a National government, but was in fact a Conservative government which openly supported rearmament. The Labour Party was split between pacifism and rearmament. Hitler's announcements had made preparation for war a higher political priority and providing a shield against the *Luftwaffe* had become paramount: the political reality was that the electorate either believed or wanted to believe that there was a defence against the bomber. In the Cabinet reshuffle that followed Baldwin becoming Prime Minister, Lord Londonderry was replaced as Secretary of State for Air by an energetic Conservative, Sir Philip Cunliffe-Lister, who became Viscount Swinton on taking up the job. He instituted regular meetings and appointed William Weir, an engineer by training who had

been responsible for increasing the output of aircraft during the Great War, to get behind progress. At the first meeting, on 30 July, Dowding revealed that the latest German bombers were capable of 270 mph, against which the Gloster Gladiator would clearly be inadequate. Swinton saw the importance of the Spitfire, but with the numbers of fighters being contemplated, he also encouraged faster development and mass production of the Merlin engine.

The Spitfire was behind schedule largely because it was complicated to build and because the company had less experience and fewer resources than Hawker. At a progress meeting on 6 February 1936, Dowding reported to Swinton that the Spitfire's first flight would be on 20 February, but when that time came, it was not ready. On 25 February, he told Swinton that the maiden flight was 'imminent', and in the first week of March, the focus finally did move from the corridors of Whitehall to the grass of Eastleigh airfield near Southampton, where the prototype Spitfire had been moved. There were no guns fitted, the undercarriage had its doors removed and been locked down and would not be retracted on the first flight, just in case of malfunction; it was fitted with a two-blade propeller to give the best performance at the lower end of the speed range during take-off and landing; it was unpainted and its bare metal finish shone except where RAF roundels had been painted on the wings and fuselage and where its number was stencilled: K5054.

On 5 March, at 4.35 pm, Vickers chief test pilot, Captain J. 'Mutt' Summers, climbed into the cockpit and, watched by Mitchell, Jeffrey Quill, Supermarine's own test pilot who had recently

78

A STAR IS BORN: on 5 March 1936, 'Mutt' Summers, Major 'Agony' Paine, R.J. Mitchell, S. Scott-Hall and Jeffrey Quill pose for an informal photograph (*above*) to mark the first flight of the prototype Spitfire, K5054 (*below*).

left the RAF, a crowd of Supermarine staff and a group of people from the Air Ministry in London, he taxied across the grass in a series of gentle left and right turns to check how it handled on the ground, finishing up on the far side of the airfield from the hangar. He turned the first Spitfire into the wind, opened the throttle almost immediately and was airborne after a short run. He flew away from the airfield high enough to check the

precise stalling speed so he could land at the right speed, and after some medium turns to get used to the handling, put the flaps down and came in to land neatly before taxiing towards the waiting crowd. That first test flight was a momentous occasion, but one carried out without fuss or overstatement.

'I don't want anything touched,' Summers said before climbing out, a comment that has subsequently been interpreted to mean that he believed the Spitfire was perfect. The truth is rather more mundane: he had not found any major problems and wanted the aircraft to have exactly the same configuration when he flew it the next time so there were would be no surprises. That the comment has passed into the myth of the perfection of the Spitfire is not surprising: there was genuine excitement, even among the professional airmen who had contributed to the Spitfire. They wanted to avoid any untoward displays of emotion or over-enthusiasm about what had been achieved, but excitement was what they felt, and it was impossible to hide it as news of the first flight was reported back to Dowding, to Swinton,

and more widely through the Air Ministry.

The excitement was not misplaced. Summers made the second flight on 10 March, during which he retracted the undercarriage in the air and put it down for landing. Dowding visited Eastleigh himself on 15 March, and reported to Swinton on 17 March that it was flying 'remarkably well' and though its speed was only 335 mph, not much more than the Hurricane's, Supermarine expected it to rise to 350–360 mph. It main drawback was that the long nose housing the Merlin made forward-vision on the ground difficult.

On 24 March, Summers handed the prototype over to the Supermarine test pilots George Pickering and Jeffrey Quill for further testing; he reported very favourably to them on the handling, particularly stressing the effectiveness of all the controls, especially the lightness of the ailerons. Between them Pickering and Quill tried various improvements, including a new, coarser-pitch propeller to increase maximum speed, with which Pickering managed to reach around 350 mph in a dive. With improvements to the rudder, cowlings and fairings and particularly to the slipperiness of its surface that came from applying a compound used by Rolls-Royce in the finish of their cars, then painting it light blue with a paint that gave it an ultra-smooth finish, and with another new propeller which had thinner tips, it reached 348 in level flight and 380 in a dive, prompting Quill to observe: 'I think we've got something special here'.

That spring, the name 'Spitfire' was firmly established, even though R. J. Mitchell had initially described it as 'bloody silly'. Once it was flying and the few glitches had been ironed out, the pressure on Mitchell was reduced. To those who knew him, he was clearly unwell and looked older than his forty-one years, but he took a huge interest in the test flying, watching from his car at

80 PUBLIC DISPLAY: photographers cluster around the point of touchdown, competing to get the most dramatic shot of the prototype, still in its blue livery, after a brief public flight at Eastleigh airfield in June 1936 (*below*). The prototype was also flown for *Flight* magazine photographers (*right*) before being handed over to the RAF.

the edge of the airfield, and talking to the test pilots in what must have been a rich but sad period in his life. As the Supermarine testing drew to a close in May, 'Mutt' Summers came one day and flew the prototype to RAF Martlesham Heath for acceptance trials by RAF test pilots; Mitchell the perfectionist was still concerned that the Spitfire did not have enough of a speed advantage over the Hurricane to justify the difference in the cost and the time taken to build it.

He need not have worried. Once again, the Spitfire's growing reputation excited enthusiasm. At Martlesham, there was a huge crowd of RAF people waiting to greet it — and these were people who were used to seeing new aircraft arrive at regular intervals. Its status as something special was enhanced because, unlike other prototypes, it was getting special treatment: it was to be flown by an RAF test pilot the same day it arrived, Flight Lieutenant Humphrey Edwardes-Jones.

82 ᴿoʏᴀʟ ᴄᴏᴍᴍᴀɴᴅ: the King inspects the prototype at RAF Martlesham Heath during his Review of the RAF that year (*below*). K5054 was later re-painted in the RAF's new camouflage scheme, and remained a favourite of photographers as it began to acquire its iconic status (*opposite*).

When Edwardes-Jones took off that evening people left their work places to watch, including secretaries, cooks and aircraftsmen. He made a short flight, and was impressed by the handling, having landed safely after nearly forgetting to lower the wheels. The Air Ministry wanted a brief report immediately and had instructed Edwardes-Jones to call a particular number once he had flown the Spitfire. He made the call, and found himself talking to Sir Wilfrid Freeman, an influential member of the Air Council and a Spitfire enthusiast who simply wanted to know if it was a fighter which the RAF's average squadron fighter pilot would be able to handle — to which the RAF's first pilot to fly the Spitfire said yes. It was a crucial endorsement by a service pilot who had not expected to be asked for such a swift and unorthodox report, but largely on the strength of it, a few days later, on 3 June 1936,

the Air Ministry placed an order for 310 Spitfires to the value of £1.25m, a triumph for Mitchell and his network of quiet, loyal, determined and knowledgeable supporters.

By 1936 the political debate over airpower had swung decisively in favour of having an effective defensive fighter force, a change represented by the first flights of the Hurricane and the Spitfire. There was no certainty that the new policy was right, but the two aircraft did articulate a sense of hope that there was an answer to the bomber, and that they were at least capable of challenging the idea that 'the bomber will always get through'.

The Spitfire, as the latest and most advanced symbol of that hope, gave people a belief, a faith almost, that they were not helpless in the face of a tyrant with a fleet of bombers. Excalibur had been forged.

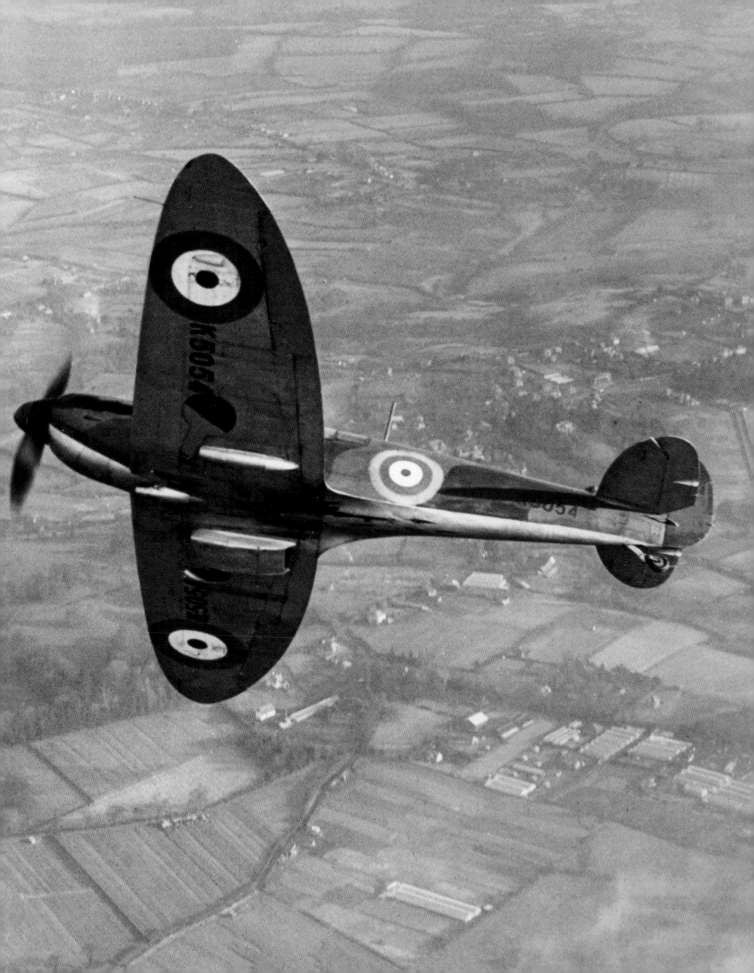

SCIENCE
AND ART

3

The late 1930s were years of scientific progress and artistic flair, characterized by the streamlined aesthetics of Art Deco. This was a prosperous time, but one in which affluent appearances were grounded by the hard reality of preparations for war: a paradoxical world that perfectly matched the beauty and menace of the Spitfire.

86

STREAMLINE MODERNE (*previous page*): the development of Art Deco in the 1930s, led by the look of racing aircraft, had a huge impact on the art and design of the period. Eric Broadbent's 'Speed Wings Over The World' heralded a new scientific age from its eyrie above the entrance to Imperial Airways Main Terminal, built in 1938 in London's Strand.

STREAMLINED DEFENCE (*opposite*): an RAF publicity photograph of the first operational Spitfire, K9787, shown patrolling the British coastline at a time of growing international tension. Its first flight, on 14 May 1938, was in dark camouflage with new roundels incorporating an additional yellow outer circle to contrast with its war paint.

THE DETAILS of the Spitfire's performance and how it had been achieved were understandably secret. However, the fact that it existed was not, and soon after its first flight, it started to develop a public, as well as a secret, profile. That dual life, half in the shadows, half in the limelight, remained a feature of its life for the next twenty years. The test flights were not announced publicly at the time, though people who lived near the Eastleigh airfield had seen it flying several times, and on 25 March 1936 they were able to read about it in the *Southampton Evening Echo*:

New Supermarine Fighter … Hush Hush Trials … Produced in great secrecy, the plane is one of the fastest of its category in the world. Like all Super-marine aircraft, the new fighter was designed by Mr R. J. Mitchell, CBE, director and chief designer of the firm who designed every British winner of the Schneider Trophy since the war. Even the uninitiated have realized when watching the streamlined monoplane flash across the sky at five miles a minute (300 mph) and more, that here is a plane out of the ordinary.

The 'streamlined monoplane' still had no official name. However, fresh from its acceptance trials at RAF Martlesham Heath, on 22 June, when a film crew from the Pathe Gazette newsreel went to Eastleigh airfield to cover its first truly public appearance, it was officially named the Spitfire. The Pathe film was seen by millions of cinema-goers that week, the opening billing announcing it as a 'vivid demonstration of Britain's latest aircraft'; for the occasion, the sonorous, authoritative tone of the commentator was almost excited:

These are some of the first pictures ever to be taken of some of Britain's new, hush-hush fighting machines, machines that set a standard that is far ahead of any of the world's aircraft. For the man in the street perhaps the most amazing machine is the Spitfire, a land version of the famous seaplanes that won the Schneider Trophy. It's the fastest single-seater fighter in the world, and although … we're not allowed to give the exact figure, we may say that it flies at something between 300 and 400 miles an hour — while it's ticking over our news plane can keep up with it, but when the pilot opens up things begin to happen …

It was a historic day, the start of a long love-affair between the Spitfire and the British press and public. There were two prototypes at Eastleigh that day: the Spitfire, which looked tiny, almost vulnerable, alongside Britain's first monoplane bomber, the rather bulbous, twin-engined monster that 'Mutt' Summers had flown down from the Vickers factory at Weybridge that morning, what the commentator could only describe as 'Vickers' long-range bomber', which had only flown for the first time that week and was later named the Wellington. The two aircraft looked very different, and had very different functions, representing the two sides of the air-power debate, but they also had things in common: they looked futuristic, shorn of all bracing wires, were fast, represented the transition from one era in aviation to another; two new monoplane species that had evolved out of a biplane-dominated past, both were the products of new technologies based on the most recent developments in aeronautical science. The Wellington was designed by Barnes Wallis, R. J. Mitchell's great competitor at the parent company, Vickers, using what he called a geodesic system of construction to make it light enough to carry a heavy bomb load, a honeycomb that was just visible through its fabric skin.

STREAMLINED AIR POWER: a Spitfire contemporary, the prototype Wellington medium bomber's geodesic construction, a latticework covered in fabric, made it light, strong and able to take huge punishment. It also entered service in 1938 but unlike the Spitfire was obsolete by 1943 as bombers increased in size.

TIME FOR CHANGE: the Hendon Air Pageant in June 1936 was among the last in which the biplane dominated the display. So swiftly did aeronautical science and technology advance during the war that by the time the pageants returned the stars of the show were jet fighters.

The all-metal Spitfire, with its uncluttered lines and modern appearance, its Rolls-Royce engine and shiny light blue paintwork, looked tame and beautiful until its mighty Merlin engine was started and the whining, throaty roar reminded any onlooker that this compact and perfectly formed aircraft was in all likelihood the fastest in the world. Unfortunately, when Jeffrey Quill started K5054 for a demonstration flight, the display had to be cut short because of an oil-pressure problem, and he had to nurse the engine round for just one circuit rather than open the throttle up for the crowd. But it still looked magnificent on film.

The Spitfire started its public life in the context of Britain's success in the Schneider Trophy five years earlier, a convenient reference point that immediately attracted the attention of the news-reel producers and the popular mass media as well as the specialized aviation press. A week after its Eastleigh debut, on 27 June, the Spitfire and its long-range bomber stable-mate made their first official appearance at the RAF Air Display at Hendon. Once again, virtually every aircraft on the airfield was a biplane, and the crowd was treated, as it was every year, to aerobatic displays by formations of biplane fighters performing low-level aerobatics while tied together with white

90

THE PACE OF CHANGE: the cockpit of a high-altitude Mk VIIc Spitfire (*opposite*). In addition to the standard flying instruments and those needed to monitor fuel, oil, electrics, oxygen, armaments, engine performance and navigation, it incorporated ducted air to pressurize the cockpit, and a clear-view panel, left, to open in case of sudden condensation.

ribbons. The antiquated fleet of front-line fighters and bombers on display only emphasized the clean, modern lines of the monoplane Spitfire, and the Hendon crowd was both thrilled and informed by the sweet roar of its engine, its small, elegant form and its sheer speed, the fruit of years of technical development that showed that the revolution in aircraft design of the previous decade had produced results. In sight and sound, the Spitfire symbolized progress. When King Edward VIII visited Martlesham Heath for the RAF Review in July 1936, he was shown the Spitfire prototype, and photographs of him peering knowledgably into the cockpit, a new and at the time modern king with a sleek, new monoplane, circulated widely, representing a big change since his late father had inspected the biplanes the previous year.

Science had also changed warfare, provoking a worldwide debate not only on the potential horrors of air power and the strategic bombing of civilians, but on the sheer cost of navies bristling with giant battleships, and armies with fleets of mechanized guns and tanks. There were doubts about the morality of poison gas and of war itself, and widespread discussions about treaties to control the spread of arms, and about disarmament and rearmament.

The Spitfire was in tune with the times, militarily and culturally. The late 1930s radiated a tremendous sense of change, of looking for new ways of seeing, understanding and doing things, and of ordering the world. It was a change based on science. As western societies came to terms with the impact of the twin catastrophes of the Great War and the Depression they saw the

potential to change the world for good or ill depending on how the legacies of Marie Curie, Ernest Rutherford, Albert Einstein and Sigmund Freud were used. Following the discovery of the neutron, helium, penicillin, and the development of the Big Bang theory, the future was an open book. In literature, the prospect of what Aldous Huxley described in *Brave New World,* published in 1932, of a scientific, consumer and permissive society, shocked his readers, while in *The Shape of Things to Come,* published in 1933, H.G. Wells speculated on the political and social systems of the future, including the idea of an end to war. New political ideas were not just to be found in books: social theories based on scientific systems were already underway under communism in Russia and National Socialism in Germany. There were new economic theories too: Keynesianism, a model for government spending to rescue capitalism; and President Roosevelt's New Deal to give Americans jobs following his election in 1933.

Just as the Spitfire was the result of the practical application of science for the purposes of war, so inventive minds found ways to exploit science in new ways to feed, heal, employ, equip and entertain people. Every year there were new things to buy and use, from frozen peas and instant coffee to sun-tan oil and nylon stockings, from X-Rays and Xerox machines to public opinion polls and electric hearing aids. The 1930s saw the beginning of the consumer society, a society attracted to the new, the utilitarian and the frivolous. It was a decade of communication, with a boom in households owning telephones, radios and the first televisions. But above all it

92 SCIENCE AND DESIGN: born in the same era as the Spitfire, American civil aircraft adopted the same science and technology of streamlining. Aircraft such as the Douglas DC-3 (*below*) and Lockheed Electra (*opposite*) changed the look and feel of air travel; seventy years and many scientific advances later, their basic shape and clean lines still define what an airliner should look like.

was the decade of the moving picture, of Hollywood, Pinewood Studios and 35mm Technicolor movies. Hollywood had suffered like all businesses in the Depression, but in 1933 RKO released *King Kong*, a box-office bonanza that rekindled its fortunes. Its producer, Merian C. Cooper, had been a Great War pilot, and he created some of the most memorable scenes in the history of the cinema as US Army biplane fighters attack Kong as he climbs one of the other wonders of the age, the Empire State Building, a symbol of the recovery of capitalism following the Wall Street Crash. Hollywood catered for the dreams of a changing society and its influence grew steadily in the 1930s, a giant engine in popular culture which dwarfed British film-making but appealed to British audiences. In the 1930s, well over sixty per cent of all the money spent on entertainment was spent in the cinema. Attendance grew throughout the decade, with many people visiting one of around 5,000 British cinemas, many of them new Art Deco palaces, every week to indulge their taste for escapism and heroes, both imaginary and real.

The typical cinema performance started with the newsreels, which were as competitive for audiences as today's television channels, and aviation was almost made for the cinema of the 1930s. Ever since 1927

when Charles Lindbergh had flown solo from New York to Paris, where he was greeted by tens of thousands of people invading the airfield, the solo aviator was a tailor-made cinema hero. Record-breaking flights and stories of new aircraft became a newsreel staple: the Schneider Trophy races, Amy Johnson's solo flight to Australia in 1930, Wiley Post's record-breaking flight round the world in eight days in 1931 and in seven days in 1933, Amelia Earhart's solo flight across the Atlantic in 1932 and Lord Clydesdale's expedition to fly over the summit of Everest — another enterprise sponsored by Lady Houston of Schneider Trophy fame.

The development of aviation and its heroes, fictional and real, fitted the new cultural and economic wave of the future, and monoplanes made of stressed aluminium alloys with stream-lined engine cowls, Perspex cockpits and retractable undercarriages became evident in civil and commercial aviation. On 8 February 1933, Boeing flew the world's first modern airliner,

its ten-seater Model 247, for the first time. It was a streamlined, 155 mph, air-conditioned, sound-proofed monoplane with an automatic pilot and an on-board lavatory for its United Airlines customers. Four months later, on 1 July 1933, the Douglas DC-1 made its first flight, and entered service with TWA in December. It was followed by the Douglas DC-2, prompting the Dutch airline KLM to drop its Fokkers and replace them with DC-2s in 1934. As a publicity stunt, KLM entered the DC-2 in the 11,000-mile London to Sydney air race, in which it came second to the specially built de Havilland Comet racer. In the same year,

Lockheed brought out the Electra, which, like the DC-2, was capable of 200 mph. By 1936, there was another Douglas airliner, the DC-3, or 'sleeper' version of its predecessors, which stressed luxury and comfort and came into service in September 1936. Britain and the US were also starting long-distance flying-boat services, the British through the Empire to the east, the Americans across the Pacific. This development would have impressed Jacques Schneider: the flying boats were fitted out in luxury and again featured the Art Deco style which lay behind their advertising.

SCIENCE AND PROPAGANDA: the Zurich International Flying Meeting of 1937 used an abstract image of the single-engined fighter for promotion; the Messerscmitt Bf 109, which had been unveiled at the 1936 Berlin Olympics, took all the main prizes — the Circuit of the Alps, speed, climb and dive and the team prize — adding to the legend of the *Luftwaffe*.

The burst of enthusiasm for aviation in the 1930s spawned a strong desire to participate as pilots as well as passengers and in Britain, de Havilland and Miles built light aircraft such as the Tiger Moth trainer, the Gypsy Moth and the Miles Master, which people could use to go touring and on holiday. The posters of the day show an idealized world of sports aircraft, autogyros and helicopters being used like cars, to commute, and supported this growing popular fascination with the world of aviation. In March 1932, the monthly *Popular Flying Magazine* started publication, edited by William Earl Johns, who had fought as a bomber pilot in the Great War. Within a few years it was selling 25,000 copies, and one of its best-loved features was the series of exploits of a character who captured the

imagination of leisure pilots of the age: the fighter pilot James Bigglesworth. When the Biggles stories were published in book form, as *The Camels are Coming* in May 1932, the fighter pilot hero immediately struck a resounding chord with a far wider audience. In fact, they were one of the most successful publishing ventures of the 20th century, and around one hundred Biggles titles are still in print today.

The Spitfire was born into a popular culture that embraced heroic stories based on a fusion of science and art. It was one of the images of the age, and like most works of art it was a one-off — not like the mass-produced Hurricane. Even from its earliest appearances, the Spitfire turned heads: in the public arena its physical appearance and sheer speed made it something special, that made its mark at air shows and through newsreels.

The Spitfire was also an advanced weapon, and just two days after its first flight there was a reminder of the real reason for its existence. On 7 March 1936 the German army, backed by the *Luftwaffe*, re-occupied the Rhineland in the first of what became a series of muscular acts of bluster and propaganda which Hitler had judged would gain Germany both status and territory but would not provoke war because neither France nor Britain was equipped or ready to fight. In reality, neither was Hitler, but he had no doubts about the value of new technologies as propaganda for the new Germany. He had seen what winning the Schneider Trophy had done for Britain, and to a lesser degree for his fascist colleague Mussolini in Italy, and how winning was effective in projecting national success both at home and abroad. He

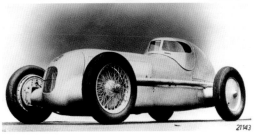

21143

S CIENCE AND SPEED: other streamlined Nazi icons of the period were the Mercedes and Auto Union racing cars, which Hitler funded as propaganda for German technology. A brilliant fusion of art and science, they dominated motor racing from 1935 until the war.

poured money into new armaments, much of it in secret, but he also financed those very aspects of the emerging consumer society which were most likely to attract attention, such as cinema, civil aviation and new public buildings. Displays of advanced technology were also ordered within weeks of Hitler coming to power, when he provided state funds to Mercedes and Auto Union to build a new generation of silver-painted, streamlined racing cars. Suddenly French Bugattis, Italian Alfa Romeos and British Bentleys looked very old-fashioned. The highly streamlined 'Silver Arrows', the Mercedes W.25 and Auto Union, started winning Grands Prix in 1934, and won nearly every one until 1939, prompting the same companies to build streamliners to challenge British domination of the land speed record too.

The idea of high technology as a symbol of national success extended to Hitler's rearmament programme, and the *Luftwaffe* was fashioned as a tool for propaganda as well as an air force. In 1936, the *Luftwaffe*'s front-line fighter was the Heinkel 51A, a biplane, and this is the aircraft that was used during the re-occupation of the Rhineland. They were not required to fire a shot, but film and photographs of a squadron of He51s flying symbolically over the Rhine in formation were distributed widely, and to give the impression there were more aircraft than there actually were they were re-painted in different markings between sorties, re-photographed and re-distributed. The *Luftwaffe*'s first modern, single-seater, all-metal monoplane fighter, the Messerschmitt Bf 109, the prototype of which had first flown six months before the Spitfire, in September 1935, was not revealed until the summer of 1936 at the Olympic Games in Berlin, where it flew over the stadium as part of Hitler's propaganda machine.

German air policy was to build up the size of the *Luftwaffe* as quickly as possible; Hitler wanted large numbers: the image of a large, modern air force, which would be valuable as part of his strategy — to intimidate rather than fight his way into power in Europe. The *Luftwaffe*, though it grew in size, was not a strategic air force in the way that the RAF was. It became highly capable in short bursts of intensive activity in support of the army, but it lacked the operational depth of its British counterpart.

Ironically, Hitler's propaganda made the RAF a more formidable opponent by influencing its modernization, expansion and re-organization in the late 1930s. On 1 April 1936, a month after the reoccupation of the Rhineland, the

SCIENCE, ART AND WAR: Dornier 17 bomber squadrons add smoke and spectacle to a Nazi rally on 1 September 1938—part of Hitler's propaganda to highlight the invincibility of the German armed forces backed up by a technically-advanced *Luftwaffe*.

Metropolitan force was split into a series of Commands based on function, reflecting the different applications of air power. Bomber Command, the offensive and strategic arm of the RAF, was equipped with the heavy bombers of the time, and with orders for the Wellington, while Fighter Command, which included barrage balloons and the Observer Corps, was responsible for home defence. After six years at the Air Ministry, Sir Hugh Dowding became Air Officer Commanding Fighter Command; he took over eighteen squadrons of biplanes, among them Bristol Bulldogs designed in the late 1920s, and the most recent of which were the three squadrons of Hawker Furys. Dowding had a profound understanding of the aircraft which would replace them and had engineered the swift approval and orders for nearly 1,000 Hurricanes and Spitfires to provide Fighter Command with a cutting edge.

Dowding had a vision for the defence of Britain from air attack. It relied heavily on technology, but having the best fighters in the world was only a start: by the time he took command, he had initiated a second, and highly secret, high technology project to detect any threat from bombers and manoeuvre the fighters to intercept them based on Radio Direction Finding (radar) and VHF radios in every fighter. In 1935 he carried out a series of experiments under the supervision of the scientist Robert Watson-Watt, who had managed to detect aircraft in flight using the echo from radio wave pulses displayed on a cathode ray tube; in 1936, as the first masts were being built on the Thames Estuary, this system could detect aircraft at twenty to thirty miles range, and plot their direction, though it was not able to provide much information on height. Radar was crucial because the speed of bombers was increasing steadily, giving less time to identify threats visually and scramble fighters to attack. Through VHF communications, the leader of each fighter squadron was also given access to an electronic representation of the vast, three dimensional battlefield. This enabled each one to act on their own initiative when it came to positioning their squadrons to attack.

The advent of Fighter Command and the anticipation of the new monoplane fighters had ensured that the fighter pilot resumed his central position in the air war as he had in the golden age of aerial combat in the Great War. As the Spitfire progressed through its acceptance trials at RAF Martlesham Heath, and more RAF pilots flew it, it became even more popular, not just because of its speed and lightness in handling, but because it met one of the primary needs of its function as a fighter: it bonded with the pilot. The fusion of the pilot with his aircraft is what makes him effective in combat, able to fly, manoeuvre, aim, lay off for the enemy's speed and position, fire the guns, and follow through, all in one, easy, flowing movement. That oneness is what wins aerial battles and it was clear from an early stage that the Spitfire had the qualities to make that relationship work.

But although the Spitfire had the qualities of a good fighter in abundance, when it came to production, it was falling behind the schedule to re-equip Fighter Command. The factory at Southampton could not possibly build the whole aircraft, it simply was not a large enough industrial concern. Instead, Spitfire components were built by up to eighty subcontracted engineering firms, some of which had worked within the aircraft industry previously and others of which had not. The parts were then assembled by Supermarine, but from the start it was management nightmare requiring skills that were not available. Having won the orders, Sir Robert McLean of Vickers, the parent company, was keen to keep as much of the manufacturing within the group as possible, adding another layer of politics between the shop floor and Fighter Command's squadrons.

The political failure to address the competing interests and priorities of the manufacturers and the Air Ministry, and work to a commonly agreed plan, had not served either the aircraft industry or the RAF well. Britain was trying to make up for time lost in the debates over what type of aircraft to order and the slower than expected pace of production coincided with a succession of RAF expansion plans which were producing the goods elsewhere: by January 1937, 2,500 new pilots had been trained and forty out of forty-nine planned new air bases had been built. The same month, the first production Gloster Gladiator flew and they started being delivered to RAF fighter squadrons the following month; the prototype Boulton Paul Defiant flew for the first time on 11 August 1937, but did not go into service until December 1939, after the war had started. The first Hurricanes were delivered to 111 Squadron in December 1937, by which time they were being produced at a rate of thirty a month; Fighter Command had five squadrons of Hurricanes before the first Spitfires even entered service in August 1938.

Reginald Mitchell was not there to see the Spitfire go into service. He died on 11 June 1937, aged just forty-two. He was a genius who had achieved a great deal in his lifetime, but who died without ever knowing the full extent of what he had created. There is still a lingering guilt that he never quite got the credit he deserved because he did not have the personality or the social prominence and because he died unfashionably of bowel cancer. To those who knew him, he was a very special man because of his integrity, his loyalty and his unflagging quest for perfection. He was not forgotten by the small group of people who had made the Spitfire possible, but only recently have modest forms of public recognition been created: a statue and a blue plaque on the house in Southampton where he lived while he was designing the Spitfire. But with Mitchell's death, the aircraft became the star.

A cutaway drawing (*far left*) of the Mk 1 released in 1940, part of satisfying the thirst for information from young and old about Britain's newly revealed success story. Such images helped the campaign to recruit aircrew, particularly pilots, by appealing to technical as well as romantic ideas of air combat.

Squadron Leader Henry Cozens, CO of 19 Squadron, the first RAF squadron to fly Spitfires, leading five Mk 1s on 31 October 1938 (*above*). Of his first flight, he said: 'It was like flying a lorry at low levels ..., but once you had reached 10,000 feet ... it was delightful to fly.'

Sergeant Bernard Jennings (*left*) scrambling during the Battle of Britain, in which he shot down four enemy aircraft; his section leader was Flight Sergeant George 'Grumpy' Unwin; both men served with 19 Squadron throughout the battle.

METAL
COVERING

THREE BLADED
VARIABLE PITCH
AIR SCREW

GLYCOL
HEADER
TANK

1,050 H.P
ROLLS ROYCE
"MERLIN" ENGINE

SPINNER

AERIAL

SLIDING
HOOD

LENGTH
29 FT. 11 IN.

FIREPROOF
BULKHEAD

ELEVATORS

PARACHUTE
FLARE

INSTRUMENT
PANEL

EXHAUSTS

FIN

UPPER
FUEL TANK.

GLYCOL
PIPE

STRINGER

TOTAL
FUEL LOAD
85 GALLONS

RADIO

LOWER
FUEL TANK

SUPER
CHARGER

ENGINE
BEARERS

DITTY
BOX

LONGERON

METAL
RIBS

UNDER-
CARRIAGE
CONTROL
HANDLE

OIL
TANK

OXYGEN
BOTTLES

BATTERY
BOX

CARBURETTOR
AIR INTAKE.

TAIL WHEEL

METAL
STRESSED-SKIN
COVERING
ASSEMBLED
COMPLETE
WITH
STRINGERS

RETRACTED
UNDER-CARRIAGE
(STARBOARD)

GLYCOL
COOLING
RADIATOR
UNDERSIDE
OF PLANE.

METAL
RIBS

BROWNING TYPE
MACHINE GUN

SPAN
OF
PLANES
36 FT. 10 IN.

GUN MUZZLES
(FOUR BROWNING TYPE
MACHINE GUNS
EITHER SIDE IN WINGS.)

THE PILOT'S COCKPIT OF THE "SPITFIRE."

GUN
SIGHT

INSTRUMENT
PANEL

CONTROL
LEVER

FIRING TRIGGER
FOR THE
EIGHT BROWNING
GUNS.

HTAVISD
1940

SPITFIRE MK I

Introduced barely a year before the outbreak of the Second World War, the original fighting Spitfire was the machine that made the Spitfire's name with both its pilots and the public. In August 1940, at the height of the Battle of Britain, Mk Is made up about a third of Fighter Command's strength, equipping eighteen squadrons in all four Groups. They were produced from 1938 to 1941, and while many Mk Is were later converted to Mk Vs, many others were sent to Operational Training Units, where they were used throughout the war to introduce newly qualified fighter pilots to the Spitfire.

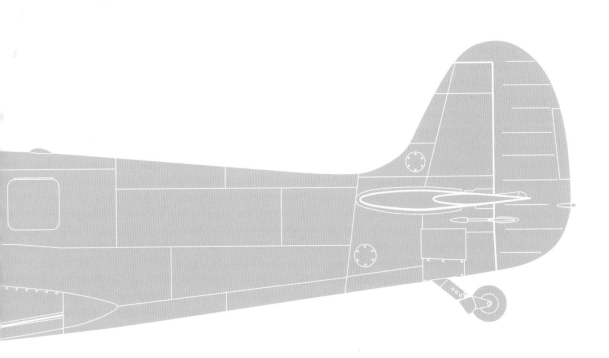

A publicity shot of a Mk I Spitfire from 1938. Even though 19 Squadron had only received its Spitfires in August that year, the pilots were recalled from leave in September 1938 during the German occupation of the Sudetenland following the Munich Crisis to be at two hours' readiness.

The 310 Mk I Spitfires ordered in July 1936 differed in detail from the prototype: the wings were stiffened to eliminate flutter at speeds up to 450 mph, provision was made to fit a three-bladed, metal propeller, a curved windscreen rather than the flat one was fitted to improve visibility, with more space above the pilot's head, the oil-cooling system was improved so it was 'satisfactory for English summer conditions' and with touching concern for the pilot, the Air Ministry required a locker for his personal belongings.

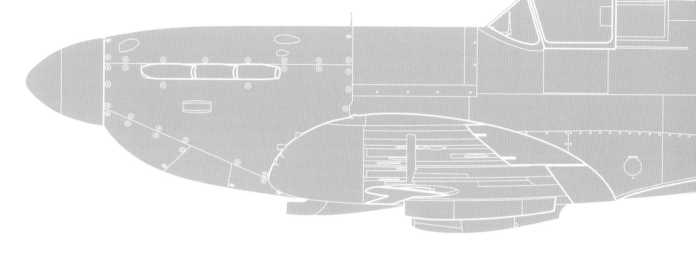

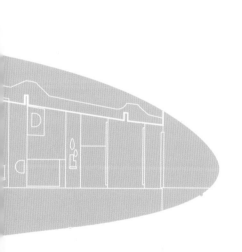

SPITFIRE	MK I (N 3171)	PROTOTYPE (K5054)
Total Built	1556	1
Wingspan	36 ft 10 in	37 ft
Length	29 ft 11 in	29 ft 11 in
Tare weight	4,713 lbs	4,082 lbs
All up weight	6,050 lbs	5,359 lbs
Power plant	Rolls-Royce Merlin III 27-litre, V-12	Rolls-Royce Merlin C 27-litre, V-12
Max power	990 hp	990 hp
Max cruising speed	353 mph at 20,000 ft	345 mph at 20,000 ft
Service ceiling	34,700 ft	35,400 ft
Time to height	7 min 42 sec to 20,000 ft	8 min 12 sec to 20,000 ft
Rate of Climb	1,840 ft/min at 20,000 ft	1,770 ft/min at 20,000 ft
Armament Mk1A Mk1B	8 x .303 Browning machine guns 2 x 20mm Hispano cannon, 4 x .303 Browning machine guns	Ballast to December 1936, then 8 x .303 Browning machine guns

Flying Officer Leonard Haines poses in his Mk I Spitfire on a press visit to Manor Farm. One of 19 Squadron's aces, he shot down eight enemy aircraft, a major contribution to the total of ninety-three claimed by the Squadron during the battle.

Flying original (left): the classic lines of the Mark I Spitfire are still exhibited at air shows today. AR213 was delivered to the RAF in July 1941; its performance had been overtaken by other marks, but it did valuable service as a training aircraft before being sold in 1947. It was restored to flying condition in 1967 for the film *The Battle of Britain*.

One-offs: the N.17 Speed Spitfire (above left) was built to break the 352 mph landplane speed record set by Howard Hughes in his H-2 (above right) in 1935. It reached 408 mph in trials, but official backing was withdrawn when the Germans produced the Me 209 (renamed as the Me 109R to identify it with the Bf 109 fighter), which broke all records at 469.22 mph.

The first Spitfire was delivered to the RAF on 4 August 1938, to replace the biplane Gauntlets of 19 Squadron at RAF Duxford. The Commanding Officer, Squadron Leader Henry Cozens, was the first front-line pilot to fly it, and as more arrived, the pilots went through an intensive flying programme, mainly to see if there were any problems which the factory and the acceptance pilots had not ironed out. There were complaints from taller pilots that their heads touched the Perspex canopy and from nearly all pilots about having to use a hand pump to raise and lower the undercarriage, but they had been noted already and modifications were in the pipeline. By November, the squadron was ready to be declared operational and to mark the occasion, the RAF had a series of photographs taken from a Blenheim, several of which were carefully staged with evocative clouds pierced by the rays of the sun — photographs which gave the Spitfire an ethereal quality, almost an otherworldliness that only added to its mystique and its public image as something special.

The RAF public relations effort for the Spitfire was puny compared with German promotion of the Messerschmitt Bf 109 at the Berlin Olympic Games in 1936. Then, in August 1937, *Luftwaffe* Bf 109s walked off with a whole range of speed and distance prizes at the Zurich International flying meeting. Later that year, on 11 November, a specially prepared Bf 109, powered for the occasion by a 1,650 hp engine, broke the world speed record for landplanes at 379 mph. The image of Germany's fighter was enhanced and there were those in the RAF who thought it might be useful to enter into a public battle for speed records. At the height of all the problems of Spitfire production, on 25 November 1937, there was a meeting at the Air Ministry which agreed to fund Supermarine to build a special Spitfire to beat the new record. A production Spitfire was taken out of the assembly line at Woolston and fitted with a special Merlin engine, which Rolls-Royce believed would produce over 2,000 hp. Flush rivets were added all round, the gun mountings smoothed over, guns removed and a four-blade propeller and streamlined canopy fitted. It was then painted blue and given a new name, 'The Speed Spitfire', and a number, N.17.

The Bf 109 had put the quest for speed back in the public domain, not in a race or for a trophy but for the absolute world speed record. In operational trim, the Spitfire Mk I had a speed in level flight of 349 mph, just 3 mph slower than the previous world record for landplanes held by Howard Hughes at 352.39 mph, though still 90 mph below the absolute record, still held by the modified Italian Schneider Cup racer, the Macchi MC.72 at 440 mph. In 1938, George Eyston drove his Thunderbolt car, powered by two Merlin engines, to a new land speed record of 375.5 mph at Bonneville, about the same top speed as the Mk 1 Spitfire in a dive.

The Speed Spitfire N.17 was progressing in secret when, on 6 June 1938, a Heinkel 100 raised the bar to 394 mph. Development of the Speed

106 FORM AND FUNCTION: the Spitfire was part of the Art Deco world of speed and streamlining. *Clockwise from bottom:* the locomotive Mallard set a record for steam of 126 mph, which still stands; George Eyston's Thunderbolt, powered by two Rolls-Royce R engines, reached 357.5 mph; the mascot for Chrysler's Airstream car was a marketing device synthesizing speed with elegance; the Hoover building indicated the modernity of its products through the design of its headquarters; the sleekness of Imperial Airways' latest airliner, the Ensign, is emphasized by the dated look of the mail van.

Spitfire continued throughout 1938, and in February 1939, it reached 408 mph at 3,000 feet, equivalent to about 400 mph at 200 feet, the height at which international records were recognized. Then the German propaganda machine had a triumph: in March 1939, Hans Dierterle, a Messerschmitt test pilot, raised it yet again, to 463 mph, in a specially prepared Bf 109, finally breaking the Schneider Trophy's hold on the absolute world speed record. The Air Ministry decided to abandon the Speed Spitfire project, while its German equivalent authorized yet another special version of Bf 109, the Bf 209, and Hans Dierterle raised his own record to 469 mph. It was the last world speed record to be set before the war. The Bf 209 was not a practical fighter, and very dangerous to fly, but the legacy of the Schneider Cup had finally been beaten by a landplane based on a fighter rather than a fighter based on a seaplane.

By the late 1930s, the streamlined form that linked speed with modernity and symbolized success though technology was in the forefront of influencing art, fashion, transport and architecture. The Schneider aircraft and the Spitfire were supreme examples of the part that aircraft played in influencing that form. Streamlining was part of the Art Deco world, the visual revolution crafted out of the shapes of the future, an exclusive world of airlines, luxury, individuality, of belonging to a coherent style that permeated the public and private spheres. It was a form that spread to other all-metal aircraft for practical reasons, to make them faster, and that influenced the design of other machines: in America streamlined trains such as the Burlington Zephyr spanned the

continent and in July 1938, the streamlined LNER locomotive Mallard set a speed record for steam engines at 126 mph that still stands — and it remains the best known locomotive in Britain. Private car ownership boomed in the 1930s in America and Europe, but streamlining was much slower to influence the shape of cars other than for the very rich. The Auburn 851 'Boat Tail' Speedster, which came out in all its streamlined glory in 1935, its radiator mascot the embodiment of Art Deco emphasis on speed and streamlining, was more a work of art than a means of transport. At the other end of the scale was the streamlined Volkswagen, heavily influenced by Hitler and the subsidies he provided.

The marriage of science and art was the look of the 1930s and gave rise to the 'Streamline Moderne' school of architecture evident in public transport, public art, and public buildings and commercial building such as at airports, cinemas, hotels, swimming pools, restaurants, garages, offices and factories, including a new office block at Woolston next to Supermarine's factory where the Spitfire had been designed. It was a look that was coherent and its appeal has lasted; genuine products that influenced and were influenced by that age, such as the Spitfire, have retained something of the positive spirit of the 1930s, the sense of modernity that co-existed with the decade's darker image as a prelude to war.

The darker side of the 1930s came in the clash of ideologies that brought about the Spanish Civil War between the Republican government, backed by the Soviet Union, and Franco's Nationalists, backed by Nazi Germany and fascist

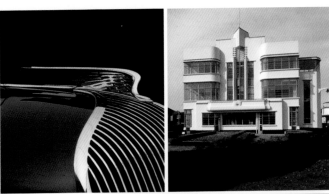

108 THE ART OF WAR: fear of the indiscriminate use and effect of air power (*below*) and faith that could bring ultimate victory (*opposite*) were evident in the propaganda of the Spanish Civil War, which saw aircraft used to terrorize the civilian population and in support of ground troops. The reality was that war showed air power was invaluable in battle, but cruel and indecisive strategically.

Italy. The war tested many of the theories about air power, starting with German Junkers 52 airliners moving Franco's forces from Spanish Morocco to the mainland. As the war escalated, *Luftwaffe* He 51 and *Reggia Aeronautica* Fiat CR 32 biplane fighters, and some Italian bombers, arrived to support Franco while Soviet Il-15 biplane fighters intervened to support the government. Both sides quickly re-learned the lessons of the Great War: that air superiority was crucial to ground operations; both sides attacked troops on the ground with bombs and machine-gun fire, and both sides deployed fighters to try to shoot the attacking aircraft down. Then the Soviet Air Force deployed its monoplane fighter, the Il-16, which for a time became the dominant fighter, and the *Luftwaffe* deployed early examples of the Messerschmitt Bf 109 to counter it. The biplane fighters on both sides were increasingly consigned to the ground-attack role as the superiority of the monoplane and the value of fast, manoeuvrable fighters quickly became apparent. The value of better technologies and good tactics also made an impression as the more advanced Bf 109s steadily

outclassed the Soviet fighters and were able to protect the Junkers 87 Stuka dive-bombers and Heinkel 111 medium bombers by providing air superiority and by escorting them to and from their targets.

The *Luftwaffe*'s participation in the Spanish Civil War was secret at first, but as its role expanded to a force of around 6,000 volunteers it was formed into a local air force in Spain, the Condor Legion. Its main task remained supporting Franco's army, but in November 1936 it bombed Madrid for three days with the intention of demoralizing the city's population as part of Franco's plan to take the city. It was a failure: 150 people were killed and many houses were destroyed, but the bombing failed to break the human spirit. The Spanish government was anxious to protect its own population and issued graphic posters of Madrid in flames, encouraging people to evacuate the city, but the inhabitants of Madrid stood fast. The government was also keen to garner support from abroad, distributing posters of dead Spanish children under stylized bomber fleets and others which called for air-raid shelters to be built rather than give in. If anything, the bombing stiffened resistance to Franco in Spain and garnered sympathetic support abroad.

The following year, art of a different kind made the most eloquent expression of the impact of air power on civilians. In April the *Luftwaffe* attacked Guernica, the capital of Spain's Basque region in what was widely seen at the time as another experiment using bombers to demoralize an enemy. The raid killed 1,600 people, a quarter of those in the city at the time, and injured 900, their numbers swelled because it was market day. This

time a *Times* reporter, George Steers, was on hand to witness the immediate aftermath and his reports outraged the world. initially, Franco's Nationalists tried to deny it had been bombed, accusing the Basques of torching their own city for the purposes of propaganda, but it was impossible to maintain the fiction. Within weeks, Picasso's 'Guernica', arguably the most famous painting of the 20th century, appeared in Paris, turning Guernica into a symbol of inhumanity, even barbarity. The name of the city still evokes the same response today.

The moral outrage at the attack on Guernica was intense, but for those who analyzed it closely, the Guernica raid was the start of dispelling the myth that bombing alone could win wars. The *Luftwaffe* had had complete local air supremacy, the city was undefended, they need not have chosen market day, there was no warning and no air-raid shelters and they dropped incendiary bombs which turned the city into a bonfire that burned for days. If, as the Germans later claimed, the target had been the stone bridge in the middle of the city, then why did they use incendiary

bombs to which the bridge would have been impervious? In any case, when the Nationalists occupied the city two days later, unopposed, the bridge was intact.

The lesson of Guernica was that its inhabitants suffered grievously because there was no defence. The bombers had came out of a clear sky, unchallenged, and had been able to hit the city almost as a training exercise. The raid outraged the world, but it failed to destroy Republican morale; when the Italians bombed Barcelona later in the war, killing 1,300 people over two days, it was not brought to the point of collapse by airpower; if anything, it made the people of those cities even more determined to resist. The two conclusions to be drawn from the final victory of the fascists in 1939 were that bombing cities was not the decisive factor in war and that unless armies on the ground were supported and protected by air superiority they were highly vulnerable. Whether fighters could defend cities and their populations against bombers was never really tested because although the Condor Legion bombed cities they did so largely in conditions of complete air superiority and never in the face of skilled and determined opposition from enemy fighters.

The *Luftwaffe's* participation in the Spanish Civil War had been valuable: its aircraft had been used in anger for the first time and serving in the Condor Legion had given its commanders and aircrews operational experience in wartime conditions, especially at a tactical level. More importantly, its impact in support of Franco's army had given it an aura of effectiveness, even invincibility, that was exactly what Hitler wanted:

the men of the Condor Legion were welcomed back to Germany as national heroes and conquerors with parades and flypasts. After that, the *Luftwaffe* was called upon in Nazi rallies: armadas of bombers and fighters flew over the crowds above troops who marched and fired guns in mock battles, in stadia ringed with Nazi flags. By 1938, it had all but abandoned the development of long-range strategic bombers because they did not seem necessary; Hitler appeared to be achieving his goals without them.

Intimidation worked. The *Luftwaffe's* effectiveness was magnified by the newsreels and other propaganda. When Hitler annexed Austria in a bloodless invasion in March 1938 and when he marched into the Sudetenland of Czechoslovakia following agreement with Britain and France in September that year, it was always there in the background. Among other factors, the Munich Agreement to dismember Czechoslovakia was influenced by the implicit threat of the use of German air power. The Agreement was publicly applauded in Britain even though it provoked some resignations from the government; in private, Neville Chamberlain, who had replaced Stanley Baldwin as Prime Minister just weeks after the Guernica raid, knew that even though the RAF was expanding, the supply of modern fighters was not what it should be. The first squadron of Spitfires had only just been formed and it would be some time before Fighter Command could mount an adequate defence.

Neville Chamberlain had been a supporter of the defensive fighter as an option for the RAF, and had pushed through increased funding for its expansion from 1935, a policy he maintained as

Prime Minister. The Guernica raid, and three months later the Japanese bombing of Shanghai, had spurred him to even greater expenditure on defence. In public, the government responded by building air-raid shelters and training all children to use gas masks. In private, the plan was to build more Spitfires, but the chronically slow output remained a closely guarded secret and British propaganda was aimed at reassuring the public rather than intimidating likely enemies.

In 1938, the Minister for Air, Sir Kingsley Wood, attended the opening of a huge new factory at Castle Bromwich near Birmingham, built at a cost of £3m exclusively to produce Spitfires, and made a speech specifically endorsing the Spitfire as central to RAF expansion. The newsreel of the event shows the Minister arriving by air to be greeted by Lord Nuffield of Morris Motors, who was to run the factory, following which they symbolically cut the first sod for building to begin. In a speech that followed he promised an order for a further 1,000 Spitfires. In another newsreel, entitled 'First Pictures of Vickers Supermarine Spitfire I, World's Fastest Aircraft, & Speech by Sir Kinglsey Wood', the opening shots emphasize the speed of the Spitfire flying towards the camera, then soaring above the clouds, setting up the Minister behind his Whitehall desk in a fireside manner to encourage men to come forward to join the RAF, which has 31,000 vacancies for pilots, fitters and other skilled trades.

As the date for the Spitfire to be delivered to 19 Squadron at Duxford approached in August, several films were made showing the first production Spitfire Mk Is. The first was *Spitfire on Trial,* shot during the aircraft's acceptance trials at

Martlesham Heath, where it is shown at speed at low level effortlessly sweeping past a Supermarine Walrus seaplane — once again to emphasize its speed. That was followed by *Britain's Latest Fighter,* a wonderful display of aerobatics against rolling cumulus cloud to show its flying qualities, all backed by stirring music and enthusiastic commentary.

Once the first Spitfires had been delivered to Duxford, a story leaked out that some RAF officers were concerned that such an advanced fighter might be beyond the capability of young pilots. To reassure the public, the Under Secretary of State for Air, Captain Harold Balfour, a pilot as well as a politician, went to Duxford to fly one for himself. He is shown climbing into a Spitfire kitted out with leather helmet, goggles, Mae West and parachute, very much the politician as Biggles. Take off, a ten-minute flight, and an

ultra-smooth landing for the cameras are followed by his assessment to the Cambridge Daily News: 'There is nothing vicious about it and the young men of the RAF will be able to do it much better than I can.'

Newsreels and newspaper coverage continued regularly throughout 1938 and into 1939, orchestrated to reinforce the idea that the government was taking air defence seriously and by its frequent appearances in that context, the Spitfire came to embody that idea. One particular shot of a Spitfire rolling above a quintessentially English village, implicitly defending it, was cut into several films. Crowds at the RAF Hendon display saw the Spitfire performing what was becoming its party piece, flashing past them with its Merlin engine at full throttle before soaring up to loop and roll among the clouds. Like the films, the displays at air shows were not militaristic or overtly propagandist,

Protecting the nation: a carefully composed photograph of Spitfires, staged for the cameras in 1938. By setting it among the clouds, wreathed in the sun's rays, this image created a vision of the Spitfire not only as a technical answer to the bomber threat, but almost as a supernatural being; a mythical saviour.

they were more lyrical and comforting, very British, like some gigantic, rather noisy, church fête.

Barely a month went by without the Spitfire appearing somewhere, particularly in the context of announcements such as the latest RAF expansion plan. The Spitfire demanded attention and had presence in person and on film; it was a star in an age of stars, in tune with the spirit of the times. Many of the newsreels had an international context: Spitfires appeared with officers of the French *Armée de l'Air* and 100 French reservists were given a conducted tour of the Supermarine factory; when the designer of the equivalent American fighter, the P-35, visited Eastleigh he flew the Spitfire. When the RAF accompanied Queen Alexandra and Queen Elizabeth to the Copenhagen Air Show, it was welcomed by a Danish women's army band and an immaculate formation flying display.

The Spitfire had become a reality because it was a political imperative. It embodied a will to resist and became part of popular culture on that basis, the purity of its form seen as necessary to fulfil its function as a fighter; it was a positive fusion of science and art which steadily became part of what people believed was a viable defensive system against what was by now the clear potential enemy: Nazi Germany.

In 1930, the air power theorists' dominant idea had been that the bomber would always get through, that it could annihilate populations, cities and industry using high explosive, incendiary or gas bombs, and that even the threat of such obliteration could bring about a military victory. That idea lived on in Bomber Command, but by 1939, while nobody really knew how effective a

fighter shield would be against bombers, and the true position as regards the production of Spitfires remained a closely-guarded secret, the idea that there was a defence was firmly established among many senior officers inside the RAF, and among politicians, and largely accepted by the British public. The embodiment of that idea was Fighter Command, a new and comforting idea: at least there was a potential means of meeting any threat, which was better than having none. It was a powerful idea, and it was built on many themes: the re-invention of the fighter pilot as a popular hero, the marshalling of science and technology in a national enterprise, the projection of that idea through the mass media, the thought that Britain had the fastest aircraft in the world, a memory of the Schneider Trophy success, and faith in the beautiful machine that brought these themes together.

The Spitfire was still untested in 1939, but a large number of different people believed in it, not only the population at large, for whom the greater part of the reason for its performance was either a mystery or a secret, not just the RAF commanders who knew those secrets, but also the test pilots and fighter pilots who could feel its sheer quality under their fingertips. That is what counted in 1939. The Spitfire was not yet the icon it would become during the Second World War, but the foundations had been laid. It was special: no overstatement was needed to bolster its image or its performance; it expressed itself in its eloquent mysteriousness, through the contrasting emotions it stirred, at the same time menacing and reassuring, functional and beautiful. The mythology of Excalibur had begun.

WAR 4

War was anticipated prior to 3 September 1939. Civil Defence worked on countering the effects of air attack: evacuating 857,000 children; testing air raid sirens; ensuring gas masks were carried and windows were blacked out. Fighter Command was there to prevent air attack: it needed fifty-two squadrons but had only thirty-five; it needed radar, but the system was unfinished; ten Hurricane squadrons were in France or ready to go, and there were 187 battle-ready Spitfires.

116

TUMULT IN THE CLOUDS (*previous page*): the Spitfire combines supreme elegance with a sense of warlike purpose. In production throughout the war, it gathered friends wherever it went and rose to every challenge to become a key character in the story of the Second World War.

TWO DAYS AFTER CHRISTMAS 1939, Muriel Green, a nineteen-year-old woman who lived in Snettisham, Norfolk, recorded an exciting day in her Mass Observation diary:

I were cooking mince pies when we heard a very loud aeroplane and saw through the window a very peculiar looking plane. We both said at once, 'I'm sure that's a Nasty'. But we both stood and watched making no attempt to take any precautions. About five minutes later we heard more aeroplanes and Jenny rushed out and said she saw three Spitfires chasing over after the other aeroplane going very fast. Mother and Jenny rushed out in the garden and then rushed back declaring they could hear gunfire. The dog barked and jumped about and I was eating my dinner and refused to get up.

Muriel Green's clear, almost off-hand, description of the British aircraft as a Spitfire is wonderful testimony to the way the modern fighter was already established in the British consciousness as a synonym for the fighter even six months before the Battle of Britain started in July 1940. Her phlegmatic response, finishing her dinner before getting excited enough to go and watch an aerial battle from her back garden, could also be taken as her placing huge confidence in the Spitfire's ability to defend her and her country from the Nazi war machine. If so, then her confidence was based on faith, for at that time Spitfires represented only a tiny proportion of RAF Fighter Command and were outnumbered nearly two to one by Hurricanes.

Maybe Muriel Green had seen the drama documentary film *The Lion Has Wings*, produced by Alexander Korda and starring Merle Oberon and Ralph Richardson, which was released in December 1939. It had been shot in twelve days and edited in eight weeks following the outbreak of war on 3 September 1939. It was clearly a propaganda film designed to show the RAF was equipped for war: after a lyrical opening evoking the British way of life, the first action comes from bombers attacking Kiel, then from barrage balloons and fighters defending London. The location for filming the fighters was RAF Hornchurch, where three squadrons of Spitfires were based. Whether Korda was influenced by the RAF hierarchy was not declared, but the emphasis given to the bomber suggests it was made with their primacy a consideration. However, the film reflected the split nature of official RAF policy at the time: the offensive character of Bomber Command and the defensive character of Fighter Command.

The RAF Chief of Staff, Sir Cyril Newall, had commanded parts of the Independent Force under Trenchard in the Great War; he would have been reluctant to see the emphasis given to air defence, believing that bombers, through their inherently aggressive nature, and not fighters, would be Britain's future salvation. However, by the time the film was released the theories about the best use of air power had already been severely tested. Two problems were apparent: accurate, or pin-point, bombing was extremely difficult, rendering 1,000-lb bombs, dropped wide of the mark, largely ineffective, and flying unescorted, relatively slow bombers over Germany in broad daylight, in the face of faster, well-armed and well-led fighters, carried huge risks. Bomber Command had four main types of bomber, the

SPITFIRES OVER ENGLAND: at the outbreak of war in September 1939, a total of 306 Spitfires had been delivered to Fighter Command, enough to equip eleven squadrons. All Spitfire squadrons were retained in Britain as defence against German bombers, their tight formation optimized for attacking the larger aircraft.

obsolescent Whitley and Hampden and the more advanced Wellington and Blenheim. To defend themselves, their tactics were to fly in close formation, in boxes, which made maximum use of their on-board armament against attacking fighters. By the end of 1939, that theory, based on those aircraft, had been tested almost to destruction, and the idea that 'the bomber would always get through' and that air power could win wars independently of armies and navies was clearly shown to be at best seriously flawed, and at worst suicidal.

On 18 December 1939, twenty-two Wellingtons flew to Wilhelmshaven to attack the naval docks in clear weather with good visibility: ten were scythed down over the target area by Luftwaffe Bf 109s, two more had to ditch in the sea on the way back having been badly damaged, two more were destroyed in forced landings at base, and the remaining eight were all damaged. The raid ultimately changed RAF strategic bombing policy: from the beginning of 1940, most bombing was to be undertaken at night, making it even more

ineffective. Despite the heroic efforts of the men who carried it out, the bombing offensive remained largely ineffective until much later in the war, and even then it continued to be carried out largely at night to avoid enemy fighters. Bomber Command was clearly not going to win the war on its own, and it was thrown onto the back foot in the opening months of the war as theories devised in peacetime met the realities of war.

Fighter Command did not face the same severe test in late 1939: contrary to some expectations, there had been no massed bombing attacks to repel: the Luftwaffe was still engaged in supporting the German army in Poland, and it had no equivalent of Bomber Command. The British government had expected a bombing offensive, and from 4 September the country was on alert, with hospitals cleared, mortuaries holding large stocks of cardboard coffins, and sites for lime pits identified. The blackout was imposed on streets, homes and even car headlamps, which had to be taped over with cardboard save for a small slit. Air-raid shelters were opened and exercises

Pᴜʙʟɪᴄ ɪɴᴛᴇʀᴇꜱᴛ (*previous pages*): the first enemy aircraft to be shot down on British soil since 1918, a Heinkel 111, fell to Spitfires of 602 and 603 Squadrons AAF on 28 October 1939, prompting a steady stream of sightseers to the moor where it crash landed.

carried out with gas masks, and the population was given rudimentary instruction in how to deal with incendiary bombs using a long-handled shovel and a stirrup pump. People were also advised to carry luggage tags with their name and address until ID cards could be issued.

Britain was on edge, and an eagerness to oppose any attack by bombers on the part of Fighter Command led to tragic consequences: on 6 September 1939, Spitfires were scrambled from Hornchurch to intercept aircraft seen crossing the Essex coast heading for London; they were led by Adolph 'Sailor' Malan, a South African who later became one of the RAF's finest fighter leaders in the Battle of Britain. When he saw the aircraft, initially he gave the order to attack, only to countermand it when he suddenly recognized they were Hurricanes. Too late: the speed of the modern fighter-to-fighter battle combined with fighter pilots' eagerness to do what they were trained to do with their Spitfires resulted in both Hurricanes being shot down and one of their pilots killed. They were the first aircraft to fall to the Spitfire's guns. Known internally in the RAF as 'The Battle of Barking Creek', it was not admitted publicly at the time, but there were other friendly-fire incidents, in one of which two Whitley bombers were shot down over the sea and one crew member was drowned.

The first blood drawn by Spitfires against the enemy was on 16 October when 603 (City of Edinburgh) Squadron of the Auxiliary Air Force intercepted an unescorted force of Junkers Ju 88 bombers as they prepared to attack warships in the Firth of Forth, the first German air raid on the British Isles. A destroyer was hit, and several

119

120

THE SPITFIRE'S EYES: RDF stations such as that at Poling in Sussex (*below*) were invaluable in detecting German aircraft. Radio signals were transmitted from the 360-foot towers on the left of the picture, then bounced back off aircraft in their path to be received by the 240-foot masts on the right.

crewmen killed, but the Spitfire pilots shot down two of the Ju 88s for no loss, the first enemy aircraft shot down over Britain and the first time the enemy had been confronted by Spitfires. Two weeks later, Spitfires of 602 (City of Glasgow) Squadron brought down a Heinkel 111P-1, which landed more or less intact but riddled with bullet holes on the moor near Dalkeith; local people flocked out to see it and photographers took pictures before the RAF took it away to see what could be learned from its equipment.

The British Expeditionary Force on the Maginot line went through a period of inactivity over the winter of 1939–40. This 'Phoney War' gave Fighter Command a welcome respite to build up its fighter force, but even as it received new Hurricanes and Spitfires, it lost four squadrons of Hurricanes to support the British Army in France and it never reached its full complement of fifty-two squadrons. The RDF-based detection system

to control the fighters was not fully operational either, and the time was invaluable in refining it into the electronic shield that made up part of what became known as the Dowding system.

Dowding's other need for time was to produce more aircraft and train more pilots. In his blueprint for Fighter Command he maintained that fifty-two squadrons of modern fighters were needed to defend Britain—about 650 fighters plus reserves. However, in early 1940, with four Hurricane and two Defiant squadrons in France, he only had thirty-eight. Dowding kept all the Spitfires in Britain as the first line of air defence. The Spitfire was one of the foremost products of Dowding's emphasis on the application of the best science and technology to the task, and though Spitfires were in very short supply, there was a strong desire for more because they were almost universally regarded as superior to the Hurricane.

Dowding's idea was that all the elements of Fighter Command would be integrated into a single entity with its nerve centre at Fighter Command's headquarters at Bentley Priory, just north of London. The country was divided into four groups: 11 Group covering the south east of England around London; 12 Group in the Midlands and East Anglia; 10 Group covering the south west of England and south Wales and 13 Group covering the north of England and Scotland. The commander of 11 Group was Air Vice Marshal Keith Park, a New Zealander who had fought in the Great War as a soldier and fighter pilot with twenty aerial victories. His bases along the coast and around London protected the capital, with 12 Group, commanded by Air Vice Marshal Trafford Leigh-Mallory, who had

THE TECHNOLOGICAL BATTLEFIELD: women played a major part in interpreting and processing the information gleaned by RDF (*above*) and continued with visual observation (*right*), giving both fighters and anti-aircraft artillery information on the position, direction and height of enemy aircraft.

not been a fighter pilot, and 10 Group providing depth to that defence and protecting the industrial heartlands of Britain.

The Groups, their airfields and even their aircraft were all linked, by the Dowding system, to the Filter and Operations rooms at Bentley Priory. Information flowed into the headquarters from various sources. There were RDF stations that could spot raids well out to sea, even over the northern French coast, giving distance, direction, and some idea of height. Observer Corps posts and anti-aircraft gun sites provided information via telephone lines, and airborne aircraft fed back via VHF radios. After informed human assessment, the key information was

displayed visually on and around a map of Britain, the continental coast of France and the Low countries, which was laid out horizontally in the Control Room, giving commanders an immediate appreciation of the complexity of the battlefield,

NERVE CENTRE (*left*): information was pooled at Dowding's headquarters at Bentley Priory, which controlled a three-dimensional battle spread over tens of thousands of square miles, all displayed almost in real time; sources included the radio transmissions of fighter pilots in the heat of the fighting.

EYES IN THE SKY (*above right*): a Blenheim Mk IV of 139 Squadron on aerial reconnaissance over northern France in April 1940 — during the prelude to the German blitzkrieg offensive on 10 May. Flying alone in clear skies, the converted bomber was vulnerable to German fighters.

with aircraft going in all directions at up to 350 mph. Which raids to intercept would be decided at the centre, and the information would flow out from Bentley Priory to the Groups and sector airfields which had their own control rooms — at which subordinate commanders, in touch with leaders in the air, decided on the best way to fight individual aerial battles. The control rooms were staffed by people chosen for their technical understanding, including science graduates, and the sector controllers were pilots themselves and knew best how to deal with pilots. They were men and women in harmony with technology on the ground in the same way that pilots were as one with their aircraft in the air.

The high technology and human input of the Dowding system was designed to find the enemy aircraft, evaluate the threat, then make the best possible use of the speed of the Spitfires and Hurricanes to intercept them. Without it, such scarce and expensive resources would have to fly standing patrols, pretty much as had happened in the Great War. This would have required more wear and tear on more fighters, which still would have been virtually blind, especially in bad weather. It was not foolproof. As the Battle of Barking Creek had shown, mistakes would happen, but such incidents led to another application of technology: the development of a small transmitter fitted to every RAF aircraft, which sent out a signal to the Control Room to identify it as friendly. This was known as IFF (Identification Friend or Foe). The Control Room at Bentley Priory was not ready until March 1940, making the respite of the Phoney War crucial.

As part of the Phoney War the RAF carried out

strategic photographic reconnaissance (PR) over the Ruhr and along the Maginot Line. The task was assigned to specialized versions of the long-range, armed Blenheim bomber, without too much success. The Blenheims could not fly fast or high enough to avoid enemy fighters, so they had to fight their way to and from any target with only their onboard armament. In forty-two sorties, eight Blenheims were lost and many of them failed to produce usable photographs. An alternative was suggested by Flying Officer Maurice 'Shorty' Longbottom, who had carried out clandestine flights to photograph Italian forces in Libya in a civilian Lockheed Hudson for MI6 in the 1930s; his idea was to rely on speed and altitude for protection rather than armament, using a single-seat fighter. The obvious choice was the Spitfire, and though they were in short supply, Dowding agreed to the experiment. It seemed fanciful at first, but with the outbreak of war, a secret flight was formed as part of Fighter Command at RAF Heston, commanded by Sydney Cotton, who had masterminded the MI6 operations in Libya: in October, two Mk I Spitfires were taken from the factory without their guns and had cameras fitted in the inboard gun positions with warm air from the engine ducted to protect them from freezing up at 30,000 feet, their undersides were painted a special duck-egg green to camouflage them from below, and they were given a smooth finish, very similar to that of the prototype and the Speed Spitfire, which made them up to 15 mph faster than the Mk 1 fighter version.

The first PR version was designated Spitfire Mk 1A, and they were deployed to Seclin in France in November 1939 as the Special Survey

SECRET SPITFIRES: in April 1940, four months after the first Spitfire was sent out on photo reconnaissance, Flight Lieutenant Maurice 'Shorty' Longbottom took this photograph (*below*) from 34,000 feet. It shows German defences near Aachen, demonstrating the Spitfire's capability for spying.

Flight — incidentally, the first time a Spitfire had flown out of the country. The first operational flight was on 18 December, over Aachen on the German-Belgian border. The workload of flying, keeping a lookout and taking photographs was high, making navigation difficult, and the first results, taken from 33,000 feet, were not of the area intended. However, lessons were learned

quickly, and within days, valuable intelligence had been gathered and the Spitfire had proved its ability to spy from the Belgian–German border right up to cities the Ruhr valley. The problem was range, but once the viability of using the Spitfire for photographic work had been demonstrated, longer-range versions were developed: the Mk 1B, which had a 29 gallon fuel tank behind the pilot, giving it a range of 325 miles; the Mk 1C, which had 30-gallon external tanks and improved cameras; the Mk 1D, which pioneered the technique of filling the hollow wings with fuel — another 57 gallons each side — with the camera moved to behind the pilot; the Mk 1E, which had very long range and used oblique cameras for low-level reconnaissance; and in July, the Mk 1F, known as the 'bowser' because it carried so much fuel, which could reach Berlin.

It was a huge testimony to the strength and versatility of the Spitfire's airframe that it could be adapted so radically, particularly with the addition of so much fuel capacity, which added to and varied the weight distribution significantly and changed its flying characteristics without making it impossible to fly. The PR Spitfire was a closely guarded secret, its contribution enhancing its usefulness and its reputation within the RAF, but not in public. Unfortunately, its qualities soon became evident to the *Luftwaffe*, which captured a short-range Mk 1A virtually intact when the German army swept through France in its spring offensive.

The Phoney War came to an end in April 1940. It was a major turning point in the story of the Spitfire and in the war. The German army subdued Denmark in twenty-four hours then invaded

CHALLENGING TIMES: the PR Mk I Type G (*right*) was adapted to take low-level oblique photographs as well as high-level shots; by adding fuel capacity inside the wings and fuselage in early 1941, its range was increased to over 900 miles — and later the same year it was upgraded to a pressurized Mk VII with a ceiling of 45,000 ft.

TURRET FIGHTER (*below*): the vulnerability of the Boulton Paul Defiant became apparent with blitzkrieg on 10 May 1940. The rear-facing dorsal turret, designed to attack bombers, left the aircraft exposed to fighter attack from below and head-on, weaknesses that *Luftwaffe* Bf 109 pilots quickly exploited.

125

Norway, Belgium, Holland and France using mechanized and armoured ground forces supported by the *Luftwaffe* with a force of 2,750 aircraft, including level bombers, dive-bombers and fighters in what became known as blitzkrieg, literally 'lightning war': an integrated system of infantry, armour, artillery and aircraft designed to shock and disorientate the enemy, operating under an umbrella of fighters to provide air superiority. It was the *Luftwaffe* at its intimidating best, a psychological as well as a physical weapon. Everything went Germany's way: the 350,000-strong British Expeditionary Force (BEF) and the French Army were rolled back, and though the Hurricane squadrons put up a stiff resistance, they were not there in sufficient strength to make a difference on their own. The Bf 109s made short work of the obsolete Fairey Battles and while the Defiants had some initial success it was only because *Luftwaffe* fighter pilots mistook them for Hurricanes and attacked from behind,

straight into their guns' field of fire; once they recognized them, and made frontal attacks, the Defiants' vulnerability and limitations became all too evident.

The number RAF of fighters supporting the BEF in France had risen to 416 aircraft, including a total of ten squadrons of Hurricanes, reducing Dowding's fighter force to twenty-eight squadrons, just over half the fifty-two that he had originally considered a minimum. The French *Armée de l'Air,* with around 1,200 aircraft, mainly fighters, lacked any technically advanced form of coordination such as the Dowding System. It also lacked a commitment to resistance — despite individuals with great courage — and a large part of its strength remained deployed outside the battle area. By mid May 1940 the French Army and the *Armée de l'Air* were on the brink of collapse and politically, France was divided between those who wanted to fight on and those who wanted to come to an accommodation with Hitler.

 AIR SUPERIORITY: two of the three Fairey Battle Mk Is of 218 Squadron shown flying over northern France (*top*) were lost in the first forty-eight hours of blitzkrieg, and a raid by sixty-three Battles on 14 May ended in thirty-five being shot down. Other British aircraft had a better rate of success. In May 1940, Hurricane pilots (*below*) achieved a ratio of two enemy aircraft destroyed for each one lost, and on one occasion shot down eleven out of twenty-four Heinkel 111s for no loss. The value of high-performance fighters was clear to both sides.

The military failure in France brought political change in Britain. Winston Churchill replaced Neville Chamberlain as Prime Minister on 10 May 1940. Among the many issues on his desk was a two-headed problem: urgent requests from the French government to send over more fighters, specifically including the Spitfires which Fighter Command had committed to the defence of Britain, and the continued slow rate of fighter production, again, specifically of Spitfires.

On the issue of production, Churchill acted promptly and decisively: four days after his appointment, he created a new government post, Minister of Aircraft Production, and appointed Lord Beaverbrook to fill it. Beaverbrook, a Canadian by birth, was the owner of the *Daily Express*, which he made the most widely read newspaper in the world, and a man of enormous energy. He was also a bully, but that was what

Churchill wanted — and importantly, he gave him the power to use that quality to increase the production of Spitfires.

The number of Spitfires reaching the RAF had been painfully low. By September 1939, 306 had been delivered, enough to equip eleven squadrons. About 184 were operational aircraft, with a further eighty-six either in maintenance or being held in reserve; thirty-six had been lost in accidents. By March 1940, the total delivered had risen to 538, a delivery rate of just over one a day, equipping nineteen squadrons, with 147 in reserve and ninety-eight lost in accidents. Production at Supermarine had been improved by using two other factories, at Eastleigh and Itchen, where finished Spitfires were assembled from parts made by sub-contractors. But Supermarine remained a small company, and the management of such a sprawling project remained a nightmare. By May, the shadow factory at Castle Bromwich had produced lots of parts, but had yet to produce a single complete Spitfire. It was partly that Mitchell's design required skilled labour which Castle Bromwich lacked. Production was further hampered by the flow of modifications from the Supermarine design office and from RAF pilots, all of which needed to be built into the production process, constantly improving the technology. The journey of technical advances from the front line to the designer's drawing board, out to the factories, tooling up, sorting out snags, through development engineers, technical testing, production adaptation, flight testing, more development, and then getting the improvements into the hands of the front-line pilots, was a huge task. In wartime conditions, it could only happen if there was

Architects of change: A new Prime Minister Winston Churchill appointed Lord Beaverbrook as Minister for Aircraft Production, with the specific task of providing Fighter Command with more Spitfires. When Churchill flew to Paris on 16 May 1940, his civil aircraft was escorted to Le Bourget airport by Spitfires of 92 Squadron.

a level of commitment by management that went beyond industrial norms. Lord Nuffield, who managed the Castle Bromwich factory, was a production engineer and he wanted everything neat, tidy and planned: his position was that he could deliver Spitfires or modifications, but not both. Lord Beaverbrook, on the other hand, wanted Spitfires and the modifications. The two men were very different personalities and within days of his appointment Beaverbrook knew there would have to be a change of management at Castle Bromwich. He simply did not believe that Nuffield was capable of making the leap of imagination necessary to produce the numbers required while keeping the improvements flowing. He phoned Nuffield and made his feelings clear; Nuffield threatened to give up the management of the plant; Beaverbrook accepted his threat as an offer and put the phone down.

Having effectively sacked Nuffield, Beaverbrook next asked Sir Robert McLean of Vickers-Armstrong, who owned Supermarine, to take over the Castle Bromwich factory and manage a production process that was dispersed through the country for reasons of security and efficiency. Beaverbrook enjoyed the power his new position gave him to make big, bold moves, and he set about increasing the production of Spitfires with style. He both bullied and encouraged the new management. He demanded ten new Spitfires from the factory by the end of June, but he also knew the value of getting people to feel involved: on one occasion he bet a group of workers £100 that they could not achieve a particular goal, which was just achievable, then paid up with glee when his target was met. But he also used tactics that were underhand, such as setting impossible targets so he could remonstrate with those who then failed. He was certainly not universally popular, but he not only started to deliver more Spitfires within weeks, in the long run he also made people believe they were not simply cogs in a wheel, that they were making something that mattered, and that in turn made them proud to be part of building Spitfires.

Sending Spitfires to France was a more complex problem for Churchill. He had promised the French premier he would send more fighters, and he wanted to be true to his word, but against him, many politicians and senior RAF officers believed that France was a lost cause and any indulgence of the French request would be folly, especially sending squadrons of the RAF's most advanced fighters, of which there was a chronic shortage. The defence of Britain was what Fighter Command had been created for, and at a meeting on 15 May between all the Chiefs of Staff and Churchill, which Dowding also attended, he stood up to Churchill's clear wish to send the ten squadrons that the French prime minister had asked for, pointing out with a simple graph how the strength of Fighter Command had diminished from the fifty-two squadrons and that the effect of dismembering it further for the benefit of France would leave him with little over half what was originally intended. He argued to preserve the most effective fighter he had, the Spitfire, in Britain, determined that it would be used as originally intended and not frittered away supporting a disintegrating French state. At the meeting Churchill agreed not to send any fighter squadrons to France, but later the same day he ordered four squadrons of Hurricanes to go and they went.

In response, Dowding applied further pressure on Churchill in a carefully worded letter to the Air Council, which he knew would be seen by the Prime Minister, summarizing his position but ending with a paragraph that placed the responsibility on those above him:

Once a decision has been reached as to the limits on which the Air Council and the Cabinet are prepared to stake the existence of the country, it should be made clear to the Allied Commanders on the continent that not a single aeroplane from Fighter Command beyond the limit will be sent across the Channel, no matter how desperate the situation may become.

It did the trick: three days later Churchill conceded the argument and the Hurricanes were brought back from France. Dowding knew that he had to give Churchill hope that saving Fighter Command and the Spitfires would contribute to victory and he did so in a historic document which concluded with his usual mixture of starkness and simplicity:

I believe that if an adequate fighter force is kept in this country and if the fleet remains in being, and if the home forces are suitably organized to resist invasion, we should be able to carry on the war single-handed for some time, if not indefinitely. But if the home defence force is drained away in desperate attempts to remedy the position in France, defeat in France will involve the final, complete and irredeemable defeat of this country.

The Air Council backed Dowding, but it was a week before he was told, and by then it was beginning to look academic: France was clearly moving towards surrendering and at the same

SPITFIRE LEADERS: Flight Lieutenant Alan Deere (*above left*) and Squadron Leader James Leathart, (*above right*), both of 54 Squadron, were among the first pilots to fully appreciate the Spitfire's fighting qualities. Both men became aces in May–June 1940. Later in the war Leathart, known as 'the Prof' because he went to Liverpool University, held many jobs in the development of tactics.

time there was a new and pressing need for Fighter Command to provide fighter cover over Dunkirk, where the BEF was gathering on the beaches to try and get back to Britain.

Operation Dynamo, the evacuation of Dunkirk, was not the battle for which Fighter Command had been designed. Fortunately for Britain, Hitler's grand strategy was to negotiate peace with Britain for an end to the war in the west, then concentrate on the east, where his main objective was invading Russia. Blitzkrieg had been hugely successful, providing Hitler, the German army, and the *Luftwaffe*, with an almost supreme confidence that they would triumph. Some wiser heads were cautious, but Goering had promised Hitler that the *Luftwaffe* could destroy the BEF on the beaches, thereby saving the German ground troops from the task.

However, the *Luftwaffe* was thirty per cent weaker in numbers than it had been at the start of the war, and many aircrews were exhausted;

Germany paused, unwittingly providing Britain with the brief respite necessary to organize the ships to bring the soldiers home. Fighter Command was expected to provide air superiority over the beaches and the Channel. The beaches were fifty or sixty miles from the nearest RAF bases in Kent and Sussex — beyond the capability of the Dowding System to provide the kind of control it could over Britain. The consequence was that the Spitfire pilots did not get as much warning of where and when German bombers would attack, and had to fly standing patrols some distance from base, reducing their time in the combat area to about forty minutes. However, working at the limit of their operational capability, in the crucial days of the evacuation between 27 May and 4 June 1940, the pilots, for many of whom it was the first taste of combat, were thrown back on their own resourcefulness and on their aircraft. It was in those few days that the Spitfire drew its first real blood against the *Luftwaffe*, proving itself superior to the

DUNKIRK: the RAF's most famous fighter pilot, Douglas Bader (*left*), had his first experience of aerial combat in a Spitfire with 19 Squadron over Dunkirk, where he shot down a Bf 109. Spitfires based in southern England played a vital, if largely invisible, role in the deliverance of the British Army from the beaches (*below*), by keeping the *Luftwaffe* at bay during the evacuation.

Bf 109; in the process, Spitfire pilots gained valuable fighting experience, and felt that superiority for themselves — which in turn gave them confidence. One of the most perceptive Spitfire pilots at Dunkirk was Al Deere, a New Zealander with 54 Squadron based at Hornchurch. He had a high regard for the Spitfire, calling it 'the most beautiful and easy aircraft to fly'. He was also gifted in being able to analyze and describe its performance in combat relative to the Bf 109 in telling detail:

Coming out of the turn when it seemed safe to do so I spotted an Me 109 diving away below me and gave chase immediately. He saw me almost at once and half rolled for the deck with me after him … from 17,000 [feet] down to ground level I hung on to his tail, losing distance slightly in the dive, finishing up about 700 yards astern as he levelled out and set course inland. Inexplicably he started to climb again, from which I assumed he was not aware of my presence behind and below. He climbed steadily but at full throttle, judging from the black smoke pouring from his exhausts, and I continued to close range until at 15,000 feet I judged that I was now near enough to open fire. A long burst produced immediate results. Bits flew off his aircraft which rolled slowly on its back and dived, apparently out of control, towards the scudding clouds below. I was taking no chances. I followed him and continued firing until flames spouted from his engine. By this time I had reached such a speed that my Spitfire was extremely difficult to control and the ground was uncomfortably close. As I eased out of the dive, I was able to watch the Me 109 hit the ground near the town of Saint-Omer and explode in a blinding flash.

Al Deere fought every day for two weeks, shooting down six enemy aircraft, including three 109s, and later flew a captured Bf 109, which confirmed his view that the Spitfire was superior:

In my written report on the combat I stated that in my opinion the Spitfire was superior overall to the Me 109, except in the initial climb and dive; however this was an opinion contrary to the belief of the so-called experts. Their judgement was of course based on intelligence assessments and the performance of the 109 in combat with the Hurricane. In fact the Hurricane, though vastly more manoeuvrable than either the Spitfire or the Me 109, was so badly lacking in speed and rate of climb, that its too-short combat experience against the 109 was not a valid yardstick for comparison. The Spitfire, however, possessed these two attributes to such a degree that, coupled with a better rate of turn than the Me 109, it had the overall edge in combat. There may have been some scepticism by some about my claim for the Spitfire, but I had no doubts on the score; nor did my fellow pilots in 54 Squadron.

Pilots such as Al Deere and their Spitfires were able to provide periods of air superiority over the Dunkirk beaches, though it was not necessarily appreciated at first by the troops on the ground when they did come under air attack. Back in Britain, the RAF was criticized for not protecting the soldiers, but that was because the RAF was seeking to engage the *Luftwaffe*'s raids well before they reached the beaches, invisible to the soldiers who only saw the raids that got through. Keith Park flew over the Dunkirk beaches to assess the

131

position himself, in a Hurricane. His analysis was that he needed to send over bigger patrols but that meant bigger intervals when the air space above the beaches would not be patrolled. He asked for more fighters, but Dowding said no. Generals are not paid to take popular decisions; it was a hard and unemotional response with men dying on the beaches, but Dowding was a general in the middle of a battle, just as much as Wellington at Waterloo or Nelson at the Nile or Trafalgar, and he remained determined to husband his resources in anticipation of an even more important battle to come.

Whether Dowding knew the extent of it or not, the Spitfire had made an impact on the *Luftwaffe* even at this early stage: German pilots were hampered to an extent by bad weather at Dunkirk, but they had not come up against the Spitfire in aerial combat before and Albert Kesselring, the commander of Luftflotte 2, Park's equivalent commander on the other side of the Channel, warned Goering that 'the modern Spitfires had recently appeared, making air operations difficult and costly'.

In fact, early June was the low point for Fighter Command: the Dunkirk evacuation was complete, 338,000 soldiers, the core of the British Army, had been rescued, but Fighter Command had lost 106 fighters, with seventy-five pilots presumed killed, and in the campaign in France as a whole, it had 320 pilots presumed killed while 115 more were prisoners of war. This left Dowding 362 pilots short of the establishment for fifty-two squadrons. Since the start of blitzkrieg, Fighter Command had lost 386 Hurricanes and seventy-six Spitfires, reducing its strength to a total of 814 aircraft of which only

565 were available for operations, including 331 Hurricanes and Spitfires, the balance being made up of Blenheims, Defiants and two squadrons of biplane Gladiators. France was surrendering, which, for Dowding, was a relief because it meant there were no more distractions for his aircraft and pilots — and he greeted the news by commenting 'thank God, now we are alone'.

Dunkirk was a low point for Britain as a whole, but as the evacuation came to its conclusion, in a speech in the House of Commons on 4 June, Churchill rallied the people by striking a defiant tone, ending with the phrase that was to become famous: 'We will never surrender.' Included in the body of the speech was a perceptively crafted passage that paid tribute to the role played by Fighter Command and dispelled any idea that the RAF had let the Army and Navy down:

We must be careful not to assign to this deliverance the attributes of a victory. Wars are not won by evacuations. But there was a victory inside this deliverance which should be noted. It was gained by the Air Force. This was a great trial of strength between the British and the German air forces. Can you conceive a greater objective for the Germans in the air than to make evacuation from these beaches impossible? They tried hard and were beaten back. I will pay my tribute to these young airmen.

Churchill's speech made a huge impression. Doris Melling, a twenty-two-year old shorthand typist in Liverpool and a diarist for Mass Observation, whose brother was serving in the RAF, wrote that evening: 'Although [Dunkirk] was a wonderful thing, we were not to look upon it as a victory —

FIGHTING SPIRIT: the King presents Alan Deere with the Distinguished Flying Cross at Hornchurch on 27 June 1940, at which time he had personally brought down five enemy aircraft. He and another Spitfire pilot were decorated for shooting down two Bf 109s while escorting Squadron Leader Leathart to rescue another squadron CO from Calais; Leathart received the Distinguished Service Order.

wars were not won by evacuations. It was indeed a wonderful speech, and even the BBC announcer got all het up about it.' She returned to it the following day: 'I mentioned in the office that I had heard we were to work another hour per day; one clerk replied: 'After that speech of Churchill's last night we can expect anything.'

Churchill set the tone by identifying the RAF as steadfast and effective at a time when all the news was of defeat. He had been careful not to single out any individuals or aircraft because it was a speech about the collective effort. In June, Al Deere was awarded the Distinguished Flying Cross at RAF Hornchurch by the King while Dowding looked on; Deere had shot down five enemy aircraft during the Operation Dynamo, making him the first Spitfire ace; he had also been shot down and made his way back from France. However, apart from his fighting contribution, his ability to analyze the combat experience contributed greatly to the RAF's understanding of the relative merits of the Spitfire and the Bf 109, and he became a great ambassador for the Spitfire, spreading the positive psychological experience Spitfire pilots gained by combat with Bf 109s and showing the *Luftwaffe*'s best were not invincible. The opposite was true for the Germans. The negative psychological

impact of losing some three hundred of their colleagues without achieving their goal was considerable: the *Luftwaffe* had committed around 300 bombers and 200 fighters to destroying the BEF at Dunkirk, and they had failed. Worse, in apportioning blame Goering did not analyze or appreciate the nature of the problem: that his air force had limitations fighting on its own. It had never before come up against a modern air force with organizational depth based on the latest technology and, above all, committed fighter pilots flying, by even a small margin, the best fighter in the world. Some of Goering's subordinate commanders did understand, in particular Kesselring, who said after the war:

… in the end it was the Spitfires which enabled the British and French to evacuate across the water. Our battered and gradually reinforced formations strained every nerve to attain their objectives. The number of overtired formations was higher than usual, with the natural result that the Spitfires steadily increased our losses.

The *Luftwaffe* still believed in its superiority, but coming up against the Spitfire had taken the edge off the arrogance of its commanders and their

ᴘOPULAR ICON: the Spitfire had not only proved itself in battle by June 1940, its natural beauty (*left*) had made its mark with the people of a nation at war. As a result, it became the focus of a gigantic appeal to the British public to support the war effort, starting with a request (*below*) for scrap aluminium to build more Spitfires.

doubts trickled down the rank structure to the people who actually did the fighting, where the idea that the Spitfire was deadly, especially when flown aggressively by men like Deere, began to take hold. The *Luftwaffe's* fighter culture was elitist, based on a warrior ethos; they were used to triumphing, and anything less hurt their pride. The psychological dent — and in June 1940 it was only a dent — which the Spitfire pilots made in that pride, had a significant effect. This was even evident in their radio transmissions: where they had used a cowboys-and-Indians idiom to warn each other of hostile fighters, '*Achtung Indianer*' became '*Achtung Schpitfeuer*'. The phrase was overheard by RAF pilots, who adopted it as part of their own culture, mimicking the German

accent and following it with machine-gun noises. It eventually found its way into popular culture in Britain, too, into school playgrounds and comic strips, reinforcing the Spitfire's status as a frightening opponent.

Possibly the most significant positive factor for Fighter Command following Dunkirk was that the Spitfire's performance in battle had lived up to the expectations of peacetime. The martial qualities displayed in the newsreels had been proved on the hardest stage of all: the battlefield. Its star qualities were recognized when a photograph of three Spitfires appeared on the cover of the *Radio Times* in the last week of June to promote a BBC radio programme, *Spitfire Over Britain,* devoted to the aircraft's contribution at Dunkirk. The radio documentary was produced by a BBC team camping out at a Fighter Command base, giving the audience a realistic idea of how it worked, spreading the credit to all the people at the base, even though the star was the Spitfire and the climax was a scripted attack on a Heinkel 111 which was shot down.

The Spitfire was a wonderful story, and, knowing a good story when he saw one, Beaverbrook became its greatest publicist. He believed that story could be turned into practical assistance to boost production. By shifting parts between factories and rationalizing the use of skilled and semi-skilled labour, the Castle Bromwich factory had delivered the ten new Spitfires he had demanded by the end of June. But he wanted more, and as a next step he decided on a national appeal for aluminium, putting out a call to the women of Britain to donate all their pots and pans, and enlisting the support of the Women's

THE SPITFIRE FUND: the price of a Spitfire was put at £5,000, for which donors could have their name painted on 'their' Spitfire. 'Red Rose III' (*above*), shown with Battle of Britain ace Squadron Leader J.A. Sanders, was one of three paid for by the Lancashire Constabulary in 1943. Individual funds sprang up across Britain and the Empire, and the RAF found ways to thank everybody from the residents of the Leeward Islands (*below*) to those who contributed in their own high street, including children (*opposite*).

Voluntary Service to collect them. These, he promised to turn into Spitfires. Collection points were established in the streets, aluminium utensils arrived individually and by the pram load, and the collections were built into piles and photographed by the press, lapel badges declaring that the wearer was a 'Shareholder in the Spitfire' were swapped for scrap metal. Jokes were also swapped: 'Out of the Frying Pan into the (Spit)fire!' was the legend on one blackboard by a pots and pans dump; 'I saw your kettle chasing a German bomber over Kent the other day' was another.

In the end, while the campaign was hugely successful in generating publicity, and collected what looked like huge numbers of pots and pans, once they were melted down, the quantity of metal was very small and most of it was not of a quality that could be used in aircraft. What the scheme had done, though, was to place the Spitfire firmly within popular culture, and once that awareness was established, Beaverbrook became even more determined to exploit its growing iconic status for the war effort as well as its fighting qualities. He recognized that many people in the country had been moved by what they had witnessed at Dunkirk and by Churchill's speeches, and that they wanted to be involved, to contribute something directly.

By the time the first new Spitfires were rolling off the production lines at Castle Bromwich, he had created an officially sponsored scheme to collect cash: The Spitfire Fund. A fellow industrialist had asked Beaverbrook how much a Spitfire cost. On hearing that it was £5,000, he had sent Beaverbrook a cheque — and with characteristic

flair, Beaverbrook extended the idea of paying for a Spitfire to the whole country, using the aircraft's growing celebrity in the air, in factories and on the Home Front as a focus around which everybody could unite and feel they had a stake in it. He used the public's emotional response to the Spitfire as a way of crystallizing national sentiment into the Spitfire Fund, getting people to contribute small amounts of money through their workplaces or their localities until collectively they had enough to pay for a Spitfire for the RAF. It worked like a dream: the Spitfire became a symbol of the contribution made by ordinary working people to the war effort as well as a symbol of the courage of its pilots. Public-spirited individuals were motivated to start funds all over the country and throughout

the Empire; in exchange they got the names of their funds painted on the side of a Spitfire. From the Outer Hebrides to Borneo and from a brass band in Southampton, who raised 8 shillings and 6 pence, to Woolworths and the Lancashire Constabulary, people were prepared to pay to adopt Spitfires and were proud to wear a variety of lapel badges in the form of a Spitfire with RAF roundels on its wings and the single word: Spitfire.

While Beaverbrook was busy bullying, cajoling and flattering the country as a whole to produce more Spitfires, and the *Luftwaffe* was pausing for breath, Fighter Command used the respite to prepare for the battle which Churchill wanted to be able to present as a battle for survival, not only to save the nation but also to save the democratic values of the Anglosphere. Hitler still believed he

could negotiate peace with Britain, and Churchill did not discourage him in that belief, buying time to make the defences better, re-focus and improve Fighter Command, time which was invaluable to Dowding. Hitler also knew that before he could switch his attention to the east and invade the Soviet Union, he had to either negotiate peace with Britain or neutralize it, and the only way to be sure of doing that was to invade across the Channel — which would mean achieving air superiority over the RAF first.

In addition to simply wanting more Spitfires, Fighter Command's other high priority was to improve the design of its star fighter by building in the results of real combat experience to maximize any advantage over the Bf 109, however marginal. In May, a Bf 109 had been captured intact in France and delivered to Farnborough, where it

MASS PRODUCTION: by February 1941, the main Assembly Hall at the Castle Bromwich shadow factory (*left*) was turning out Spitfires on a truly industrial scale compared with Supermarine's much smaller production line at Southampton (*below*). Nearly 23,000 Spitfires were built in all, about a quarter of them with money donated through the Spitfire Fund.

was flown in mock combat against the Hurricane and the Spitfire. The results showed that the Bf 109 was superior to the Hurricane except in its turning circle and low-level manoeuvrability. The Spitfire came out ahead on manoeuvrability against the Bf 109, thanks largely to the lower wing loading, a key Mitchell design feature, and was superior in all aspects above 20,000 feet, though the Bf 109 was initially slightly faster than the Spitfire in a dive. However, the tests also showed that by changing from a two-speed to a constant-speed propeller, the Mk 1 Spitfire would be only fractionally slower. Dowding leapt on any technological advantage he could give his pilots and ordered urgent trials with constant-speed propellers. By the middle of June, the evidence showed improvements in take-off and climb performance, a higher operational ceiling, better endurance and, crucially, a higher diving speed than the Bf 109. In a matter of days rather than weeks — evidence of a new urgency and a new relationship between industry and the RAF — all Mk 1 Spitfires were fitted with de Havilland constant-speed propellers, and the Mk II, which was about to start emerging from Castle Bromwich, was fitted with the superior American Rotol system. Other improvements were built into both the Mk I and Mk II: harmonizing the guns to a closer range; using de Wilde incendiary ammunition that flamed when it struck, confirming the pilot's aim; fitting rear-view mirrors, armour plate behind the pilot's seat and a laminated glass shield in front of the Perspex canopy to protect the pilot in a head-on attack.

While the Spitfire was being improved and Beaverbrook and the Vickers management were busy revolutionizing the management at Castle Bromwich to produce more Spitfires, Fighter Command was speeding up the training system by scrounging fighter pilots where it could. Pilots were a fairly heterogeneous fraternity: the RAF itself included regulars, many of whom had come from the Dominions and joined in the late 1930s, including Al Deere from New Zealand, Adolph 'Sailor' Malan from South Africa, and ninety Canadians out of whom whole squadrons were formed, including No. 1 Squadron RCAF, which later became 401 Squadron RAF. They included men from the established British officer class, such as Douglas Bader and Dowding's own son, Derek, a Spitfire pilot with 74 squadron at Hornchurch, but they were not all the classic public-school types. In fact, of 2,945 men who took part in the battle only around seven per cent came from that background, while over forty per cent were non-commissioned pilots, Sergeants and Flight Sergeants, like Ginger Lacey, who had joined through the RAFVR. There was an exclusive element in the Auxiliary Air Force squadrons, who adopted a highly selective attitude to

membership, rather like that of a golf club, and in which Lord Beaverbrook's son, Max Aitken, served with 601 Squadron at Tangmere. Dowding asked for, and got, Royal Navy pilots too, though Churchill had to personally instruct the Royal Navy to release its pilots to the RAF. Then there were 141 Polish pilots who had escaped following the invasion of their country the previous September; these made up 302 and 303 squadrons, which were in training in June 1940, as was a Czech Squadron, 310, and five Free French pilots who took part in the Battle of Britain, forming what later became a Free French air force. There were also three Americans, Gene Tobin, Vernon Keogh and Andrew Mamedoff, who flew Spitfires from Middle Wallop with 609, and William Fiske, who flew with 601 Squadron. Americans were forbidden by law from enlisting in foreign armed forces, so these airmen made a sacrifice in crossing the Atlantic — they did so for ideological reasons, but also because they simply wanted to fly the Spitfire.

Making fighter pilots out of people who can fly aeroplanes is a long process, and like in the Great War, many had to learn the skills on the job. Achieving a unity of energy and purpose between pilot and aircraft was crucial, as a Pilot Officer, William 'Smithy' Duncan Smith wrote after his first flight in a Spitfire in September 1940:

I indeed felt part of the Spitfire, a oneness that was complete … I chanced some aerobatics and found the aircraft's response sweet and positive … one of the features of the Spitfire I discovered was how beautifully she behaved at low speeds and at high G close to the stall … with full power in a steep

BROTHERS IN ARMS: two men who distinguished themselves in the Battle of France and the Battle of Britain. Sergeant James 'Ginger' Lacey (*above left*), was an RAFVR pilot who flew Hurricanes and Spitfires and finished the war as the second highest scoring RAF pilot with twenty-eight victories. Flight Lieutenant The Honorable Max Aitken (*above right*), Lord Beaverbrook's son, flew Spitfires with 601 Squadron Auxiliary Air Force, the so-called 'millionaires squadron' and became a Wing Commander with eight victories, then an MP.

turn and at slow speed she would judder and shake, rocking to and fro, but as long as she was handled correctly, she would not let go and spin … I was to bless these qualities when it came to the real thing: they got me out of trouble more times than I can remember.

The Spitfire would become an instant and lasting friend to the pilots who flew and fought in it during the Battle of Britain. They loved it because it did the job it was designed for superbly. Uniquely among warriors, fighter pilots fight, kill and die alone, often in lonely tracts of hostile sky with only their aircraft for company. Pilots fly into battle together, and plan to fight as a team, but they do not have the soldierly bonds of close comradeship to give them courage in battle; aerial combat has always involved individuals fighting at the limits of human and technical capability, the outcome dependent on quick responses to changing circumstances, where fractions of a second make a difference. Each battle is finely judged, and finding tiny advantages in combat that increase their effectiveness depends on establishing an emotional and physical bond between man and machine, an intimate relationship that enables them to operate as a single entity, the pilot an extension of the aircraft's controls, the aircraft an extension of the pilot's very being.

Establishing that bond was one of the keys to the Spitfire's success as a fighter and this is something that William Duncan Smith expressed in ancient, resonant, almost mystical terms: 'You don't just strap yourself in, you buckle the Spitfire on, like girding on armour … the Spitfire became an integral part of and an extension of one's own sensitivity.'

Pilot Officer H.G. Niven, who flew Hurricanes with 601 Squadron and Spitfires with 602 Squadron, also found the Spitfire's handling remarkable:

Flying the Spitfire was like driving a sports car. It was faster than the old Hurricane, much more delicate. A perfect lady; it wouldn't do anything wrong. The Hurricane would drop a wing if you stalled it coming in, but a Spitfire would come wafting down; you couldn't snap it into a spin. Beautiful to fly … and so fast … if you shut the throttle in a Hurricane you'd come to a grinding halt; in a Spitfire, you just go whistling on.

The Spitfire was not, as some of its detractors had believed, 'too fast for dogfighting'. RAF fighter pilots who had exchanged their Fury and Gauntlet biplanes adapted their skills to flying the much faster Spitfire relatively easily; it seems extraordinary now, but there were no two-seater Spitfires at the time and most pilots made their first flights after just a briefing from somebody who had flown it before. There were the Spitfire quirks, such as the narrow undercarriage and the hand pump to put it down, and the flaps to reduce landing speed, but once they became routine, pilots found they could establish that all-important bond with their machine that made flying and fighting a single, flowing experience, based on trust.

The problem for most pilots was tactics rather than flying the Spitfire: the RAF official Manual of Air Tactics specified a series of standard attacks as the basis of aerial combat, carried out with the kind

of parade-ground precision and formation flying that thrilled the crowds at air displays. They were known as Fighting Area Attacks, or FAAs, the whole idea being that fighters would be attacking bombers together, at speeds well over 300 mph, and each one might not have enough time to hit the bomber hard enough on its own. To bring the maximum firepower to bear on the target, fighters took off, climbed and fought in a basic unit of three, flying in a 'vic', the leader ahead of two wingmen. Once a target had been identified, and on the order of the leader, they moved into line astern or echelon port or starboard, each fighter effectively joining a queue to fire at the same target. The vic was an inflexible formation which made keeping a look-out difficult in the air, presented a closely packed target for enemy fighters and gunners, and if it came under attack from escorting enemy fighters, any fast move could result in collision. Nor did the theory take any account of escorting fighters, or the bomber crews' efforts to weave all over the sky in an attempt to escape, not to mention firing their own guns. Worst of all, the FAAs robbed the fighter pilot of his initiative.

The *Luftwaffe*'s fighters flew in a much looser, more flexible formation, based on four aircraft operating as two pairs some 200 yards apart which meant they could operate as four or split into two groups of two, each one based on the idea of a leader and a wingman whose job was to keep a lookout behind. The RAF pilots spoke with one voice having encountered the Bf 109s and steadily adapted to a variation on the German system they called the 'finger four' from the spread of the finger tips of the hand. At whatever speed, aerial combat, especially against

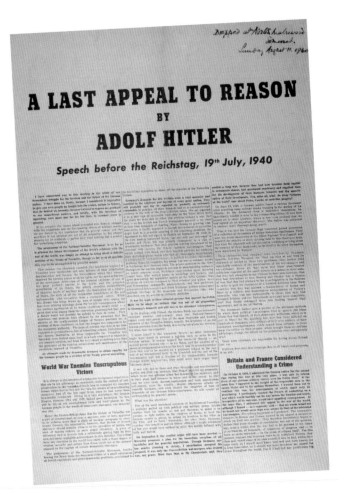

other fighters, was infinitely fluid and individual; it relied on seeking and using any advantage, just as it had done in the Great War; it relied on the fighter pilot's training, but also on his spatial awareness, aggressive instincts and ability to judge the immediate situation and how to make best use of the small advantages of speed, manoeuvrability and, above all, confidence in his aeroplane, something the Spitfire gave him.

After two months of defeats in Europe, Britain was alone: from Norway through the Low Countries to the South of France, the Nazis were installing their forces of occupation; Mussolini had allied himself with Hitler and declared war on Britain; any decisive Bomber Command offensive was a long way in the future and Fighter Command had too few fighters. However, production was on the increase, civilian and RAF engineers were

carrying out improvements to the Spitfire at squadron level to make them as ready for battle as possible, the RAF was scouring the country for fighter pilots to fly the new Spitfires and Hurricanes and to fill the gaps left in its ranks after Dunkirk, and those pilots, and the British public, were embarking on a love affair with the Spitfire on whose performance so much hinged.

On 18 June, Churchill made a speech in the House of Commons that prepared the British people for the battle ahead. It was a speech that defined and created a mood of defiance in preparation for the Battle of Britain: 'Let us therefore brace ourselves to our duties, and so bear ourselves that if the British Empire and its Commonwealth last for a thousand years, men will still say, "This was their finest hour".' Excalibur had been unsheathed.

5 BATTLE

In the Battle of Britain, as in the war as a whole, a few brave men fought and died while millions of others—whole economies—were harnessed to give them the weapons to do so. The human cost of the battle was high: of 2,945 airmen who fought, 507 were killed and 500 more wounded.

146

THE BATTLE OF BRITAIN was the defining episode
in the evolution of the Spitfire as a national icon.
It was fought through the long days of high
summer 1940: on some days Spitfire pilots raced
after their prey dragging their vapour trails across
brilliant blue skies with southern England spread
out like a quilted map beneath them; on others
they flew low, close to a choppy, grey sea to
protect convoys, stalking their quarry in opaque
rain, always on the lookout for predators among
the towering clouds. It was on days like those that
Tubby Mayne found his Spitfire cockpit comfort-
ingly snug: '… the Spit and the Merlin engine, they
were superb. They were what gave us confidence.
You could get into that cockpit and shut the

THE FEW (*previous pages*):
Pilot Officer Keith
Gillman was just nineteen
years old when he failed to
return from a mission over
the Channel on 25 August
1940, having posed for one
of the most iconic images
of the human dimension to
the national struggle.

IMAGE OF INNOCENCE
(*right*): this image, entitled
'children in Dover watch
a dogfight between
the *Luftwaffe* and RAF
Spitfires', was taken by the
Magnum photographer
George Roger, who found
them straining to watch
the Battle of Britain taking
place above their heads.

canopy and feel you were in a fortress and no one
could get you.'

From July to September the daily life of Britain
went on as normally as it could with a battle for
national survival going on overhead: people still
went to the factory, the office and the pub; they
read books and they tended their gardens. But
the battle brought distractions: trips to the air-
raid shelters, eking out the tea ration, collecting
money for the Spitfire Fund, and every night tens
of millions of people joined the nightly ritual of
listening to the news on the BBC Home Service.
The daily round-up of events was as much a
collective national experience as a source of information, the newsreaders crystallizing the mood
of the day: thoughtful if the news was bad; elated
if it was good and inspiring; anticipatory when
Churchill's voice was about to boom defiance out
of the family radio set. Churchill delivered his own
running commentary on the war and a constant
theme was to leave no doubt about the sheer
scale of what was happening:

*The Battle of France is over. The Battle of Britain
is about to begin. Upon this battle depends the
survival of Christian civilization, upon it depends
our own British way of life and the long continuity
of our institutions and our Empire.*

His speech on 18 June made sense to the British
people but not to Hitler. The Führer found it
incomprehensible that Churchill was not going
to negotiate peace terms, which meant that Hitler
would have to invade Britain. The mood in Berlin
changed: he had tried to get his way by threat, but
now Goering and the *Luftwaffe* would have to
make good that threat and use force, fighting the

THE BATTLE OF BRITAIN: the apparently random patterns of contrails left by British and German aircraft in a dogfight on 18 September 1940 (*right*) seem to have inspired the Official War Artist Paul Nash's masterpiece of composition (*top*). It is a fierce, chaotic view of the threat posed by high-level bombers over Kent, seen from peaceful countryside north of the Thames where, in the foreground, Spitfires take off to join the fray.

RAF for control of the skies over the Channel and southern England. Goering accepted the challenge, asserting confidently that the *Luftwaffe* would beat the RAF, and on 2 July, Hitler approved Directive 16, authorizing his Chiefs of Staff to start planning to invade Britain in September.

In the meantime, as a prelude to the battle, Goering set about a more immediate plan: to close the Channel to British shipping. The *Luftwaffe* had

around 2,600 aircraft, including 1,200 medium bombers, Heinkel 111s, Dornier 17s and multi-role Ju 88s, 280 Ju 87 Stuka dive-bombers, and 980 fighters, mostly modern Bf 109s, but also Bf 110s — twin-engined fighters designed to destroy bombers but highly vulnerable to Spitfires and Hurricanes.

By July, Fighter Command had its establishment of fifty-two squadrons. Eight of them were made up of Defiants, Blenheims and Gladiators, all of which had been shown to be highly vulnerable to the Bf 109, but the remaining forty-four were equipped with modern fighters — nineteen with Spitfires and twenty-five with Hurricanes. However, not all were up to strength: the total serviceable aircraft numbered around 600, although the deficit in pilots had been reduced from 362 just after Dunkirk to seventy-nine. Bomber Command also deployed its Whitleys and Wellingtons to attack airfields and ports in northern France which could serve to embark an invasion force.

ODERN EXCALIBUR: bathed in sunlight from a clear sky, a Mk I Spitfire over the English countryside evokes the deadly purpose in the midst of tranquillity that characterized the summer of 1940.

In July, Castle Bromwich produced another twenty-three Spitfires, taking total production to twenty more than had been planned. Dowding and Beaverbrook were both key figures in the Spitfire story, very different people who got on because both were both single-minded and knew how to get results. Beaverbrook's ruthless pursuit of increased output of fighters was working: in a six-week period between June and early August, the industry turned out 166 Spitfires and 322 Hurricanes. The Castle Bromwich workforce, forty per cent of whom were women, underwent a transformation, the Vickers management was as ruthless as their boss in streamlining the production process — which had involved the widespread sacking of people who would not change to a more flexible pattern of work and respond to the needs of war. There was still much to do, but integrating improvements and modifications into the production while also increasing output was beginning to work, and a team spirit was developing as people recognized the importance of their contribution. When the Supermarine test pilot Jeffrey Quill, another key person in the Spitfire story, went to collect the first Castle Bromwich Spitfire, after a frustrating day waiting for it to be finished, he took off and immediately went into an aerobatic display over the airfield so that the people who had made it could see what they had done and feel that they were playing a part in the coming battle against the *Luftwaffe*. The uncanny ability of the Spitfire to inspire confidence and affection, and its proven fighting quality, added to the improved production prospects, brought an order for yet another 1,000 Spitfires.

The Battle of Britain started on 10 July. As its first target the *Luftwaffe* chose a westbound

149

ATTACK ON A CONVOY SEEN FROM THE AIR (*above*): the war artist Richard Eurich's vivid impression of the opening stages of the Battle of Britain, when the *Luftwaffe* tried and failed to close the English Channel to merchant and naval shipping.

convoy of merchant ships and their destroyer escorts codenamed 'Bread'. It was just off Folkestone when radar picked the first indications of a large raid heading to attack it. The first engagement of the battle came just before two o'clock: a force of twenty-four Dornier 17s escorted by thirty Messerschmitt Bf 110s and Bf 109s was intercepted by one squadron of Spitfires and two squadrons of Hurricanes. One Hurricane squadron took on the bombers while the other Hurricanes and the Spitfires took on the fighters; the *Luftwaffe* lost two Dorniers and ten Bf 109s while 11 Group lost one Hurricane, which collided with a Dornier, and five Hurricanes and four Spitfires were damaged. One merchant ship was sunk. It was a Fighter Command victory by any standards.

The following day, radar picked up a raid heading for an eastbound convoy in Lyme Bay. Six Hurricanes and six Spitfires intercepted about ten Stukas, but as they were about to attack, they were bounced by around twenty Bf 109s; the Spitfires split, three going for the Stukas while the other three and the Hurricanes took on the Bf 109s. The result was one Hurricane and two Spitfires lost for two Bf 109s shot down, a much more sobering outcome than the previous day. However, no ships were hit and in other engagements that day, the *Luftwaffe* lost eleven aircraft to Fighter Command's four.

On 14 July another westbound convoy was attacked just off Dover. It was a sunny day and the press had gathered on the cliffs in the afternoon anticipating they might see the fighting at first hand;

they included the Pathe cameraman J.F. Gemmell and the BBC reporter Charles Gardner. With no warning, suddenly Gardner realized that the convoy was being attacked by Stukas. He was unable to identify all the aircraft but just started recording what he saw and in so doing produced what became a classic eye-witness account of an aerial battle:

The Germans are dive-bombing a convoy out to sea … there's one going down on its target now — Bomb! No, he missed the ships — it hasn't hit a single ship … There are about ten ships in the convoy but he hasn't hit a single one … there are one, two, three, four, five, six German machines dive-bombing the British convoy … but now the British fighters are coming up … here they come — the Germans are coming absolutely steep dive and you can see the bombs actually leave the machines … but I can't see our Spitfires … Oh, here's one coming down … there's one going down in flames … somebody's hit a German … a long streak of smoke … the pilot's bailed out by parachute … and he's going slap into the sea … and there he goes, Smash!

Oh yes, I can see one, two, three, four, five, six, seven, eight, nine, ten Germans haring back to France now for all they can go … Now there are the Spitfires, there are about four fighters up there and I don't know what they're doing: one, two, three, four, five fighters fighting, fighting, fighting, right over our heads now. There is one down right on the tail of what I think is a Messerschmitt and I think a Spitfire behind him … there are three Spitfires chasing three Messerschmitts. Oh boy! … Oh this is really grand … and there is a Spitfire just behind the

first two, he's got them. The RAF fighters have really got these boys taped … our machine is catching up the Messerschmitt now … now right in the fight … Now go on George you've got him.

Gardner's report was played to the nation about four hours later, to a huge and overwhelmingly positive radio audience; it was just what people wanted to hear, and its eyewitness quality, and the sheer excitement in his voice, conveyed a sense of truth and of victory. Churchill sent the pilots a message of congratulation and that evening, in a speech broadcast immediately after Gardner's report, he stirred their hearts again with images of a Britain 'shielded from above by the prowess and devotion of our airmen.'

However, there were those who objected to the populist tone of the report, including one correspondent to *The Times* who described it as 'revolting … Where men's lives are concerned, must we be treated to a running commentary on a level with an account of the Grand National or a Cup Final tie?' Such views were challenged by others who found it '… inspiring, for I felt that I was sharing in it, and I rejoiced unfeignedly that so many of the enemy were shot down and the rest put to ignominious flight.' The BBC defended its decision to broadcast vigorously. Given the huge popularity of the report on radio, the following week, an edited version of Gardner's commentary was put together with Gemmel's footage of the same incident, and other footage, and released by Pathe as a cinema newsreel, adding to its impact. The Spitfire was at the heart of both reports.

Unfortunately, the report was not as accurate as the millions who listened to it assumed: the attacking force of about thirty Stukas, protected by thirty Bf 109s, was initially attacked by just three Hurricanes, one of which was shot down, and the parachute Gardner assumed was a German pilot was almost certainly that Hurricane pilot, Pilot Officer Michael Mudie, who was rescued by the Royal Navy but died of his wounds the next day. Six more Hurricanes and twelve Spitfires arrived and two Stukas and one Bf 109 were shot down, with two more crash-landing in France; the convoy was undamaged. That Gardner had misidentified some aircraft was understandable: he simply assumed that all aircraft shot down were German and that all British fighters were Spitfires, suggesting that was the way it seemed at the time and that he instinctively saw the Spitfire as the protector.

If evidence of the importance of having fighters of the Spitfire's quality was needed, and how different the battle might have gone had those who believed in Mitchell's genius not persevered in building truly modern fighters, it came tragically

on 19 July. Nine Defiants of No. 141 Squadron were scrambled to patrol south of Folkestone when they were bounced by twenty Bf 109s flying cover for a raid on Dover Harbour; within minutes, six of the Defiants had been shot down with four pilots and five air gunners killed, and two pilots injured.

At 8.15 on the morning of 24 July, one of the biggest battles so far took place off North Foreland; it became known as the Battle of Thames Estuary. Radar had identified a large raid setting out from Calais towards two convoys in the estuary, prompting the Spitfires of 54 Squadron at Hornchurch, just across the estuary, to be scrambled. When they arrived they found two waves of Dornier 17s, each of eighteen aircraft, protected by more than forty Bf 109s: initially twelve Spitfires against sixty or seventy German bombers and fighters. Al Deere, who was leading a section, reported the size of the raid to the control room, then 'got among them' and he managed to open fire on a Dornier, but was

Casualty: the two-seater Defiant was withdrawn from daytime service in the Battle of Britain, though it continued to operate at night. It later had on-board radar fitted and had some success when attacking from below at night.

forced to break off for fear of colliding with it just as the Bf 109s attacked the Spitfires. Two more squadrons of Spitfires then arrived, and in a matter of seconds, the sky was filled with aircraft trying to shoot one another down and avoid colliding at the same time. The Dorniers broke off their attack and headed back towards France with the fighters trying to protect them, but three were shot

NEMESIS: Germany's most prolific fighter, the Messerschmitt Bf 109. More than 30,000 were built — almost half of all German aircraft production — and like the Spitfire, its performance and capability was developed throughout the war. By 1944, however, it was overwhelmed by long-range American fighters such as the Mustang.

down over the estuary and four Bf 109s were shot down in the ensuing fighter-to-fighter battle. Then the sky was empty, but Fighter Command had succeeded: the attack had been broken up and the convoys protected.

The battle illustrated that Fighter Command's job was to shoot down the bombers or at least break up the raids and prevent them from doing any damage; fighters were only taken on to stop them protecting the bombers and though there was no rule, increasingly where the RAF fighters included Spitfires and Hurricanes, it was the Spitfires who took on the Bf 109s. During July, the *Luftwaffe* had hoped to clear the skies of British fighters as a prelude to gaining air superiority; they tried to tempt the Spitfires into combat by flying high above the bombers, but Dowding and the Commander of 11 Group, Keith Park, were

clear: the priority was hitting the bombers. Goering, and some German commanders, believed they were on top, and that the RAF was far weaker in numbers than was the case: in the month of July, Beaverbrook had managed to squeeze 488 fighters out of the factories; in contrast, the *Luftwaffe* had only received 220 new Bf 109s.

By the end of July the *Luftwaffe* had little to show for its efforts: the Channel was not closed and Britain's sea-trade had not been damaged; the Germans had sunk four destroyers and eighteen, mainly small, merchant vessels and they had destroyed 148 RAF fighters; however, they had lost 286 aircraft, 105 of them fighters, and the Ju 87 Stuka and Bf 110 fighter had been shown to be very vulnerable. The effectiveness of the Bf 109 had been demonstrated, but so had the effectiveness of the Spitfire.

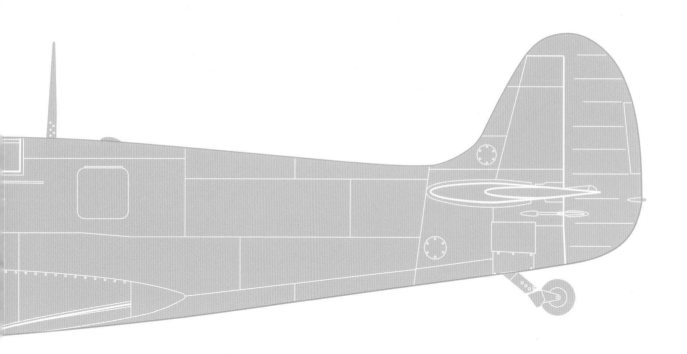

PROTOTYPE (K5054)	
I	
37 ft	
29 ft 11 in	
4,082 lbs	
5,359 lbs	
Rolls-Royce Merlin C 27-litre, V-12	
990 hp	
349 mph at 16,800 ft	
35,400 ft	
8 min 12 sec to 20,000 ft	
1,770 ft / min at 20,000 ft	
Ballast to December 1936, then 8 x .303 Browning machine guns	

A Mk IX delivered in April 1944 (*above left*), it remains in flying condition in California. Later models of the Mk IX were fitted with the Merlin 66 engine which was tailored to match the FW 190 and had their wing tips removed to increase their rate of roll in combat.

The main difference between the Mk IX and its predecessors was the more powerful engine. The Merlin 61 came with the negative-G carburettor with automatically controlled, two-speed superchargers. The engine required two radiators compared with one on previous Spitfires, and they were thermostatically controlled rather than operated by the pilot; to cater for increased fuel consumption, the tanks were enlarged and pressurized, and though the cockpit was not pressurized, the pilot did have an improved heating and cooling system.

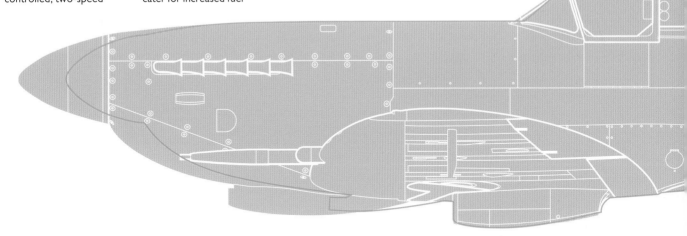

SPITFIRE	F MK IX (AB 505)
Total Built	5665
Wingspan	36 ft 10 in
Length	31 ft 4 in
Tare weight	5,800 lbs
All up weight	7295.5 lbs
Power plant	Rolls-Royce Merlin 61 27-litre, V-12
Max power	1,565 hp
Max speed	408 mph at 25,000 ft
Service ceiling	43,000 ft
Time to height	5 min 42 sec to 20,000 ft
Rate of Climb	3950 ft / min at 20,000 ft
Typical armament	2 x 20mm Hispano cannon and 4 x .303 Browning machine guns

A Mk IX showing its two radiators and central carburettor air intake (left); also visible are the blanked-off ports, which were standard in the universal wing, enabling two more cannon to be fitted.

SPITFIRE MK IX

The Mk IX Spitfire set a new standard in fighter performance in the middle of the Second World War. It was built to counter the latest German fighter, the Focke-Wulf 190, and the high-altitude bomber and reconnaissance variants of the Junkers Ju 88. The urgent need for a new air-defence Spitfire was met initially by adapting the Mk V airframe to take the more powerful Merlin 61 engine. Performance improved dramatically, but accommodating the engine meant extending the nose and fitting a four-bladed propeller —

Spitfire IXs of 241 Squadron (*far right*) flown by Flying Officers H. Cogman and J.V. Macdonald over mountainous terrain south of Rome, 27 January 1944. They carried out tactical and shipping reconnaissance, escort and ground-attack duties over Italy and continued in these multiple roles until the end of the war. *Right*: Mk IX Spitfires of 443 (Canadian) Squadron taking off from Ford airfield on the Sussex coast. The squadron was equipped with Mk IXs in March 1944 in preparation for D-Day and during the landings it flew low-level cover over the beaches using 44-gallon drop tanks for added range and endurance; 443 moved to the continent on 15 June to carry out deep penetration ground-attack sorties using 90-gallon drop tanks, and moved with the ground forces right up to VE Day.

The Mk IX, like all Spitfires, was a gift to photographers. This study, of a pilot mounting his aircraft to go to war, shot against a vivid, sunlit sky, attended by his airman rigger, was commissioned by the Royal Aeronautical Society.

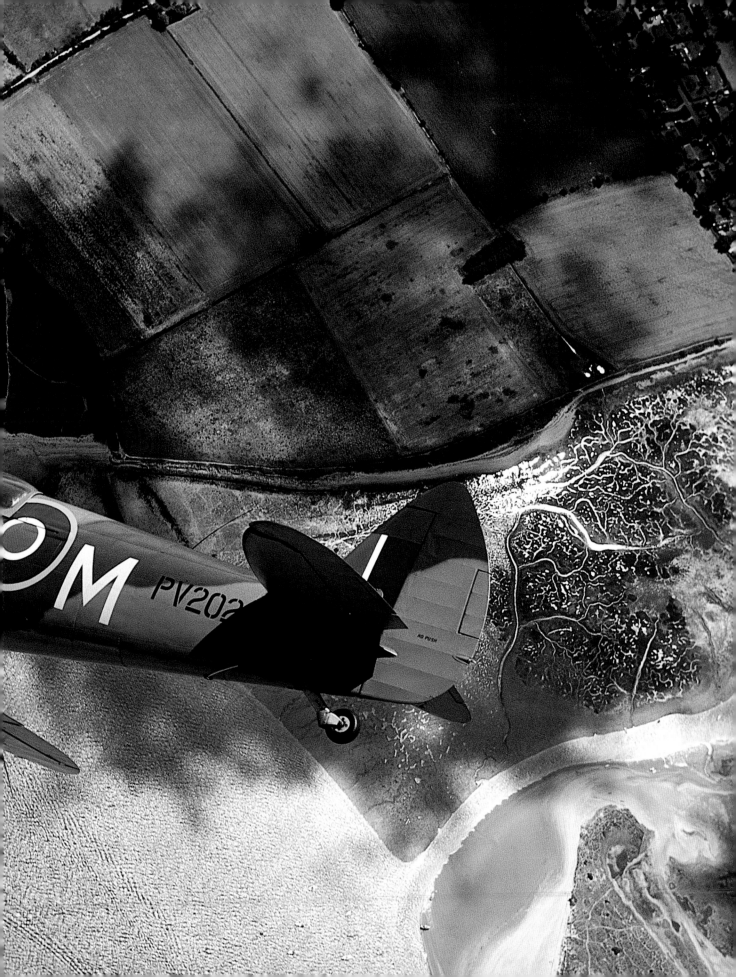

S PITFIRE APPEAL: Douglas Matthews, aged two, was taken to a Sunderland department store in August 1940 dressed in his mini-RAF uniform (*above*). He played with model aircraft in the store window as a way of helping to boost the collection for the Spitfire Fund.

A SPITFIRE MADE FOR TWO: the Mk IX Spitfire (*left*) was delivered to the RAF in 1944, flying with 33 Squadron and 412 Squadron RCAF. It was sold back to Vickers-Armstrong in 1946 for conversion into a Tr9 training machine for the Irish Air Corps before being restored to enable non- military pilots to experience the thrill of aerobatics in the Spitfire.

On 1 August Hitler issued Directive 17, which ordered the *Luftwaffe* to destroy the RAF 'with all means at its disposal and as soon as possible.' On the same day, Goering held a conference with his senior commanders in The Hague to pass on Hitler's orders: 'the Führer has ordered me to crush Britain with my *Luftwaffe*. By delivering a series of heavy blows I plan to have this enemy, whose morale is already at its lowest, down on its knees in the nearest future so that our troops can land on the island without any risk.'

The overall head of the *Luftwaffe*'s fighters, Colonel Theo Osterkamp, saw the validity of Dowding's concentration on attacking bombers. He told Goering he believed that Fighter Command had eleven new Spitfire squadrons, which he believed were as good as the Bf 109, but Goering dismissed his comments: 'This is nonsense. Our information is excellent and I am perfectly aware of the situation. The Messerschmitt is much better that the Spitfire because the British are too cowardly to engage your fighters.'

Having failed to close the Channel to shipping, or to destroy the RAF in the air, Goering had a new plan for the *Luftwaffe*: he decided to attack British fighters on the ground by bombing Fighter Command's airfields. This new plan went under the grand title of *Adlerangriff* (Eagle Attack) and the start date, set for 5 August, was to be known as *Adlertag* (Eagle Day). While the *Luftwaffe*'s planners worked, the weather intervened, and *Adlertag* was delayed until 13 August, a delay that was to Fighter Command's advantage: on 1 August, Dowding had 245 serviceable Spitfires and 341 serviceable Hurricanes; in those two weeks the number of aircraft at his disposal increased and

Dowding made two Polish squadrons and one Czechoslovak squadron operational.

In the heat of battle, the Spitfire Fund was booming. Its success on the ground was largely down to the energy and commitment of women: in Newcastle, the mother of a two-year old boy, Douglas Matthews, made her son a tiny RAF uniform and took him to a department store in Sunderland to collect money from shoppers; the Ladies' Hairdressers combined to collect enough to present the nation with a Spitfire they chose to name 'Permanent Wave'; another Spitfire had the name 'W.D.F.U.N.Z.' on the side, having been paid for with £5,000 raised by the Women's Division of the Farmers' Union of New Zealand. There was even a fund set up by a lady called Dorothy, who collected money from other women called Dorothy and had a Spitfire named after them. In Kent, during the plum harvest, the Pathe Gazette newsreel showed a group of schoolgirls picking baskets full of ripe fruit and setting up a roadside stall to sell them for the local fund. There was huge national awareness of the scheme, but it was at a local level that the support of the local press turned many small contributions into larger sums: the *Worcester Evening News and Times* presented a Spitfire called 'The Malverns' and, not to be outdone, the *Kidderminster Shuttle* presented another, 'Kidderminster, Bewdley & Stourport'; in Northern Ireland, the *Belfast Telegraph* raised enough to present seventeen Spitfires, all named after parts of the province.

Another route was through business: The miners of Bolsover Colliery raised over £13,000; Woolworths presented two Spitfires, 'Nix Six Primus' and 'Nix Six Secundus' from their

162 NOTHING OVER SIXPENCE: the directors and staff of Woolworths funded the purchase of two Spitfires, which were painted with the store's 'Nothing Over Sixpence' logo.

marketing slogan Nothing Over Sixpence. On 9 August, Frank Edwards, 32, a factory buyer, recorded in his Mass Observation diary:

Well, today started off in good style for on arrival at the office we all found on our tables a sheet of paper folded into three, bearing on the outside the words: Important to every worker. On the inside was an announcement that our company was going to present a Spitfire to the Air Ministry and that £5,000 was needed. Subscriptions were to be made during the four pay days of this month. Everyone seemed to be very enthusiastic about the idea and in the course of the day, a poster showing a Spitfire with suitable wording was displayed.

People from all walks of life wanted to be associated with the Spitfire and they used its image on envelopes, advertising on leaflets, on National Savings Stamps, postcards, posters, seed packets, clocks and stamps, and above all on lapel badges. Many individual Funds had their own badges made, finding the opportunity to associate their locality, business or organization with the Spitfire irresistible: Cheadle Rural District Council, Vauxhaul-Bedford Motors, whose badge made wearers 'Shareholder', The Flying Doctor Service and the Barrier District Pastoralists in Australia. Tiny models were made by Meccano to be worn in buttonholes, and were exchanged for millions of contributions. What had started out with collecting scrap had turned into one of the most successful appeals of the 20th century, in the course of which the act of giving involved people in what the Spitfire was doing — and with it began a lasting bond of affection.

HARD EVIDENCE: the remains of a Bf 109 shot down in 1940 are paraded through Parliament Square in London, drawing attention to the effectiveness of the Spitfire Fund in supporting the war effort.

If people worldwide expressed their confidence in the Spitfire by raising money to buy more of them, the RAF expressed its confidence by ordering them. Fighter pilots and test pilots, ground crews, engineers and technicians, senior commanders, draughtsmen, development engineers and designers all played their part in creating its status as an invincible weapon by increasing its effectiveness. For example: one of the disadvantages of the Merlin engine compared with the

Daimler Benz engine in the Bf 109, which had fuel injection, was that the Merlin had carburettors. The result was that in a negative G manoeuvre in combat, such as pushing over into a high-speed dive, the Bf 109 had an advantage because the power continued uninterrupted while the Merlin briefly cut out as the carburettor was starved of fuel. The reason was that when the Merlin had been designed and developed, dogfighting had not been anticipated as the primary function of the

164

new fighters. They had been seen as gun platforms to fly in a standard form of attack on an obliging bomber flying straight and level, not twisting and turning and changing direction every few seconds at over 350 mph. The problem was fixed by an enterprizing scientist at Farnborough, Miss Beatrice Shilling, who suggested putting a thin diaphragm with a small hole in the centre in the float chamber to prevent the fuel being flung by centripetal force to the top of the carburettor. It worked, and another little disadvantage over the Bf 109 was ironed out. In her honour, pilots christened the device 'Miss Shilling's orifice'.

The Spitfire was evolving in the heat of the battle. On 5 August, Jeffrey Quill rejoined the RAF briefly, in part because he wanted to fight, but also because he wanted to learn first-hand how the Spitfire performed in combat and how it could be improved. He was posted to 65 Squadron at Hornchurch, which had three squadrons of Spitfires, and flew routinely during August, being credited with one Bf 109 shot down and sharing in the destruction of a Heinkel 111 before being recalled to Supermarine where his test-pilot skills were required. It was a valuable insight into the practical problems faced by the fighter pilots, and one of his major recommendations was to improve the visibility from the cockpit to enable the pilot to twist and turn his head more. Other visibility problems occurred at high level: the coolant in the water often boiled above 20,000 feet and the steam escaped only to form ice on the outside of the canopy immediately and when diving suddenly the inside of the canopy became covered in condensation; the problem was overcome by diverting hot air from the engine

into the cockpit before diving. Many pilots had also discovered a marked stiffening of aileron control at airspeeds around 400 mph in a dive; as a result of Quill's work, the fabric ailerons were found to bulge at very high speeds and fitting alloy replacements made a huge improvement.

One of the most pressing needs was to give Spitfire pilots better armament and in early August, 19 Squadron was equipped with the Spitfire Mk IB, which had two 20mm Hispano cannon fitted instead of the normal eight Browning machine guns. They were not ready for combat: the cannon were mounted on their sides to fit them into the Spitfire's thin wing, on mountings that were not sufficiently rigid and that prevented the spent cartridge cases from being ejected properly so that they frequently jammed under combat conditions. When they did jam, the recoil made the aircraft yaw towards the side on which the gun had failed. Some improvements, such as increasing the amount of armour plate around the pilot's seat and the fuel tank, could be incorporated swiftly, but others took time to reach the front-line squadrons, and many of them were not available until after the Battle of Britain; others were built into the Spitfire Mk II, which retained the eight Brownings, the first of which were delivered to 611 Squadron in August as the battle moved up a gear.

Poor weather had delayed *Adlertag*, but on 12 August it began to improve as a large high-pressure weather system moved over Britain from the Azores. The *Luftwaffe* launched a series of attacks on Fighter Command airfields and radar stations at Hawkinge, Manston, Lympe and Ventnor, designed to force the fighters into the air

REASSURING IMAGE: 65 Squadron during the Battle of Britain. One of the three Hornchurch Spitfire squadrons that used Manston as a forward base, they never spent the night at Manston, but flew in each morning from Rochford, deliberately overflying Deal, Margate and Ramsgate to let the townsfolk know that the Spitfires had arrived.

or face being destroyed on the ground. The attack on Manston was carried out by a force of mixed fighters, Bf 110s and Bf 109s, using improvized bomb racks carrying a single bomb; they damaged two hangars, runway areas and other ground installations. The three squadrons of Spitfires at Manston got airborne quickly, and fought a series of battles, but were then ordered to land back at their home base of Hornchurch because of the damage done to Manston, which they could see smoking. Hawkinge and Lympne were damaged too, and Ventnor radar station was put out of

commission. The *Luftwaffe* claimed to have shot down forty-six Spitfires and twenty-three Hurricanes. In fact they had shot down twenty-two aircraft in all, killing eleven pilots, and lost thirty-one aircraft themselves. Dowding realized immediately that what he saw as the real battle was just about to begin.

August 13 promised to be a fine day, but the morning was cloudy. Goering had planned massive raids, but as a result of bad intelligence and his own indecisiveness, and despite detailed planning, the *Luftwaffe*'s morning operations were a

AIR FIGHT OVER PORTLAND 1940, WITH CONTRAILS AND AIRCRAFT IN THE SKY: Richard Eurich's study of air warfare from the spectator's viewpoint captures the contrast between the peace and tranquillity on the ground and the desperate struggle going on overhead. The layers of the battle are evident from the decaying contrails at high altitude, the smoke dragged by a stricken aircraft, the wreckage and the lone Spitfire over the harbour heading for the melée.

shambles: orders for bombers to take off were received and acted on; then Goering ordered the attack postponed until the afternoon but only the fighters received the order, leaving bombers to head for England unprotected. The *Luftwaffe* had identified Royal Navy, Coastal and Training Command airfields as fighter stations; they were attacked, but damage to Fighter Command was slight. In the afternoon, Goering put his largest force to date in the air to bomb targets in the Thames Estuary, Kent, Portland and Southampton. It claimed seventy Spitfires and Hurricanes were destroyed, plus eighteen Blenheims, when in fact Fighter Command lost a total of thirteen aircraft and shot down forty-five.

The attacks continued that night against the aircraft industry, including the Spitfire factory at Castle Bromwich, but only eleven bombs were dropped and production was not affected. The following day, the *Luftwaffe* attacked in smaller numbers, hitting Manston again, and seven other airfields, but with small raids, some of which were against maintenance and training airfields. A single Heinkel 111 attacked the Spitfire Operational Conversion Unit at Hawarden in North Wales, way beyond the range of escort fighters, prompting two senior flying instructors and one of their pupils to scramble and shoot it down near Chester. The *Luftwaffe* lost nineteen aircraft to eight RAF fighters.

It was evident to *Luftwaffe* pilots that Fighter Command had not been crushed. German intelligence overestimated the damage caused, assuming the raids had been devastating when in fact the damage they inflicted was limited. Aircraft on the ground were dispersed around the perimeter and given individual blast pens and, thanks to the Dowding System, many pilots were given enough warning to get into the air before the attack; damage was also swiftly repaired. The *Luftwaffe* commanders failed to appreciate how Dowding had integrated radar stations with the network of control rooms that kept functioning even when parts of it were hit and put out of action. The radar stations were attacked but rarely put out of action; the masts were hard to damage with bombs and the buildings were small targets and needed a direct hit to knock them out. Goering did not understand their importance, and in his order for the day on 15 August, he told his

commanders to stop attacking them because such attacks were clearly not effective.

The *Luftwaffe* committed every fighter it had and most of its bomber force to the attack on 15 August. By not committing his whole bomber force, Goering was effectively admitting that the *Luftwaffe* had so far failed to gain air superiority. It was also clear that the Bf 110 Zerstörer twin-engined fighter and the Ju 87 Stuka dive-bomber were just too vulnerable. Goering believed in fighters protecting bombers, and he issued orders that each Stuka squadron be protected by three Bf 109 squadrons: one to provide close protection around them, even to the extent of diving with them on their bombing runs, one to fly ahead and take on any attacking fighters, and one behind to protect the rear. Goering was trying to achieve superiority by two means: by destroying airfields with bombs and by fighter-to-fighter battles in the air. The Bf 109 pilots were stuck between the two, and taking on the Spitfires at the extreme limits of their range while also trying to protect the bombers proved to be too much. However, the tactics came from the top. Goering denied the Bf 109 pilots what they longed for, the freedom to use the whole sky to take on the Spitfires. Instead, flying close protection meant waiting to be attacked, putting them at a disadvantage from the start. And whenever Goering did come up with a new tactic, Dowding seemed

SPITFIRES AT SAWBRIDGE-WORTH: a watercolour by the war artist Eric Ravilious shows the individual blast pens built to protect aircraft from anything but the most accurate bombing, a lesson learned from the *Luftwaffe*'s attacks on RAF airfields in the Battle of Britain.

to have an answer. The other problem was self-deception: the *Luftwaffe* based it tactics on poor intelligence, believing it had reduced Fighter Command to 300 aircraft when the real figure was more than twice that, at around 700.

That day was decisive. The bombers attacked RAF airfields at Lympe, Hawkinge, Croydon, West Malling, Biggin Hill, Kenley and Martlesham Heath in the southeast, and Driffield and Acklington in the north. Dowding was able to adjust his response to the greater threat and ensured they were met with the same stern resistance by sending fifteen squadrons from all four Groups into the battle. That night, the RAF claimed 153 German aircraft shot down, the highest daily total to date. Both sides exaggerated their successes and minimized their losses; in fact the figure was seventy-five. The *Luftwaffe* claimed eighty-two Spitfires and Hurricanes and nineteen other aircraft shot down, when in fact Fighter Command lost thirty-four, with seventeen pilots killed and sixteen wounded.

The next day, the *Luftwaffe* once again concentrated on Fighter Command's airfields and managed to take out Ventnor radar station, but they lost

forty-five aircraft to Fighter Command's eight. On 17 August the *Luftwaffe* paused for breath, making no attacks, but on the following day made its maximum effort again, against Fighter Command's airfields. It was the most gruelling day of the battle so far: three waves of bombers attacked in an attempt to finish Fighter Command off; a combined high- and low-level raid on Kenley put the control room out of action and set many of the hangars on fire; a similar raid on Biggin Hill caused extensive damage, but failed to stop the airfield operating. Croydon and West Malling were also hit, and that day, sixteen RAF personnel on the ground and forty-four civilians were killed and more than a hundred injured. In fierce battles in the air, the *Luftwaffe* lost seventy-one aircraft, with more damaged, while the RAF lost twenty-seven fighters and ten pilots.

Goering believed he could break Fighter Command in a week, but on the evidence of the *Luftwaffe*'s losses that day he had a long way to go. The nature of the battle was changing: *Adlerangriff*, far from being a clean, quick kill by a bird of prey, had become a cockfight.

GRAVEYARD: *No.1 Metal and Produce Recovery Depot, Morris Works, Cowley, Oxford, November 1940*: Frances MacDonald's painting shows German aircraft reduced to scrap — yet more evidence for the public of the effectiveness of Fighter Command in defending the nation.

A HOUSE DIVIDED: the Air Officer commanding 11 Group, Air Vice Marshal Keith Park (*left*), whose airfields and squadrons in Southeast England took the brunt of the attacks by the *Luftwaffe*, frequently felt unsupported by the Air Officer in charge of 12 Group in the Midlands, the offensively-minded Air Vice Marshal Trafford Leigh-Mallory (*right*). History has largely vindicated Park's tactics.

The following day, a newsreel called *Aerial Blitzkrieg* was released with pictures of Spitfires taking off, flying in formation and landing, and ending with shots of a huge scrap yard of German aircraft. There was stirring commentary which began:

Another instalment of the greatest aerial story of all time; a story of continued heroism of our marvellous air force. Hitler promised to come to Britain in mid-August but sent 1,000 aircraft instead. And what a warm welcome he received … the Battle of Britain is fought out in British skies with increasing intensity … Hitler's much-vaunted air force is receiving the soundest thrashing it's ever had … hundreds of miles of countryside are littered with the smashed and burnt out planes of Nazi Germany …

Behind the scenes both sides took stock; there were tensions. On 19 August, Keith Park held an 11 Group conference to reiterate the importance of protecting the airfields by going for the bombers who were doing the damage, even though that meant avoiding combat with the Bf 109s which, so some believed, might go against the grain of naturally aggressive Spitfire pilots. Park and

Dowding also had to counter a growing belief put forward by Trafford Leigh-Mallory of 12 Group that larger formations, so-called 'Big Wings' of up to five squadrons at a time, should be scrambled to meet the bigger raids. At a *Luftwaffe* conference called by Goering on the same day, he blamed his fighter pilots for not being aggressive enough, when in fact it was their lack of range and his tactics that were the problem. That, and the psychological impact of the Spitfire.

The British fighter's reputation for effectiveness had spread to the *Luftwaffe,* creating a negative effect on the confidence and morale of German aircrews — a development that only increased its value as a weapon, giving it a psychological advantage that particularly affected inexperienced *Luftwaffe* pilots. On believing he had seen one, a German fighter pilot told all his colleagues over the radio: '*Spitfire hinter mir! Spitfire hinter mir!*' (Spitfire behind me!) Then, moments later: '*Spitfire immer noch hinter mir! Wass soll ich tun?*' (Spitfire still behind me, what shall I do?) The reply, from Adolf Galland, arguably Germany's best fighter leader since Richthofen, was aimed at restoring morale: '*Aussteigen! Sie Bettnasser!*' (Bale out, you bed-wetter!).

The idea that every opponent was a Spitfire

LIFE OF EXTREMES: the routine of battle produced a collective experience that demanded fighter pilots live between grabbing moments of tension-filled relaxation (*top*) and the sudden scramble into action (*bottom*).

170

has been described as both 'Spitfire snobbery', a form of excuse for coming off worst, and as the 'Spitfire complex', that they were superior, invincible and to be feared. Going into battle against a Spitfire which you believed was superior did not help morale and this is evident in the testimony of Heinrich Meyer, a Bf 109 pilot:

Suddenly we were jumped on by a squadron of Spitfires; until we got our flaps up and increased speed we were no match for the RAF. I was hit and smoke billowed from my plane, I tried to make it back but a Spitfire on my tail gave me no rest, I weaved this way and that ... until another 109 came to my rescue.

Galland paid the Spitfire possibly its greatest tribute when famously, at the height of the Battle of Britain, in response to being asked by Reichs-marschall Goering, who had just rejected a change of tactics to counter the Spitfire's greater manoeuvrability, what he wanted, replied: 'I would like an outfit of Spitfires for my squadron.'

In fact, the Bf 109 was similar in overall performance to the Spitfire — technically superior in some aspects and inferior in others. It was the *Luftwaffe*'s flawed tactics that made the difference. The order to stay close to the bombers irritated the Bf 109 pilots, such as Gunther Ball of 8/JG52, mainly because of the opportunity it gave their opponents to use the Spitfire's qualities to the best advantage: 'We could not use our altitude advantage nor our superiority in a dive ... the Spitfire had a marvellous rate of turn, and when we were tied to the bombers and had to dogfight them, that turn was very important.'

SPITFIRE MAN: the son of a miner, Flight Sergeant George 'Grumpy' Unwin joined the RAF as a clerk in 1929 before training as a pilot. He was one of the first Spitfire pilots, serving with 19 Squadron from 1938 to December 1940; in August 1940, having shot down one Bf 109 over London he climbed back to the fight to shoot down two more; his final total was thirteen. He died in 2006, aged ninety-three.

The Spitfire's fighting reputation made it a formidable opponent, technically and psychologically. However, if *Luftwaffe* aircrew blamed the Spitfire for their lack of success, it was only because they failed to recognize Fighter Command's greatest asset: its pilots. In the ten days up to 18 August, the RAF lost 154 experienced fighter pilots, and sixty-five raw trainees arrived to fill their places. Many of them flew up to four sorties a day, their lives a routine that included only combat and sleep, a glass or two of beer after dark and the regular death of close friends. On 18 August Churchill visited the Operations Room at Bentley Priory to see the battle unfold under its gentle lights, watch the WAAF plotters move their markers to show the latest positions of hostile and friendly forces, their

subdued conversations punctuated by the clipped, urgent jargon of the battle and bursts of static feeding the reality of the fighting through the Tannoy system, pilots in the act of killing or being killed. Whether or not the young men who died ever knew the true historic significance of the battle they were fighting at the time, the older men listening to them did. There had never been a battle like it before: Churchill knew they were witnessing a finely balanced battle for national survival and he saw and heard for himself just how stretched and committed the pilots of Fighter Command were. Being driven home that night, he was emotional and unable to speak. When he did speak, it was in the House of Commons two days later, his words an inspired echo of his experience in the Operations Room which has summed up

172 SPITFIRE LEADER: born in South Africa, Squadron Leader Adolph 'Sailor' Malan was promoted to command 74 Squadron in August 1940. Just days later, Spitfires under his command shot down thirty-eight enemy aircraft in a single day; his own score was twenty-seven enemy aircraft. He went on to command Biggin Hill before returning to South Africa after the war, where he died of cancer in 1963.

the Battle of Britain ever since: 'Never in the field of human conflict has so much been owed by so many to so few.'

Churchill's words sprang from his profound sense of history. He evoked the British narrative of Harfleur, the Armada and Trafalgar, the high price paid by individuals as part of a small, special, warrior group, and linked it to the mood and the events of August 1940. Through the courage of Battle of Britain pilots, the Spitfire and the Hurricane were both absorbed into that narrative as well, the Spitfire in particular becoming a modern symbol of defiance against the odds and of ultimate victory.

The battle continued. The end of August saw a struggle between Keith Park's 11 Group and Field Marshal Albert Kesselring's Luftflotte 2, which continued to bomb Park's airfields in Kent, Sussex, Surrey, Essex and Hampshire. The next major assault came on 24 August, with German fighters packed tightly around the bombers, making it hard for the Spitfires to get at them. Park's Group was stretched across the whole of southern England when more raids were detected going for his bases north of the Thames: Debden, North Weald and Hornchurch. Park asked Leigh-Mallory of 12 Group to cover them and a wing of Spitfires and Hurricanes was scrambled, led by Douglas Bader, already a famous fighter pilot and leader who had artificial legs. It was a failure: it took valuable time to coordinate and assemble, and only one of the five squadrons, No. 19, with their cannon-equipped Spitfires, arrived anywhere near. When they did, jammed cannon reduced their effectiveness and by the time the rest of the wing arrived, Hornchurch and North Weald had been bombed. Fighter Command lost twenty-two

aircraft and the *Luftwaffe* lost twenty-six.

Compared with the previous week, losses were down, but it was clear to the Germans that they had still not won the battle in the air. While the bombers were damaging the airfields, it was at the expense of destroying fighters, which continued to exact a price and showed no sign of weakening, and the Stuka had been effectively withdrawn from the battle. Meanwhile, pressure mounted on Goering as the German army and navy pressed for air superiority as they prepared to invade: Hitler's deadline of 10 September was only two weeks away, and could not be postponed indefinitely as the Channel would become too choppy for the invasion barges. Following the raids on Kenley and Biggin Hill, the *Luftwaffe* sent around a hundred bombers to targets in southern England that night; for whatever reason, one of them bombed London by mistake. The next night, Churchill ordered retaliation against Berlin: eighty-one British bombers attacked the German capital. They did little damage, but the raid roused Hitler's anger.

The *Luftwaffe* continued to attack Fighter Command airfields, but Kesselring still followed a policy of seeking to lure the Spitfires in particular into the air, where he believed he would meet them with superior numbers: if the Spitfires could be knocked out of the battle, the Hurricanes would have to deal with the Bf 109s alone and the German bombers would be less vulnerable. To carry out the policy, around eighty per cent of the *Luftwaffe*'s fighters were assigned to Luftflotte 2, about 600 aircraft, and during the last week of August, as well as bombing raids against airfields, Kesselring sent massed fighters over southern England on their own. In the dogfights that

174 PERSONAL COURAGE: WAAF Sergeant Joan Mortimer, Flight Officer Elspeth Henderson and Sergeant Helen Turner outside the bombed control room building at Biggin Hill, where they stayed at their teleprinters during the bombing attacks of 1 September 1940 — an act of gallantry for which they were awarded the Military Medal.

followed, Hurricanes and Spitfires were represented in a ratio of roughly 2:1, as they had been throughout the battle, and they shot down enemy aircraft broadly in proportion to their numbers. However, in combat with Bf 109s, the slower Hurricane's only defence lay in its ability to out-turn an attacker, while the Spitfire had a small speed advantage as well, making it more difficult to shoot down.

On 30 August, Fighter Command flew over 1,000 sorties in the day for the first time. However, Biggin Hill was bombed twice, thirty-nine people were killed on the ground, part of the electricity grid was hit by a bomb, and seven radar stations were put out of action. The following day, Biggin Hill and Hornchurch were attacked again, and at Hornchurch, Spitfires were still scrambling

into the air as the bombs fell on the airfield. Al Deere's Spitfire was blown upside down on takeoff, the aircraft running along on its back for quite a distance, but he escaped with minor damage to his head and was back in the air the next day. Biggin Hill was attacked twice and the 12 Group wing again failed to provide cover; the operations room was put out of action and two of the three squadrons based there had to land at other airfields. Fighter Command was under real pressure, but the system was still able to respond: Beaverbrook worked aircraft repair crews round the clock, damaged airfields were also repaired, new phone lines installed and makeshift operations rooms set up again in other buildings. Biggin Hill was raided for the sixth time on 1 September and there were heroes on the ground now, as well as in the air. RAF, WAAF and civilian personnel were undeterred and kept as many Spitfires and Hurricanes flyable as possible; WAAF telephonists who kept the system going during raids received medals for gallantry. And at the top of this pyramid of activity was the Spitfire.

The battle of attrition went on. Fighter Command lost 103 pilots and a further 128 were wounded in just two weeks. To strengthen the ranks, Dowding hadmade the Czech and Polish squadrons operational. However, for the first time in the battle, production of new fighters fell below losses: between 24 August and 6 September, 466 Hurricanes and Spitfires had been destroyed in the air and on the ground against only 269 replacements. By juggling the stocks, Dowding managed to keep the number serviceable each day at around 600. The first Mk II Spitfires with the more powerful Merlin XII engine were starting to arrive

92 EAST INDIA SQUADRON

DESTROYED 129
PROBABLE 60
DAMAGED 70
TOTAL 259

175

TEAM EFFORT: an official photograph of the pilots and non-operational officers of 92 Squadron with a Spitfire in February 1941, celebrating their 130th enemy aircraft destroyed. Of the ten pilots, eight were Spitfire aces: Sergeant E. Havercroft, Flight Lieutenant Brian Kingcome, Squadron Leader J. Kent, Flight Lieutenant J. Villa, Pilot Officer C. Saunders, Flight Officer R. Holland, Flight Officer A. Wright and Sergeant D. Kingaby.

from Castle Bromwich, but would take a few weeks to become operational. In the meantime, on 4 September, 19 Squadron flew its cannon-equipped Spitfires to Hawarden and swapped them for older eight-gun training Spitfires as a way of increasing their effectiveness.

British intelligence learned on 6 September that Kesselring planned to concentrate on bombing aircraft factories — in particular Supermarine's factory at Southampton and Hawker's at Brooklands. Fighter shields were put round Surrey and Southampton, supported by 10 Group, for each of three successive *Luftwaffe* attacks, none of which did any real damage. The *Luftwaffe* lost thirty-five to RAF twenty-three, of which twelve pilots were saved. It was the last day of the sustained attacks on Fighter Command, and a crucial turning point in the Battle of Britain.

Outraged at the raid on Berlin, Hitler made a public speech on 4 September, in Berlin, promising to raze British cities to the ground by way of revenge. Just as Fighter Command was on the back foot, Hitler decided to give the *Luftwaffe* a task for which it had never been equipped: a strategic bombing offensive against one of the largest and best-defended cities in the world. It came as a surprise and for that reason, initially, it was successful: on 7 September, as Park was preparing to defend his airfields, the raids by-passed them and reached London, where 448 civilians were killed and more wounded, mainly in the East End. A second attack on 8 September killed another 412 Londoners. On 9 September, radar identified several *Luftwaffe* raids going for London again, but Park had used the respite to work out a defensive plan, putting two squadrons

176

SUPREME LEADERSHIP: King George VI and Queen Elizabeth are welcomed to Bentley Priory by Air Chief Marshal Sir Hugh Dowding in September 1940 (*below*), representing national support for the Spitfire and Hurricane pilots. Despite the Spitfire's greater profile and glamour, the two fighters (*opposite*) have always, and rightly, been given joint honours for their different contributions to victory.

together as a small wing which held off until the escort fighters reached the limit imposed by their fuel, leaving the bombers unprotected. Then the RAF fighters pounced in force, physical evidence to the bomber crews that Fighter Command was far from finished. Many jettisoned their bombs well short of their targets and turned to go home; no sooner had they done that than they were confronted with more squadrons cutting off the line of retreat to the coast. Not one bomb was dropped on London. The *Luftwaffe* lost twenty-eight and the RAF lost nineteen fighters, but the damage to the German crews was significant: there seemed to be more Spitfires and Hurricanes than ever.

The *Luftwaffe* came back at night, and the death toll among Londoners rose, but to very little military purpose in a sprawling city, and just as the raids on Madrid and Barcelona had stiffened rather

than weakened civilian morale, so London buried its dead and developed a quiet, defiant attitude to the attacks. Many had witnessed the raids turn away, and seen the Spitfire's vapour trails high above the city, and even though they may not have appreciated it, by taking the brunt of the attacks they were giving the RAF just the respite it needed.

With the last date for invasion just over a week away, Goering planned a final massed effort to bomb Britain and destroy its air defences on 15 September; it was reported that he told his crews that Fighter Command was down to its last fifty Spitfires. British intelligence was able to warn Dowding that it was seen as a decisive day by the German High Command and that the attacks would come in two waves, morning and after-noon. The first wave crossed the coast at 11.30, to be met by three squadrons of Spitfires and seven squadrons of Hurricanes — numbers which made the fight much more even, and a surprise to the *Luftwaffe*, who believed Fighter Command was close to being a spent force. The 11 Group fighters returned to refuel and rearm and were back in the air to meet the second wave, this time with the 12 Group Wing, again led by Douglas Bader, which brought the grand total of RAF fighters to around 300 in the air at the same time. Churchill, accompanied by his wife, was at Uxbridge, 11 Group Headquarters, in the operations room. He asked Park: 'What reserves are there?', to which Park replied 'There are none.'

The Bf 109s duly had to turn back from the outskirts of London leaving the unprotected bombers to take huge punishment. That night the BBC reported the score as 185 Germans shot down for the loss of thirty British fighters, from

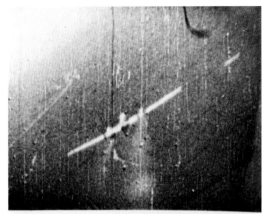

Direct leadership (*opposite*): Reichsmarschall Hermann Goering addressing German air crews during the Battle of Britain (*top left*); he insisted on the superiority of the *Luftwaffe*, contrary to the experience of the men bombing London (*top right*) in the face of determined opposition from the RAF. A Spitfire (*below*) has just completed a rear attack on a Heinkel 111 before undershooting the bomber.

The face of battle (*this page*): a camera gun showing tracer from a Spitfire flown by Flight Lieutenant J.H.G. McArthur of 609 Squadron hitting a Heinkel 111 (*above*) that had just bombed the Filton aircraft factory on 25 September 1940. Tracer helps a Spitfire pilot aim at a Bf 110 (*right*) as its port engine catches fire.

which ten pilots were safe, and the newspapers blazed with the news the following morning. The truth was more prosaic: sixty Germans shot down, but it was still one of the greatest losses suffered by the *Luftwaffe* in a single day.

It was the Germans' final effort and the turning point in the Battle of Britain. With hindsight, it can also be seen that it was a turning point in the war. Hitler, Churchill and their respective Chiefs of Staff knew that without the air superiority for which the *Luftwaffe* had been fighting for over two months, the immediate threat of invasion was over. Two days later, intelligence photographs brought back by Spitfire PR Mk IAs confirmed that Hitler had called off Operation Sealion. Switching the *Luftwaffe*'s bombers and fighters from Fighter Command airfields to London was arguably Hitler's biggest mistake of the whole war, but that should not obscure the fact that by resisting as it did, by defending Britain, Fighter Command had won the Battle of Britain. The decisive day was 15 September, and it has been celebrated as Battle of Britain Day ever since. It was what Trafalgar Day was to the Royal Navy, and Waterloo Day to the Army.

The victory was taken by the narrowest of margins, and criticism of the conduct of the battle by Dowding and Park followed swiftly. It was not aired in public, but the burden of that criticism was the small number of fighters they sent in to tackle much larger numbers of bombers and escorting fighters. The feeling was that by committing a greater proportion of the forces at its disposal in the beginning, Fighter Command could have inflicted greater damage on the *Luftwaffe* earlier. However, the fact remains that Fighter

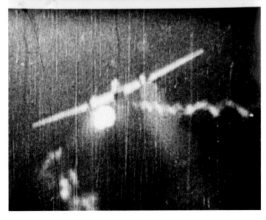

PRESS VISIT: Squadron Leader Brian 'Sandy' Lane (above left), who commanded 19 Squadron at Manor Farm, Fowlmere, a Duxford satellite airfield in Cambridgeshire, with one of his flight commanders, Flight Lieutenant W.G. Clouston and a Spitfire (*above*).

ARMOURER: Fred Roberts re-arms a 19 Squadron Spitfire at Manor Farm (*right*) while the pilot, Sergeant Bernard Jennings, has a word with his mechanic.

Command's tactics won the battle — and that it did so without knowing day-to-day what to expect, and husbanded resources accordingly. Dowding had created the system that made victory possible by supporting the Hurricane and the Spitfire, radar and control rooms, and by linking them all together in the teeth of political parsimony. The evidence showed that the quick responses and flexibility of their policies were the best way to fight the battle, and that getting the big wings airborne in time meant scrambling them before the enemy's intentions were clear — but it was a defensive policy and therefore wrong as far as its critics were concerned.

Dowding and Park were shabbily treated by the RAF after the Battle of Britain. The feeling that its senior officers listened to less gifted but more aggressive men persists to this day: in October Dowding was replaced at the head of the most advanced defensive fighter system in the world by Air Chief Marshal Sir Sholto Douglas, and Keith Park was replaced by Leigh-Mallory at 11 Group. Dowding, who had extended his service beyond his retirement date as recently as July 1940, was asked to look at RAF waste, and Park was moved to a training post. Dowding had made many enemies in the RAF by being blunt in his views and dogged in seeing them through into action. If he was unhappy about either the fact or the manner

Public interest: the wreckage of a Bf 109 that crashed in flames in southern England on 29 August 1940 (*above*) is examined by Home Guard and farm workers for the benefit of the camera. A more intact Bf 109 that crashed into a haystack just outside London on 9 October has its engine cowling removed for a more detailed examination by an expert (*right*).

of his departure, he did not show it: he was as self-effacing as he was blunt and dogged, a tough-minded man who took difficult decisions and saw them through. Wars are not about fairness, but the feeling of injustice that a man of such talents was cast aside was felt widely among the pilots who served him, among whom there was a strong bond of mutual loyalty and understanding. Dowding expected a huge amount from his pilots; he understood how important their expertise and fighting qualities were to making his system work, and the sheer quality of the men he was leading was part of the overall equation he had to balance. He protected their interests vigorously, once provoking Churchill to remark that they were 'his chicks'. Dowding could not have been paid a more eloquent compliment. Fighting men know instinctively when they are being well led.

Al Deere, who flew Spitfires over Dunkirk, and whose powers of analysis had been demonstrated in his combat reports, was clear on Dowding's policy and decisions, and on the counter arguments:

The tremendous odds faced by the pilots of the 11 Group squadrons gave rise to criticism of Air Vice Marshal Park's tactics. I am in a position to comment at first hand on one aspect of these, and that was the policy of using selected Spitfire squadrons to draw off the enemy escort fighters, thus enabling the remaining squadrons, and this included 12 Group Hurricanes, to concentrate more effectively on the bombers. Though this decision means a much tougher and unrewarding job for the Hornchurch Spitfire squadrons, I do not recall a single

pilot saying other than he thought it was an excellent idea. I strongly support this view, and on numerous occasions witnessed the rewards reaped when enemy bombers, shorn of the majority of their escort, were set upon by the defending Hurricanes which, excellent as they were, could not have coped so effectively without the intervention of the Spitfires.

One of the key advantages the RAF had over the *Luftwaffe* was the quality of its leaders, from Bentley Priory through Group, station, squadron and flight level. Ever since the Great War, the RAF had operated a policy of not singling out individuals for special status, and that ethos worked well

PRIVATE INTEREST: On 28 August 1940, Winston Churchill was travelling between Dover and Ramsgate, touring invasion defences, when a Bf 109E was shot down at Church Whitfield. He ordered his car to halt and walked over to view the wreckage, much to the consternation of his personal bodyguard (on the right) as German aircraft were active above.

Public demonstration: armourers firing a Spitfire's eight Browning .303 machine guns in the butts. This was almost certainly a shot set up for publicity purposes or for the press, in order to impress upon the nation the Spitfire's deadly firepower and accuracy.

for the most part. There was a highly individual-istic culture among fighter pilots, and personal scores against the enemy fuelled that individualism, but squadrons were very tightly knit and it was to their immediate squadron colleagues that first loyalties were given, rather than to wider notions of King and country; they were anonymous, one of The Few, and consequently they were all heroes.

Nothing will ever alter the deep admiration felt for those pilots, not just in Britain but worldwide, but to put them in the air and keep them there took leadership on the ground and in the air. Tens of thousands of people contributed, some of whom flew, such as the Bomber, Coastal and Training Command crews, but most of whom worked at airfields: armourers, fitters, instrument technicians, airmen whose job was simply to manhandle the aircraft on the ground, refuel them, cannibalize parts from those that crashed, build blast pens, drive trucks — a host of jobs required to keep the aircraft flying. There were those who worked endless shifts at Bentley Priory, at RDF stations, headquarters, filterers, plotters, training bases, in operations rooms, on switchboards, civilians who repaired telephone cables round the clock, the German speakers who monitored radio traffic and interviewed captured aircrews at a special centre at Cockfosters, and the chaplains who had to inform relatives that a loved one had been killed or injured in the air or on the ground. In the midst of the battle they were not forgotten, especially where they were in the front line. The Station Commander at Hornchurch, Wing Commander Cecil Bouchier, became famous for his running commentaries on

the battle from the station's control room, relayed over the station's Tannoy system to everybody on the base, from cooks to intelligence officers, who cheered his words as one: 'Blue leader has got a Dornier, Blue One has got a 109 on his tail; he's diving, yes, he's left … now right … a Spit … yes a Spit has got the 109 …'

The sense of collective effort went far beyond the RAF: there were the volunteers of the Observer Corps, the soldiers who manned the Army's anti-aircraft batteries, the Royal Navy's ships' crews who guarded the Channel, the Royal National Lifeboat Institution which rescued pilots. And there were thousands more, from Lord Beaverbrook himself to factory cleaners in the hundreds of industrial plants and factories which made the fighters; there were hundreds of thousands rising to millions who collected money for the Spitfire Fund, and tens of millions of people who had no involvement and went about their daily routine of work and home, reading papers, going to the cinema and listening to the BBC news.

There was a clear public mood of subdued triumph, of relief gradually turning into hope even as the bombing of cities continued. On 4 September, Doris Melling wrote in her Mass Observation diary:

Everyone getting very mad about these raids. Apparently we are just here to be hit at. It said in one of the papers that it was a fine sight to see the Spitfires taking off after the Germans. I dare say it is. I would like to see it round here. I feel strongly that there is too much fuss being made about London. Liverpool is a very important place and I don't think it's being defended as well as it might be …

Doris Melling wanted Spitfires. For all manner of reasons, not least the media, which magnified its sheer presence, it was the Spitfire that inspired confidence: as long as Spitfires were in the skies overhead, Britain was beginning to seem safe and though Fighter Command's pilots were clearly the individual heroes, they were anonymous, The Few. The visible heroes were the Spitfire and the Hurricane. And though twice as many Hurricanes took part in the battle as Spitfires, and Hurricane pilots shot down more German aircraft than Spitfires, it was the Spitfire that became embedded in the public consciousness, the Spitfire that people loved and with which millions identified.

Even under the constraints of the war, and the restrictions imposed on the use of paper and ink, a series of books about the battle was published starting early the following year. The official account, published in a small blue pamphlet by His Majesty's Stationary Office in 1941, was called simply *The Battle of Britain: August–October 1940*. It was written in wartime, and understandably, it is an account that emphasizes the collective effort and the courage of the fighter pilots. The Hurricane and the Spitfire both feature, but it is the Spitfire that gets the one bit of humour, with a small section headlined '*Achtung Schpitfeuer*', clearly intended to convey something of the status the Spitfire gained in the battle. The story of the Spitfire Fund also appeared in book form under the title *Birth of a Spitfire: The Story of Beaverbrook's Ministry and Its First £10,000,000*, by Gordon Beckles. In the introduction, an unnamed Flight Lieutenant is interviewed about his Spitfire and how he keeps in touch with the people who have contributed to paying for it;

then a Hurricane pilot tells a story about his Squadron Leader and how he put all the winnings from a darts match in the pub into the Spitfire Fund box on the bar. By way of explanation, the Squadron Leader then sums up: 'I think it must be the name that caught on. It gives Jerry something to think about. You can hear them shouting at each other in the air '*Spitfieren! Spitfieren! Achtung! Achtung!*'

There were also personal accounts by fighter pilots published in 1941, some of them classics. *Fighter Pilot* is by Paul Richey, who flew Hurricanes in France in April 1940, was wounded in a Spitfire in the Battle of Britain, then served as a controller before returning to Spitfires in 1941. Others include *Spitfire Pilot, A Personal Account of the Battle of Britain* by Flight Lieutenant David Crook, DFC, *Squadron 303: the Story of a Polish Spitfire Squadron in the RAF and Battle of Britain* by Arkady Fielder; and *The Last Enemy* by Richard Hillary, a Spitfire pilot who was shot down and badly burnt, but was driven to fly again and did so only to be killed later in the war. *The Last Enemy* was reprinted virtually monthly in 1942 and is still in print today. Hillary spent a day in Brighton just after the Dunkirk evacuation and he recalled in *The Last Enemy* having a drink with two French soldiers and a Belgian despatch rider. It was a time when many British soldiers had a dim view of the RAF, who they believed had let them down at Dunkirk, and Hillary, who was about to convert to Spitfires, recorded the following story:

But it was our Belgian despatch rider who surprised and delighted us by endorsing everything we said.
'How could we expect to see many British fighter

FROM BATTLE TO BLITZ: Spitfires intercepting German fighters over London on 6 September 1940. The official date for the end of the Battle of Britain was 31 October 1940, by which time the RAF had beaten the *Luftwaffe* by day; unable to invade, Hitler turned his bombers to nightly attacks which lasted until summer 1941.

planes?' he asked. *There was a heavy fog over the beaches and they were above.*

One fight however, he had seen — a lone Spitfire among four Junkers. For him, he said, it had been symbolic, and he admitted having prayed. If that Spitfire came out on top, then they would all be rescued. His prayer was answered. It shot down two Germans, crippled a third, and the fourth made off.

Fighter Command's victory in the Battle of Britain demonstrated that the succession of predictions that air wars would bring the world to an end, or put omnipotent power in the hands of dictators and tyrants, was untrue. Benign defensive aircraft such as the Spitfire were part of the redemption

from that appalling prospect. Fighter-on-fighter combat for air superiority was crucial and had a simple purity of spirit about it: high in the sky, their vapour trails visible evidence of their dangerous but protective work. The bomber would not always get through, and even though in the autumn of 1940 the Blitz was becoming a nightly experience, the bomber had not cowed the people into submission; humanity and civilization could survive this and even come out enhanced by it, and the Spitfire had bought the time to make that possible. It wasn't rational, but the Spitfire filled a need in millions of people for something to bind them together at a time of peril in a shared national experience, something to believe in, something almost sacred: a true icon.

6

The Second World War was fought on an industrial scale, using weapons from the bouncing bomb to the atom bomb and from midget submarines to computers. But one weapon found its way into the war's soul by always rising to the challenge in a huge range of tasks: the Spitfire.

FIGHTING MACHINE

Fighting machine (*previous page*): a Spitfire Mk Vb of No 92 Squadron based at Biggin Hill in May 1941; the superficial resemblance to the Mk I is unsurprising since it was converted from a Mk I that had served with 19 Squadron — the cannon barrels extending from the wing's leading edge and the bulges at the rear that house the guns' working parts are the giveaways.

The battle of britain had demonstrated that the Spitfire was one of the two fastest and most technically advanced fighters in the world. It was arguably the best all-round fighter, the only other contender for that accolade being its opponent in the battle: the Messerschmitt Bf 109. The difference was that the Spitfire had just played a central role in winning the battle, while the Bf 109 had finished up on the losing side. In the evolutionary process that determined which fighters would survive and which would pass into history, that placed the Spitfire ahead of its rival. They were both cutting-edge machines, natural predators capable of asserting themselves against other fighters and also of destroying those lower down the food chain.

Aircraft of many different kinds were going to have a central role in the conduct of the Second World War — not by winning it alone, as some air-power theorists had predicted, but by being integrated into land and sea operations at many different levels. Just a few months previously, two-seater fighters such as the Defiant and the Messerschmitt Bf 110, and light bombers such as the Fairey Battle and the Ju 87 Stuka, had been in the front line — but their savaging at the hands of fast, modern fighters such as the Bf 109 and the Spitfire had rendered them so vulnerable that they had been withdrawn from the battle. As the range of tasks multiplied, these aircraft found new roles lower down the natural order. As an interim measure, the Defiant became a night fighter fitted with on-board radar, a role which the Bf 110 also performed later in the war. The Battle and the Stuka were employed in offensive roles in support of the Army, but only under the protection of air

superiority fighters like the Spitfire. As the war widened, aircraft found their way into every nook and cranny, doing all kinds of jobs for which specialist aircraft would ultimately be built, but which in 1940 had to be covered by the existing inventory. They were adapted to perform in different climates, particularly in the Mediterranean, North Africa and the Middle East, and without the operational support and technical facilities that were available in Britain.

The Spitfire demonstrated its quality and adaptability by providing the backbone of Fighter Command. Its primary role would remain air defence, if for no other reason than that the Air Staff anticipated and planned for another onslaught on the British homeland by the *Luftwaffe* at some time in the future. If that day ever came, Fighter Command wanted only the best. Having seen the Spitfire and the Hurricane in action, and in order to rationalize fighter production, the Air Staff made the important decision at a meeting on 14 October 1940 — even before the Battle of Britain was formally over — to concentrate fighter development on the Spitfire and not the Hurricane. It recorded starkly in its minutes: '… the Hurricane is found not a match for the Messerschmitt. The Spitfire retains its superiority.'

The Spitfire was already a fighting legend. R.J. Mitchell's emphasis on perfection had paid dividends in combat, where the Spitfire used its marginal, but crucial, advantages over the Bf 109 to inflict, and just as importantly to take, punishment. It was not an emotional decision; it was based on analysis of the performance of the two aircraft that demonstrated Spitfires shot down

THE PRIME MINISTER CALLS: Winston Churchill talking to Alex Henshaw during a visit to the Spitfire factory at Castle Bromwich on 28 September 1941. Henshaw, the factory test pilot and a pre-war racing pilot, had just given Churchill a demonstration of the Spitfire's speed, a point emphasized when the photo was distributed to the press.

more of the total German losses in proportion to their numbers than the more numerous Hurricane: for every twenty-two German aircraft shot down by Hurricane squadrons, Spitfire squadrons shot down twenty-seven; for every Spitfire lost, they shot down 1.8 Germans while for every Hurricane lost, they shot down 1.3 — which translated into the Spitfire surviving in battle nearly thirty per cent longer than the Hurricane. For air defence, the Air Staff clearly made the right choice.

Their choice also had to meet the need for the policies of the new regime at Fighter Command following the departure of Dowding and Park. In 1940 Britain stood alone, giving poignancy to what had been achieved: the Dunkirk operation had brought the British Army home and the Battle of Britain had prevented invasion by denying the *Luftwaffe* air superiority. However, while victory in the battle had bought Britain breathing space,

as Churchill had pointed out, wars were not won by evacuations, however bravely carried out, and victory in the wider war was still a long way off. In 1941, there was no immediate way to hit back at Germany. The RAF's bombers and their very brave crews bombed at night, but they were largely ineffective at hitting specific targets, and did not have any more effect on morale than the *Luftwaffe* had on London. The Spitfire, for all its many qualities, was a defensive fighter, and it lacked the range to escort bombers to Germany's industrial heartland in the Ruhr, let alone to Berlin. As German naval activity started to increase in the Atlantic, Bomber Command was increasingly used to bomb port facilities in Germany and on the French coast.

Once the Battle of Britain was over, senior RAF officers were eager to launch offensive operations, and from early 1941 Fighter Command's Spitfires were used to strike across the Channel, up to five squadrons at a time escorting small numbers of bombers on daylight raids to the railway yards at Lille, operations known as a 'circuses'. Later, pairs of Spitfires went looking for trouble, shooting up military targets such as troops or parked aircraft or trains on the ground, and tempting *Luftwaffe* fighters into the air, known as 'rhubarbs'. Other than as an outlet for the aggressive theories of the new AOC of Fighter Command, Sholto Douglas, and the new commander of 11 Group, Leigh-Mallory—and the aggressive instincts of some pilots—the military objectives of these raids were unclear. Though they increased in the summer of 1941, they were not particularly effective, and most pilots found them exciting but fairly pointless: the damage done was minimal and the number of aircraft and pilots lost was high. Douglas Bader was among the losses, shot down in a Spitfire and taken prisoner in August.

At the same time, military planners began to develop a British form of blitzkrieg, integrating aircraft with ground operations and providing air cover for amphibious warfare in preparation for the day when the European mainland could be invaded. The idea of Combined Operations was developed, and one of its key prerequisites was air superiority over the planned battle area. In a newsreel shown on 6 April 1942 called *Attack from the Air*, 7,000 British soldiers gathered to witness the tactical use of airpower, delivered right into the battlefield by a variety of aircraft. Among them, cannon-firing Hurricanes had been assigned to a ground-attack role, and Douglas Boston medium bombers to strafe and bomb the targets. The newsreel was a vivid demonstration of tactical airpower; the version shown to the soldiers

lasted three hours, and was designed to give them confidence that aircraft could help ground troops. However, as a prelude, a squadron of Spitfires led by Squadron Leader Brendan 'Paddy' Finucane flew over the mocked-up battlefield at the head of 402 Squadron, to signify that air superiority had been gained and that the protective umbrella had been provided. Unusually, Finucane is named in the commentary because he was already well known; he had joined the RAF from the Irish Republic, had fought through the Battle of Britain, and was at the time the best known of Fighter Command's aces after Douglas Bader, who had been shot down the previous year. Finucane was a hugely popular figure: models of his Spitfire, with a shamrock emblazoned on the side, were sold by traders in Oxford Street and Piccadilly, such was the power of the image he and his aircraft represented. For the soldiers, it would have been reassuring to know that the RAF took protecting them seriously enough to commit the best pilots and aircraft it had to the job.

The decision to develop the Spitfire as the RAF's principal fighter had major implications for Supermarine at a time when the production system was going through major reorganization. A bombing raid on 26 September 1940 had destroyed the Woolston design office and the factory next door, where wings were made; there was increased demand for the air defence Spitfire, including upgrading it, while at the same time photographic reconnaissance versions were being built. All of this had to be achieved while gearing up for mass production. Fortunately, the final assembly plants at Eastleigh airport and the Castle Bromwich factory were unaffected by the

FROM DEFENCE TO OFFENCE: Brendan Finucane, a great fighter leader who served his entire career on Spitfires, in October 1941 when still just twenty-one years old. The youngest Wing Commander in the RAF, with the Distinguished Service Order, the Distinguished Flying Cross and 2 Bars, he led two Spitfire squadrons and accounted for twenty-six enemy aircraft, but died in 1942 returning from an offensive over France.

bombing and most of the jigs and machine tools were intact. There was no point in rebuilding the factory: it was far too attractive a target for the *Luftwaffe* to return to. Instead, Beaverbrook ordered the whole process to be dispersed to whatever facilities could be requisitioned within a reasonable distance of each other.

What followed was industrial improvisation based on human genius, ingenuity and team spirit. The man in control was Len Gooch, the engineer in charge of Spitfire production. He pored over maps of southern England, then sent out small teams from his workforce to examine any sites that might prove suitable for small-scale production work. Within days, bus depots, garages and small factories as far away as Reading, Hungerford,

Salisbury and Winchester had been requisitioned, jigs and tools installed, workers accommodated locally and work started again. The design office moved to Hursley Park, a country house just north of Southampton: initially to the house itself then to a well-camouflaged building in the wooded grounds. Production fell to a low of forty-two aircraft in December 1940, and it took nearly a year to get output back up to 130 a month—but Spitfire production was more secure. With the possible exception of the design office, there was no part of the process that represented a decent-sized target, and if anything was hit, it could be replaced quickly.

The process for dealing with upgrades and modifications was even more complex, and relied

194

heavily on Mitchell's original foundations of team-work and communication—involving everyone from front-line pilots to designers, manufacturers and testers. Supermarine also had to work with Rolls-Royce to make the best use of the growing power of the latest Merlin engines, which were being produced in ever more variants to power the range of new aircraft on order, from the multi-role Mosquito to the later models of the Halifax and Lancaster heavy bombers.

The gearing up and dispersal of Spitfire production put it at the centre of public consciousness; it could hardly be otherwise with wings and fuselages being collected from and delivered to familiar local premises in the High Street. In April 1941, a newsreel showing Spitfires being made was released in support of the activities of the Spitfire Fund. The workforce is shown as largely female, with pictures of women at lathes and other machine tools; the commentary very carefully interweaves the Spitfire, the women workers and the Fund:

The constant drone of machinery in our aircraft factories is the music of victory. Over acres of floor space men and women are turning the money from the thousands of Spitfire Funds into machines for the RAF. From government training centres, these girls have come to take their place at lathe, miller and drill. With the confidence of experts they set about the job of shaping raw metals from the foundries into the components of more than 1,000 hp demons of the air; from factories to assembly sheds, where skilled men and expert fitters and riggers begin to bring the planes to life. Here is where your salvage, your saucepans and

Aʀᴛɪsᴀɴs ᴀᴛ ᴡᴏʀᴋ: *Fitters Working on a Spitfire, 1940* (*top*) by Raymond McGrath and *Building Spitfires* (*below*) by Norman Wilkinson both focus on Spitfire construction. As demand for Spitfires grew and the production process became more complex, skilled labour was thinly spread.

Mass production: aircraft components like these fabric-covered rudders were made at small factories and at Castle Bromwich, where most Spitfires were finally assembled. Up to forty per cent of the workforce were women, and at its peak in 1944 the factory delivered six new Spitfires a day.

shillings and pence have, under the magic wand of industry, become part and parcel of the finest fighting machine in the world. Every plane is a mechanical masterpiece.

Women made up 61 per cent of cinema audiences during the war, many going twice a week. Another newsreel, in November 1941, called more overtly for women workers: *The Call for Women* was a series of interviews with women about what part of industry they would like to be in and when it came to aircraft factories, the woman interviewee said: 'I'd like to help build Spitfires; my boy's in the RAF; I'd like to do my bit to help him.'

An important part of the Spitfire's history and mystique was that the finest fighter in the world was produced by artisan engineers, draughtsmen, and machinists, but also by skilled female labour trained on the job. The parts they made were assembled and parked under trees until they could be flight tested. Women also flew Spitfires: members of the Air Transport Auxiliary (ATA) would deliver aircraft to front-line squadrons, but also ferry them between different parts of the dispersed production system for work to be done on them. The first woman to fly a Spitfire was Margie Fairweather, who had been a flying instructor before the war. She was a reserved character and recorded the experience poignantly to her father in a letter: 'I'm sure you will appreciate the great honour [I] have brought to the family by being the first woman to fly a Spitfire.' Fairweather was killed in an air crash in 1944 when the fuel system in the aircraft she was flying malfunctioned. Another member of the ATA was Ann Welch. In February 1942, a Spitfire needed to be flown from a small airfield to RAF Colerne, where it was to be fitted with weapons prior to urgent shipment to Malta, but the weather was so bad that nobody was flying into Colerne. She

INDOMITABLE: Air Transport Auxiliary pilots Lettice Curtis (*left*), who flew thirteen days on, two days off from July 1940 to September 1945 without a break, and Jackie Sorour (*right*) who believed her life had led inexorably to her first flight in a Spitfire. Of the 164 women who flew with the Air Transport Auxiliary, Lord Beaverbrook said: 'They were soldiers fighting in the struggle as completely as if … engaged on the battlefront.'

managed to get airborne, and by flying low and slow, using roads and railway lines to guide her, she made the journey success-fully—the only aircraft to do so that day. One of her colleagues, Lettice Curtis, was lyrical about the Spitfire:

In the air the Spitfire was forgiving and without vice, and I never heard of anyone who did not enjoy flying it. It had a personality uniquely its own. The Hurricane was dogged, masculine and its undercarriage folded inwards in a tidy, businesslike manner. The Spit, calling for more sensitive handling, was altogether more feminine, had more glamour and threw its wheels outward in an abandoned, extrovert way. From the ground there was a special beauty about it. The cockpit of any single-seater aircraft is a very snug private world, but to sit in the cockpit of a Spitfire, barely wider than one's shoulders, with the power of the Merlin at your fingertips, was sheer poetry—something never to be forgotten by those who experienced it.

Being part of the team that produced Spitfires was about pride; the men and women were not simply cogs in a wheel: the work they were doing mattered. Directly and indirectly, the man who had the energy and the faith to create such a system was Beaverbrook, and Churchill never forgot the creative drive which Beaverbrook

provided as Minister of Aircraft Production in 1940 and 1941. By spring 1941, the Spitfire Fund had raised between £13m and £14m, enough to pay for 7,000 Spitfires—or one in eight of all the Spitfires ever produced. Beaverbrook joined the list of characters who had contributed to the Spitfire legend; by maintaining the quality of the original aircraft, and producing variants for specialized work, and by producing the sheer numbers needed, the Spitfire became ubiquitous in the war. Through its growing celebrity on the Home Front it became a symbol of the contribution to the war effort made by ordinary working people in factories, and through the Spitfire Fund, millions of people bought into its production, believing they shared in its success: something of which they were very proud.

Later in the war, in 1943, 'Wings for Victory Week' was opened in Trafalgar Square on 6 March 1943. Frank Edwards went along, to find two bombers on display, a Lancaster in the square

L ONG-RANGE SPIES: Spitfire PR Mk IG of 1 Photographic Reconnaissance Unit (*right*), flown by Pilot Officer J.T. Morgan on low-level missions over French ports in search of the German Navy; a Spitfire PR Mk IV at Benson, Oxfordshire (*top*) showing a camera with a 20-inch lens being loaded into the vertical position for high-altitude work.

itself, and a Halifax in Dorland Hall in Lower Regent Street, intended to gain support for the bombing campaign nightly over Germany. However, 'in a lower hall, [there was] a Spitfire which went through the Battle of Britain. I joined a very long queue to gain admission to the hall, which I estimate has been visited by some thousands of people today.'

It was a curiously British story. Theory had taken second place to practicality and maximum common sense: the result was a high-technology fighter produced along a trail that meandered over southern England as RAF requirements, pilots' experiences and ideas about new ways to use the Spitfire were brought together and developed by individuals such as Joe Smith, Len Gooch and Jeffrey Quill—who between them had designed, produced and tested almost every part. Even as

the process became steadily more complex, and the Spitfire began to widen its activities in a variety of guises, it seemed to emerge from semi-secret communities in hideaways buried deep in the British countryside.

After air defence, the Spitfire's most significant contribution to the war was in photographic reconnaissance. During the Battle of Britain, the early PR Mk 1s had regularly flown over the Channel ports to monitor the progress of the build up of German troops and ships getting ready for the invasion of Britain. Later models had photographed bomb damage on targets hit by Bomber Command in Germany, collecting evidence of the effectiveness or otherwise of the bombs in the target areas. On 29 October 1940, Flying Officer S. Millen flew a round trip to Stettin on the Baltic coast, taking five hours and twenty minutes, in an unheated Spitfire PR Mk 1 Type D, the super-long-range version. It was the longest reconnaissance flight to date. A total of 229 Type D PR Spitfires were built, and from early 1941 they were re-designated the Mk IV, with the very efficient Type 45 Merlin engine, wing tanks and cabin warming for the high altitudes. This was the

HIGH AND LOW LEVEL: this vertical photo taken over Cap de la Hague, France in January 1941 (*above left*), was the first to provide evidence that the Germans were using early-warning radar. The ringed circular objects were thought to house 'Freya' aerial arrays, a fact confirmed by subsequent low-level sorties. The oblique photo of a Würzburg radar installation near Bruneval (*above right*) was taken from a Spitfire on 5 December 1941. A classic low-level photograph, it led to a Commando raid in February 1942, which dismantled the system and brought the vital components back to Britain for analysis.

variant that became the mainstay of the RAF's Photo Reconnaissance Unit (PRU) in 1941.

The PRU at Heston had been moved from Fighter to Coastal Command in June 1940, in part at least because there was an almost daily demand from the Royal Navy for intelligence about the whereabouts of the German capital ships. In November, the German battleship *Admiral Scheer* managed to evade the Royal Navy and reach the Atlantic, setting off a frantic search of ports along the Atlantic seaboard from Norway to southern France.In the space of a week, PRU Spitfires flew to Marseilles, Trondheim and Toulon to check the whereabouts of other German ships. In early 1941, the cruiser *Hipper* and the two German battle cruisers *Scharnhorst* and *Gneisenau* also managed to get into the Atlantic, and between them they sank forty-seven merchant ships in seven weeks.

In late March 1941, the Navy believed the *Scharnhorst* and the *Gneisenau* were in the French port of Brest, and was anxious for confirmation. The weather was very bad, but on 28 March Pilot Officer Gordon Green of the PRU flew over at 30,000 feet, to find Brest obscured by cloud. He

waited for a gap in the cloud, and when he found one he took photographs which showed the two ships in port. Having established their whereabouts, the PRU flew to Brest three times a day to see whether they would break out. During the first week of April, Bomber Command flew over 200 sorties, but failed to hit either ship. On 5 April 1941 Green flew a Spitfire Type G, which had guns and an oblique camera so it could be used at low level. As he came close to Brest Harbour, the ships' guns opened up on him, enabling him to report that they were still there, but without the photographic evidence. Next day, a Coastal Command Beaufort torpedo bomber flew into the same fire, but pressed home the attack and hit the *Gneisenau,* damaging a propeller before crashing into the water. The pilot, Kenneth Campbell, was awarded a posthumous Victoria Cross; Green returned on 7 April and managed to get evidence of the damage.

The same basic qualities that had made the Spitfire ideal for photo reconnaissance—speed and the ability to operate at very high altitude— also made it ideal for carrying out 'Met Flights', lonely flights early each morning to gather weather information, on types of cloud, wind

STOP GAP SPITFIRE: built to counter the German Focke-Wulf 190, the 'clipped wing' Spitfire Mk Vb had more than four feet removed from each wing. This produced a marked improvement in the speed of roll, giving it a combat advantage over the standard Vb at lower altitudes, although above 20,000 feet they were on equal terms again; the Mk V was no match for the FW 190.

strength and direction, which was then compiled with information gathered from ground stations into briefings for aircrews on operations later in the day. These aircraft flew daily to around 40,000 feet over the British mainland, depending on the weather, or sometimes just went on climbing until the aircraft stalled in the thin air.

The almost nightly bombing of British cities, the Blitz, continued through the winter of 1940–41, maintaining the concern that the *Luftwaffe* would try to overwhelm the RAF again in the summer of 1941. To meet that threat, a new air-defence version of the Spitfire had been in development since 1940, but it would take time to produce. The need for a new, more powerful high-altitude fighter was considered so urgent that the planned new design was shelved in favour of a quicker solution based on the Mk I modified for the Merlin 45 engine — to be known as the Mk V. Jeffrey Quill flew the Mk V for the first time on 20 February 1941, and it went into squadron service the same month; by end of 1941, all day-fighter squadrons in the air-defence role were equipped with Mk Vs. Using 30-gallon and 45-gallon external tanks, the Mk V was the mainstay of the fighter sweeps over the Channel throughout 1941.

Initially, the Mk V came in two versions: the Va, which had eight Browning .303 machine guns, and the Vb, which had two 20mm cannon and four Brownings, but as production geared up and the cannon were deemed reliable, the Va was dropped in favour of the Vb. By October 1941 a universal wing had been developed that could house either eight .303s, a mixture of four .303s and two 20mm cannon, or four 20mm cannon — testimony to the Spitfire's ability to meet the needs of the moment.

The threat of a second Battle of Britain did not materialize, in fact it receded after 22 June 1941 when Hitler invaded Germany's former ally, the Soviet Union, bringing Russia into the war. Later the same year, on 7 December 1941, the war became fully global when the Japanese attacked Pearl Harbour, involving the United States as well.

But the globalization and industrialization of the war would take time to turn the tide in the Allies' favour, and meanwhile Germany and her ally Italy were threatening British interests elsewhere, particularly in the Mediterranean. Mussolini intended to establish a new Roman Empire here, threatening the British Empire in the Far East, East Africa and its source of oil in Persia. From its headquarters in Cairo, the RAF's Middle East Air Force covered not only Egypt, but to the north Palestine, Jordan, Iraq, Cyprus, Turkey, Greece, and the Balkans, and to the south Sudan, Somaliland and Kenya. It had 300 aircraft, most of them obsolete, and in 1941 it had no Spitfires. What was needed in the Middle East was an air force that could take on the Germans and Italians in the air, winning battles for air superiority, but which could also support British troops on the ground. From the beginning of 1942, as the war spread across Russia, the Middle East and the Far East, many more potential battlefields opened up, each with a network of supply routes, all of which would have to be fought for and protected from the air. The lack of air power was seen as central to the collapse of the British naval and military forces in the Far East which culminated in the surrender of Singapore in February 1942.

The winter of 1941–42 was another low point for British fortunes. On 2 December 1941 Hitler had issued another Directive requiring air superiority over, and sea supremacy in, the Mediterranean, as a prelude to the German–Italian offensive along the African coast—aimed at taking Egypt, the Middle East and the Suez Canal, and opening the way to the oil in the Persian Gulf and British India. Britain was no longer alone, but there had been nothing but defeats for more than two years. Aircraft production was increasing, including new, advanced models in America, but in 1942, there was nothing to match the Spitfire and the widening war was imposing ever-increasing demands on the RAF.

Britain was in crisis again, and, not for the last time, the Spitfire rose to the occasion. Its first overseas deployment was in the Mediterranean, where it will always be associated with one battle in particular: Malta. In the summer of 1941, Malta had been under siege as first Greece and then Crete fell to the Germans. Hurricanes had been sent to the eastern Mediterranean to reinforce MEAF Gladiators, but by early 1942 the Italian air force was able to bomb Malta on a daily basis. The German army under General Erwin Rommel had established itself in North Africa, but relied on supply by sea from Italy. Malta was a perfect base from which the RAF could both defend British convoys to Egypt and attack Axis shipping supplying Rommel, but it was rendered ineffective by aerial bombardment from the Italian mainland. It was also starving: the attack on Malta was more intensive than on London two years previously, with over 1,000 islanders killed and thousands more homeless, and for its people's stoicism, the island was awarded the George Cross. But what Malta needed was a viable air defence or it would be either starved into submission or invaded.

Workhorse: around 6,700 Spitfire Mk Vs were built, either from scratch or by converting Mk Is and IIs. They did a huge range of jobs, especially in the Mediterranean — including air defence and high-altitude interception, as an escort for Allied bombers, and even as a fighter-bomber; bringing the Spitfire close to troops on the ground both protected from air attack and supported them as flying artillery.

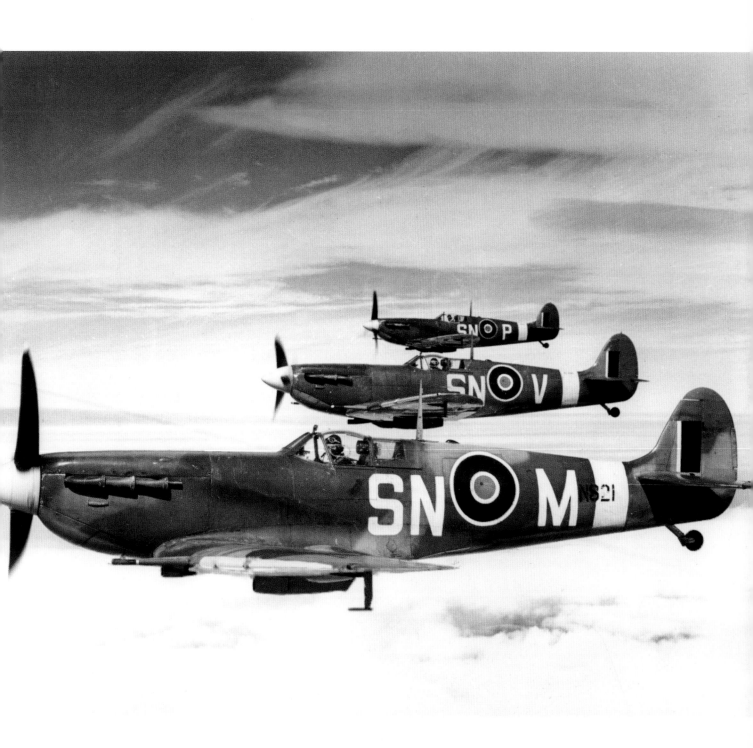

Defending Malta:
Squadron Leader E.J.
'Jumbo' Gracie taking off
from the flight deck of
HMS Eagle in his Spitfire
Mark Vb on 21 March 1942,
the first of nine reinforce-
ments for the hard-pressed
island. The Spitfires used
90-gallon ferry drop tanks
to reach RAF Ta Kali,
where Gracie took
command of 126 Squadron.

That meant Spitfires, but delivering them by sea would be impossible as no ships were reaching Valetta unscathed. They would have to fly in.

Another chapter in the Spitfire's story opened with an extraordinary series of secret operations. In early 1942, fifteen tropicalized Spitfire Mk Vs were delivered to Gibraltar in crates, where they were reassembled and loaded onto the aircraft carrier *HMS Eagle*. Operation Spotter started on 7 March from a position off Algiers: the Spitfires took off from its deck and flew the 660 miles to Malta. They were a valuable addition to the island's defence, but a single squadron was not nearly sufficient to make a difference. *HMS Eagle* made another trip on 27 March, but even two squadrons would not work, so Churchill asked Roosevelt to lend Britain the *USS Wasp*, which could deliver nearly fifty Spitfires at a time. The first contingent from the *Wasp* landed in the middle of an attack on Malta's airfields by Bf 109s and Ju 88s based on intelligence reports that the Spitfires were coming. Over the next week, the number of Spitfires was halved by the *Luftwaffe*, though they mounted a vigorous defence, shooting down 200 German

aircraft. Under that pressure, the RAF simply lacked the numbers to knock the *Luftwaffe* and the *Reggia Aeronautica* out of the battle. The RAF on Malta was building a replica of the defensive shield that had worked against the *Luftwaffe* in 1940: a control room and radar system, which had been delivered earlier in the year. To command it, Group Captain Woodhall, who had been station commander at Duxford in the Battle of Britain, was brought to Malta. At one point there were no serviceable fighters when an attack showed on the radar, but Woodhall began directing a non-existent squadron of Spitfires towards them while another officer pretended to be leading the squadron; true or not, the story is told that in the confusion, two German fighters shot each other down.

The next attempt to supply Malta with Spitfires was better planned. On 9 May 1942, *HMS Eagle* and *USS Wasp* jointly delivered sixty-four aircraft, many of them flown by veterans of the Battle of Britain. As soon as the Spitfires landed, they were refuelled and armed in thirty-five minutes, then back in the air to shoot down seven enemy aircraft and damage many more. Through May and June,

BATTLE OF MALTA: ground crew refuelling a Spitfire Mark V from petrol cans at RAF Ta Kali (*right*) at the height of the battle; *Fighters take off from Luca's bombed runway* by the war artist Leslie Cole (*below*) captures the unique mixture of order and chaos in which the Spitfires had to operate.

the combination of radar and sufficient numbers of Spitfires established periods of air superiority over the island—enough for servicing and airfield repair. The Axis attacks, which had been keeping a force of around 600 aircraft tied down, were reduced in the second half of June, and the German and Italian pilots lost the supremacy they had previously enjoyed, giving the RAF some respite. The Spitfire's success over Malta was marked in a series of newsreels that chronicled the Battle of Malta: on 11 June a newsreel called *Malta Shows She Can Take It* appeared, the high point being a Spitfire shooting down a Stuka that had just bombed Luqa airfield. In Britain, the Spitfire was seen at the heart of a crisis, having helped take the fight to the enemy and a key part in defending not just Malta but the hard-pressed British army in North Africa.

In late June, that army was in orderly retreat towards Egypt, its position fast developing into a crisis: Rommel's armoured divisions continued to push towards the prize of Cairo and by 1 July had reached El Alamein, 150 miles from the city. In support of Rommel's offensive, Field Marshal Kesselring, who had commanded Luftflotte 2 in the Battle of Britain, renewed the attack on Malta to either crush the RAF on the island or at least neutralize its airfields as bases from which German ships could be attacked and British convoys from Gibraltar protected. On 1 July there were 200 aircraft on Malta, more than half of them Spitfires, of which ninety-five were serviceable; during the next two weeks, the RAF shot down forty German aircraft, just over half of them bombers, and lost thirty-nine fighters, from which twenty-six pilots were rescued. The tide of battle was beginning to change. Then Kesselring's old adversary, Air

Marshal Sir Keith Park, arrived to command the RAF on Malta and the pace of progress quickened: Park's rapport with the pilots, many of whom had served him in 11 group in 1940, and the confidence they had in his understanding of a battle for air superiority using radar and Spitfires, only increased their confidence. By 14 July, Kesselring had lost forty-four aircraft and the sense of replaying the Battle of Britain increased. Park moved the Spitfires onto the offensive, over the sea between Malta and Sicily, where from altitude they dived on the *Luftwaffe*'s attacks. The Germans fell back on the tactics of 1940 too, sending over high-level fighters to take on the Spitfires and low-level fighter-bombers to attack the airfields.

By August, the Spitfires had established a level of air superiority and on 10 August, a convoy of fourteen merchant ships left Gibraltar with food, oil and military supplies. Kesselring deployed 150 medium bombers and eighty torpedo bombers and fighters to stop it. An air battle took place around the convoy as it sailed east, which cost the Allies eighteen aircraft; HMS *Eagle,* three other escorting warships and nine merchantmen sank, but five ships, including a tanker, made it to Valetta and enabled Malta to fight on. Kesselring could not sustain the level of assault or the losses, and from 15 August, he called off mass attacks. On 31 August, a newsreel film called *Malta Convoy* was released, showing the relief of Malta and concluding with shots of Spitfires protecting the ships as they arrived and were unloaded. The Spitfire had weathered another crisis, damaged the enemy again, and bought crucial time.

On the same day, Beaufort torpedo bombers based in Malta, protected by Spitfires, sank

a German tanker that was trying to deliver fuel to Rommel, who could not mount an attack against Cairo without it. Three days later he called off his offensive. Spitfires became fighter-bombers: improvized bomb racks under their wings had been used to bomb targets in southern Sicily, taking the fight to the enemy, but also showing adaptability, the ability to switch between air defence and ground attack. In September, more convoys arrived at Malta, and many more managed to reach Alexandria with supplies for the Eighth Army as it prepared for the battle of El Alamein. For ground attack, they included more Hurricanes, American fighters such as P-40 Kittyhawks and Tomahawks. Huge Liberator bombers arrived in Malta to keep up the pressure on Rommel's supply lines, beefing up the Middle East Air Force ready for a British counterattack.

Kesselring mounted attacks against Malta in the autumn, which intensified during the Battle of Alamein; on 10 October, five attacks of 120 bombers attempted to penetrate the island's defences, but they were intercepted by Spitfires well north of the island and not a single bomb dropped on Malta. Intensive raids, involving 250 aircraft, continued to 19 October, but the Spitfires intercepted them all, shooting down forty-six for the loss of thirty Spitfires. Once again, the *Luftwaffe* had failed to crush Malta, the crisis had been averted, and Spitfires had been in the thick of it. Several times during the battle, invasion had been delayed due to lack of air superiority or because convoys were getting through, and the arbiters had been the island's 367 Spitfires.

While the battle for supply routes across the Mediterranean was raging in the autumn of 1942,

208 Tropical spitfire: a Spitfire Mark V on a landing ground in the Western Desert showing the 'beard' filter fitted to protect the radiators from sanding up — an example of the way the Spitfire could be adapted to meet any challenge the fortunes of war threw its way.

there had been a parallel battle to gather intelligence using aircraft. In May 1942 the *Luftwaffe* introduced a very high altitude, pressurized Ju 86P reconnaissance bomber which could carry out photographic reconnaissance over Egypt from a base in Crete. These aircraft could fly at over 40,000 feet. To counter them the RAF modified Mk V Spitfires locally in Egypt, stripping out any extra weight — including all the armour plate and four of the eight guns — altering the engine to give it a higher compression ratio, and fitting a four-bladed propeller. The first interception was made at 42,000 feet on 24 August 1942, but though it scored hits on the Junkers, the improvized Spitfire did not shoot it down. More weight was taken out, including the radio, and the fuel load was reduced, then on 29 August it took off again, accompanied by a second Spitfire riding shotgun complete with a radio to follow ground control; this time two Ju 86Ps were shot down. The *Luftwaffe* did not try again.

By mid-October, General Montgomery had built up his forces sufficiently to challenge Rommel at El Alamein. The Middle East Air Force had some 1,200 front-line aircraft in sixty squadrons ready to support the army: officially they were the 1st Tactical Air Force, but known as the Desert Air Force. The *Luftwaffe* was down to just over 600 aircraft in Africa, only half of them serviceable, and it was short of fuel. The British preparations took place in conditions of total air superiority thanks to the arrival, from August 1942, of more Spitfires. When the battle of Alamein began on 23 October, Montgomery had complete surprise: the army had tactical bombers, largely American Bostons, Mitchells and Baltimores, to work alongside the artillery barrage and over the front line with the tanks and infantry. It was another turning point: the first time the Allied equivalent of blitzkrieg had been unleashed on the Germans — who could not move under the shield provided by Spitfires, beneath which fighter-bombers and medium bombers pounded Rommel's troops. Montgomery knew the value of air superiority:

On 28 October, the enemy made a prolonged reconnaissance of Kidney Ridge, probing for soft spots while the two German Panzer divisions waited in the rear. In the evening, they concentrated for attack, but the Desert Air Force intervened to such effect that the enemy was defeated before he had completed his forming up.

El Alamein was the first unequivocal Allied victory. Just as the Battle of Britain, between July and October 1940, had been the first turning point of the war, by stopping the German war machine, preventing invasion, and buying time, the Battle of Malta and the Battle of El Alamein, between July and October 1942, saw the turn of the tide towards victory begin. Unlike in the Battle of Britain, the Spitfire was not central to the turnaround in North Africa and the Mediterranean, because it was just one element in a victory that involved hundreds of thousands of soldiers, sailors and airmen — but the Malta Spitfires were crucial in making that victory possible. The breakthrough at El Alamein was the result of the integration of air power and the concept of air superiority into sea and land battles. However, the media did turn to the Spitfire for an image of victory: posters aimed at raising money for the war effort showed Spitfires triumphing over German bombers in Libya and on 26 November

a victorious note was sounded with more than an echo of the BBC *Spitfires over Britain* radio programme: *Spitfires over Malta.* Churchill found a phrase for the mood: 'This is not the end. It is not even the beginning of the end. But it is, perhaps, the end of the beginning.'

In 1941 and 1942, the Mk V Spitfire was the backbone of the RAF's air superiority fighter force both at home and abroad. But from late 1941, Spitfire pilots on fighter sweeps over Europe started bringing back reports of a new German fighter: the Focke-Wulf 190, which proved faster than the Mk V and was able to out-climb, out-turn and out-roll it too. Losses on the fighter sweeps started mounting and they had to be suspended, but fortunately, the stretched German industry was at that time concentrating, on Hitler's orders, on bombers rather than defensive fighters — perversely, the opposite of what was needed — and so there were only small numbers of the new German fighter in operation.

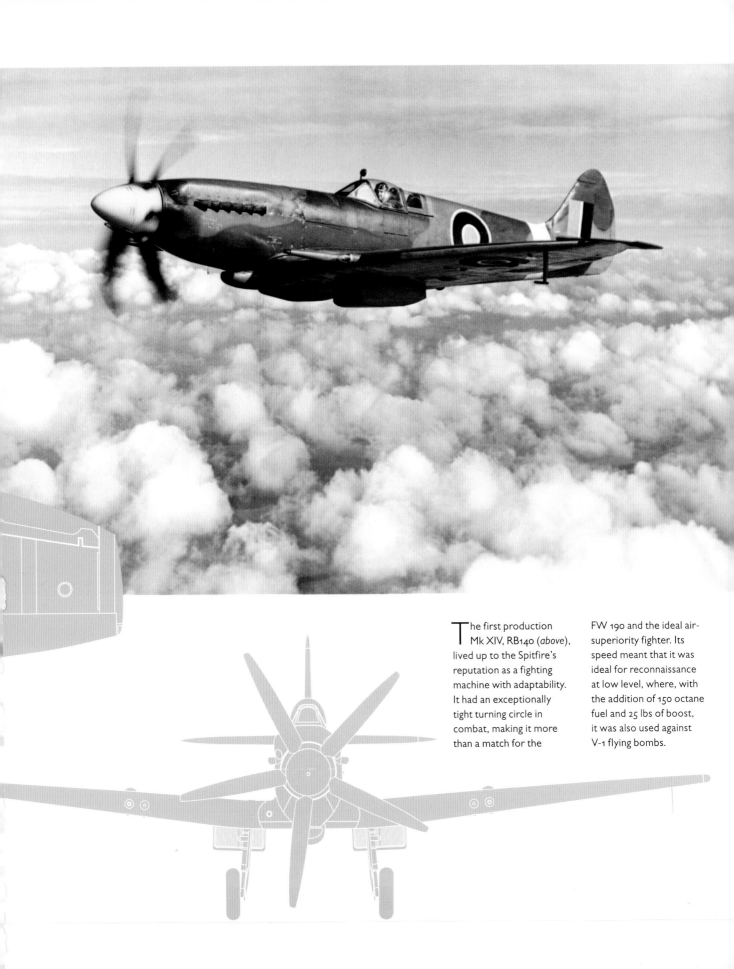

The first production Mk XIV, RB140 (*above*), lived up to the Spitfire's reputation as a fighting machine with adaptability. It had an exceptionally tight turning circle in combat, making it more than a match for the FW 190 and the ideal air-superiority fighter. Its speed meant that it was ideal for reconnaissance at low level, where, with the addition of 150 octane fuel and 25 lbs of boost, it was also used against V-1 flying bombs.

The Mk XIV cooling system retained two radiators, both bigger than previously. There were radiators for both coolant and oil under the left wing, and an intercooler radiator under the right wing. The biggest improvement from previous marks was the 30–35 mph increase in speed, which made this Spitfire a formidable opponent.

From the pilots' point of view, the most obvious change was that the Griffon engine turned the propeller in the opposite direction to the Merlin and the torque pulled the Mk XIV to the right, especially on take-off. This led to experiments with a six-bladed contra-rotating propeller; the solution ultimately was increased fin and rudder area and rapid re-trimming by the pilot.

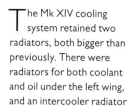

SPITFIRE MK XIV

The Mk XIV was an important landmark in the evolution of the Spitfire: the first to forego the trusty 27-litre Merlin engine in favour of its cousin, the 36-litre Griffon. It was not just a matter of engine power, it was a change in the experience of flying the Spitfire; greater take-off, operational, and climbing speeds made increasing demands on the pilot, especially when changes in speed induced changes in direction because of the huge torque that resulted from the extra power. With its longer nose and, in the later models, 'teardrop' canopy, the Mk XIV was visibly different, but no less beautiful

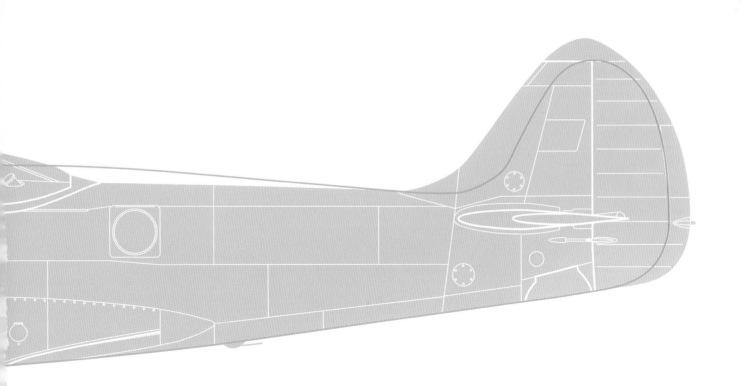

A restored Mk XIV of the Battle of Britain Memorial Flight flying in the 1990s: later models were fitted with the E Wing incorporating two 20-mm cannon and two .5-in machine guns, a shorter rear fuselage and the more elegant 'teardrop' canopy. A total of 957 were built, making the Mk XIV the last major Spitfire production run of the Second World War.

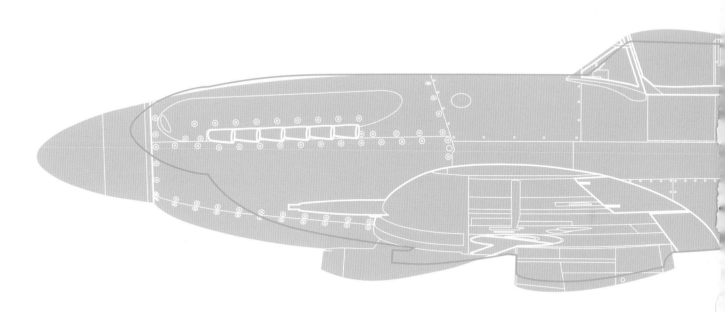

SPITFIRE	**F MK XIV** (JF 319)	PROTOTYPE (K5054)
Total Built	957	1
Wingspan	32 ft 10 in	37 ft
Length	32 ft 8 in	29 ft 11 in
Tare weight	6,376 lbs	4,082 lbs
All up weight	8400 lbs	5,359 lbs
Power plant	Rolls-Royce Griffon 65 37-litre, V-12	Rolls-Royce Merlin C 27-litre, V-12
Maximum power	2035 hp	990 hp
Maximum speed	446 mph at 25,400 ft	349 mph at 16,800 ft
Service ceiling	43,000 ft	35,400 ft
Time to height	5 min 6 sec to 20,000 ft	8 min 12 sec to 20,000 ft
Rate of Climb	3600 ft / min at 20,000 ft	1770 ft / min at 20,000 ft
Typical armament	2 x 20mm Hispano cannon, 4 x .303 Browning Mk II machine guns	Ballast to December 1936, then 8 x .303 Browning machine guns

QUANTUM LEAP: the bulging engine compartment of the Mk XIV, built to house the Griffon engine that powered its five-bladed propeller, gave the Spitfire (*left*) a more aggressive appearance compared even with the relatively recent Mk IX (*below*), which had already grown a longer nose to accommodate the bigger Merlin 61 engine.

The Supermarine design office was working on a more advanced Spitfire, the Mk VI, but suddenly, in a situation similar to that at the end of 1940, there was an urgent need for an answer to the FW 190, which indicated the *Luftwaffe* might be pulling ahead in the quality of its fighters. There was a new engine available, the Merlin 61, which had a two-stage supercharger initially intended for a high-altitude bomber. As a stop gap, rather than wait for the Mk VI, production was shifted to a hybrid, strengthening the Mk V Spitfire airframe to take the Merlin 61 engine. The result was the Mk IX, which RAF test pilots began trialling in April 1942. It was a superb machine: the fastest Spitfire yet. The power of the Merlin 61 was harnessed through a four-bladed propeller, giving it greatly improved performance at altitude, with a cruising speed of 409 mph at 28,000 feet. The engine was fitted with a new carburettor, which overcame the negative G problems of previous Spitfires.

The first deliveries of Mk IXs to squadrons started in June. In the same month, in a stroke of extraordinary luck, an FW 190 pilot lost his way and landed in Britain. Through mock combat, the RAF established that the FW 190 was 20–25 mph faster than the Spitfire Mk V, could climb at an extra 450 feet per minute and had better fighting characteristics. As a stop gap within a stop gap, while Mk IX production was geared up, a standard Mk V with its wingtips clipped by more than two feet and a more powerful Merlin 50 engine, fitted with a modified supercharger to improve performance at low level, was tested in mock combat with a standard Mk V: the clipped version

218

SEA SPITFIRE: following the Spitfire's success in 1940, the Royal Navy wanted a version. After changes to the undercarriage and landing speed, the Seafire was operational from 1942, but it was not until the folding-wing Mk III (*above*) that it became fully navalized.

FIGHTING SPITFIRE: in July 1942, in simulated combat between a Spitfire Mk IX (*opposite*) and a captured FW 190, pilots found the two aircraft evenly matched in speed, climbing, diving and manoeuvrability. The report concluded that victory in combat would be down to the Spitfire pilot's initiative.

was found to have a 5 mph advantage and a much better rate of roll. In July, the first Mk IXs were trialled against the captured FW 190: it had a slight speed advantage, but overall, its fighting characteristics were similar. Once again, the Spitfire had stepped up to the mark in a crisis.

Among the first threats the Spitfire Mk IX was used to counter was the pressurized, high-altitude Ju 86R bomber. Like the Mk V in Egypt, two Mk IXs were stripped of their armour plate and guns, leaving just two cannon. On 12 September, one Mk IX special intercepted a Ju 86R approaching Southampton and pursued it from 41,000 feet to 43,000 feet, managing to hit it before one cannon jammed; the recoil from the other immediately skewed the Spitfire, allowing the Ju 86R to escape. Once the *Luftwaffe* realized that Spitfires were capable of operating at such altitudes

they abandoned further attacks.

Measured in terms of production, the Mk IX was the most successful version of the Spitfire: a total of 5,710 were built. Counting in the upgrading of some Mk Vs and the Mk XVI, which had a different number because it used an American-built Merlin engine, but was otherwise the same aircraft, total production was around 7,000, or nearly a third of all the Spitfires produced.

The more the Spitfire did, the more was required of it, and in 1942, a very different and badly needed variant was introduced: the Seafire. The Royal Navy had wanted a naval version of the Spitfire since before the war, but the RAF had always been given priority. However, by the end of 1941 the obsolete Fairey Fulmar, the Navy's interceptor, and the Swordfish biplane torpedo bomber were still in frontline service, and an upgrade was urgently needed. The Admirals demanded, and got, the go-ahead for a Spitfire Mk V with foldable wings and an arrester hook. The first deck landings were made early in 1942, and, inevitably, the long, high nose made things difficult. The Spitfire had not been designed to survive being thrown on to a steel deck at flying speed and other more rugged aspects of naval aviation—it was a delicate thoroughbred compared with most naval aircraft—but the Spitfire pedigree went a long way to assuaging its pilots, who loved it as much as its RAF counterpart. The Seafire entered naval service in June, and by August there were four squadrons; their first combat came in the 'Torch' landings in North Africa on 8 November, where its first victim was a Vichy French Dewoitine fighter, yet another contribution to the fighting in the Mediterranean.

SCHNEIDER SPITFIRE:
the idea of a floatplane
fighter came after defeat in
Norway, where runways
were sparse. Built in 1942,
three Mk V floating fighters
were shipped to Egypt in
a plan to operate from
uninhabited Greek islands
against *Luftwaffe* transports
—which was abandoned
when the Germans occu-
pied the islands. A Mk IX
was also converted
(*above*) for possible use in
the Pacific, but that plan,
too, was dropped.

SPITFIRE MAILPLANE: this
sleek PR Mark XI, flown
by Jeffrey Quill for the
cameras (*opposite*), was
modified as a high-speed
mail carrier in June 1945.

In the same month another important photographic reconnaissance variant, the PR Mk XI, was
introduced. As the scale of the war widened and
the Allies moved onto the offensive, the demand
for battlefield reconnaissance increased. The
Mk XI was essentially a PR version of the Mk IX;
it had no pressurized cockpit, but the Merlin 61
engine gave it a nominal ceiling of 38,000 feet—
though they frequently reached 40,000 feet. In May
1943, a Spitfire reconnaissance flight brought back
the photographs of the Dam Busters Raid, which
were all over the front pages of the newspapers
the following day. Further versions included the
Mk XIII, a low-level version with oblique cameras,
which was used extensively to photograph
hundreds of French beaches as the Allies looked
for a suitable place to land their armies on D-Day.

In addition to the major variants, other, smaller
adaptations took the Spitfire into other areas:
they were adapted to carry air-sea rescue kit of

dinghy, food and water, stowed in the bottom
of the fuselage in two containers which could be
dropped to downed aircrew floating in the sea.
There was even an experiment with two containers rather like sleeping bags over each wing,
designed to carry passengers. One of the most
unusual modifications harked back to the late
1920s and the Schneider Trophy racers: a floatplane. It started life as way of developing a fighter
that could be operated without an airfield; trials
showed that the Spitfire was suitable, but plans
were shelved until 1942 and Japan's entry into
the war. Jeffrey Quill flew the first example in
October 1942, a strangely evocative image over
Southampton Water. A total of five were built,
and three were shipped to Egypt in crates, where
a scheme had been hatched to operate them
from inlets on the Greek islands in order to
shoot down German transports supplying the
occupation forces on other islands—but the plan
was abandoned. The RAF also sent Spitfires to
Murmansk, as part of the effort to protect the
convoy system, and the Russians wanted Spitfires
for their own air force; they used some in their
navy too, but, having no carriers, launched them
along rails.

On 14 May, in a newsreel that opened by
showing Spitfires shooting down an FW190,
the Air Officer Commanding Fighter Command,
Sholto Douglas, then went on to announce from
behind his desk a change of direction in fighter
operations: 'In the Battle of Britain, Fighter
Command was on the defensive; now the
initiative is ours and every day with our sweeps
and escorted bomber raids we are carrying the
war to the enemy. We like it better that way.'

SPITFIRE ADVANTAGE: gun-camera footage showing the end of a Focke-Wulf 190 in May 1942 — note the pilot bailing out. A month later the Spitfire Mk IX came into service, with performance to match the FW 190. Since German pilots found it difficult to tell the difference between a Mk V and a Mk IX, all Spitfires were treated with equal care.

The announcement was well ahead of a plan to conduct the first major Combined Operation, the Dieppe Raid on the coast of northern France. It had been originally planned for June, but because of a combination of bad weather and changes to tactics, was delayed until 19 August. The idea was to land 6,000 troops on the Dieppe waterfront as a practical experiment in coordinating land, sea and air forces, gathering intelligence on German capabilities and, having established air superiority over the battlefield area, to damage the *Luftwaffe* by drawing it into the air for a large aerial battle. The air forces were commanded by Trafford Leigh-Mallory of 11 Group and Spitfires made up forty-eight of the sixty-six squadrons of fighters. In addition, there were Hurricanes and Typhoons in the ground-attack role and eight squadrons of bombers. It was the biggest single aerial battle since the Battle of Britain two years previously, and the Spitfires had two jobs: to maintain air superiority, and to escort a raid o USAAF B-17 Flying Fortresses to bomb the *Luftwaffe*'s main base in the area at Abbeville.

The ground operation was a disaster: it did not take many of the objectives; there were serious deficiencies in command and control, and more than half the ground troops were killed, wounded or taken prisoner. In the air, the one notable success was that the *Luftwaffe* failed to penetrate the Spitfire screen over the town. However, Fighter Command lost 106 fighters, more than half of which were Spitfires. The public and official line after the raid was that valuable lessons had been learned; the reality was that a great deal of work was needed before combined operations could be mounted, let alone an invasion and liberation

of Nazi-occupied Europe. On the positive side, the need for air superiority over any such operations was still very clear, and the ability of the Spitfire to provide it had been demonstrated to the full.

The Spitfire's evolution during the war, its increasing complexity and its broadening influence in the expanding theatre of the conflict was largely a result of rising to the challenges that the war threw up, and adapting Mitchell's basic design to the new tasks. Most of that development took place out of necessity, and in secret, but throughout 1941 and 1942 the Spitfire's reassuring presence pierced the darker days of defeat and uncertainty with a sense of hope and national purpose. The idea that the Spitfire did actually make a difference was not just propaganda, it was true. Any review of the newsreels shows that it was sometimes centre stage, the star of the show, and at other times part of the setting—but always present. When Churchill visited RAF pilots, they were Spitfire pilots; when Lady Cox presented a Spitfire to the nation in July 1941, the newsreels were there to show her doing so; in November it was Australian pilots in the RAF carrying out a sweep in Spitfires and when the second Eagle Squadron of American pilots was formed in December, it was a Spitfire squadron.

The Spitfire featured in the newsreels almost monthly: in January, there was a film called simply *Another Spitfire Squadron is Formed*; in March, the focus was on Merlin engines, which were powering a range of aircraft by that time in the war, but the film opened and closed with Spitfires; in April, it was a film about teaching Spitfire pilots to shoot, using gun-camera footage of FW 190s under attack, and in May, there was a double-bill

AMERICAN SPITFIRES: members of 121 (Eagle) Squadron look on as three Spitfire Vbs come in to land at Rochford, Essex after a fighter sweep over northern France in May 1942 (*above*); then Flying Officer K.M. Osbourne shares his experience of a dogfight with his CO, Squadron Leader W.B. Williams DFC and other members of the squadron of American volunteers who served in the RAF (*right*).

of Spitfires being tested in the United States and King George VI visiting a Spitfire squadron.

In 1942, the Spitfire moved from the newsreels to the main feature with its first full-length film: *The First of the Few*. It was essentially a biopic about R.J. Mitchell: the uplifting story of the Spitfire, intended to brighten the darkest days of the war. William Walton was commissioned to write a special musical score, which became *The Spitfire Prelude*, a musical celebration of the Spitfire in the Battle of Britain. The film was a drama rather than a documentary, and as such it was not a factually accurate account: all the pilots who were involved in the Schneider races and in

MERLIN POWER (*right*): fitters about to marry up the supercharger to a Merlin engine. As with the Rolls-Royce R racing engines of the Schneider Trophy days, the supercharger was the key to the Merlin's performance. Around 150,000 of these engines were produced, for use in Hurricanes, Lancasters, Mustangs, Mosquitos and other aircraft as well as in Spitfires.

the birth of the Spitfire are brought together in one man, Geoffrey Crisp, a test pilot and fighter pilot played by David Niven; R.J. Mitchell is played by Leslie Howard, but Howard played him as a middle-class gent who shared a public-school background with Crisp, while the real Mitchell had been a working-class hero. Niven and Howard had both been in Hollywood when war broke out, and had come back to take part; Niven, who was twenty-nine at the time, as a soldier, Howard, who was forty-nine and fresh from appearing in *Gone With the Wind*, simply as a patriot. These inaccuracies, which have been criticized by historians and film reviewers, are misplaced: firstly, *The First of the Few* was intended from the outset to be an entertainment rather than a historical exercise, and secondly it was designed to evoke emotional patriotism at a dark time in the war. It was a fictionalized version of the Spitfire's story and an attempt to explain its unique qualities and its unique place in the war to an audience that knew very little about the detail. One of the myths at the time was that Mitchell sketched the broad outline of the Spitfire in twenty-four hours, and the film provides a valuable service in that it debunks that idea, putting Mitchell's genius and hard work right at the centre of the plot. It also carries the theme of the quest for perfection over many years, starting with the Schneider Cup and evoking the shared memory of that national success. The theme of perfection is summed up by Mitchell: 'It's tiring stretching for something that's just out of reach.'

The First of the Few was a huge success in Britain, and in the United States—where it was released with the title *Spitfire*. It added to the feeling of an emotional bond between the Spitfire and many people. More importantly, it set the tone and parameters of the Spitfire story, gave it a historical context, created a single narrative, a common idea of what the Spitfire meant. Both actors portrayed their characters as heroes with

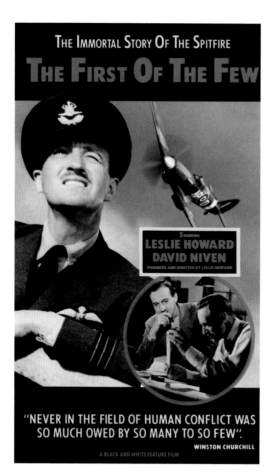

226　WARTIME TRIBUTE TO R.J. MITCHELL: *The First of the Few*, produced in 1942 and starring David Niven, Leslie Howard and Rosamund John, acknowledged the debt the nation owed Mitchell—and in doing so, it cemented the Spitfire's special place in public consciousness at a time when the war was increasingly industrialized and fought by mass-produced machines.

values that they wanted to protect—those same values that Niven and Howard, who also directed the film, had returned from Hollywood to defend. The brave, youthful ideals of RAF pilots were reference points which everybody understood, particularly in the opening and closing sequences, which show a wartime Spitfire squadron commanded by Crisp as an RAF Group Captain in scenes indistinguishable from the newsreels. The film was a landmark in the development of the Spitfire as an icon in the war. It made people believe what they wanted to believe, that the Spitfire was historically integral to the war; that it had been willed into existence as a great protector.

Playing R.J. Mitchell was Leslie Howard's last starring role. He continued to work as an actor, voicing films and travelling to lend his stardom to the war effort, and he died in that context. In a sad conclusion to his career, he was flying from neutral Portugal back to Britain in a KLM/BOAC DC-3 on 1 June 1943, when the airliner was shot

down by the *Luftwaffe*. His death was a national tragedy, and it was widely held during and after the war that the Germans had known he was on the flight and targeted him.

The dark days of 1942 were also the context of Humphrey Jennings' classic twenty-minute wartime documentary, *Listen to Britain*. It is a masterpiece of very British propaganda, and apart from the opening words, the power of the film is achieved entirely through editing. The scenes are of daily life, of routines, juxtaposed brilliantly to produce exactly the opposite effect from Nazi propaganda: the sights and the sounds of popular Britain, with no voiceover, suggesting that the images themselves and the everyday sounds that go with them are enough to make the British public feel good about themselves—and among them is 'the roar of the Spitfire'.

The tide of the war was changing. Britain and America were moving towards re-occupying Europe in the west, while in the east, the Soviet Union had turned Germany back at Stalingrad. The production of a whole range of new, specialist aircraft was evolving and the Spitfire's position of primacy among single-seater fighters slowly began to wane, though its image did not. The Hawker Typhoon, originally conceived as a high-level interceptor to take over from the Hurricane and Spitfire—altogether a more brutal aircraft, with more power—suffered teething problems, and production was halted in 1940 as Hurricanes and Spitfires were the priority for the Battle of Britain. The Typhoon was faster than the Spitfire at low level, but it was not as effective at high level, and finished up as a superb ground-attack fighter. The high-speed, high-altitude, multi-role de Havilland Mosquito, originally ordered as a two-engined bomber before the war, became the jack of all trades *par excellence*: in the high-altitude PR role, as a night fighter, as a pathfinder to mark targets for bombers, and even as a way of delivering spies into Europe.

Early in the war, the RAF had purchased an American fighter, the P40 Kittyhawk, but it had always been used in the ground-attack role. When the British Air Purchasing Commission was in the United States in April 1940, it prevailed on North American Aircraft to build a fighter for the RAF in a hurry: the P-51 Mustang. The prototype was built in 117 days and flew for the first time forty days later, in October 1940. The key to its speed and overall performance was the laminar flow wing, which produced very low drag, and at low level it was faster than the Spitfire powered by an Allison engine. Deliveries to the RAF of the first of 620 started in 1942, and it became operational in a fighter reconnaissance role on 27 July, taking part in the Dieppe raid. The Mustang's two great characteristics were speed and range, but when it was matched with the Merlin engine, produced by Packard in America, its combat qualities improved, especially at high altitude, and it was purchased in large numbers by the USAAF. A close cousin to the Spitfire, sharing an engine and built to an RAF specification, the Mustang was the only Allied fighter that stood up against the Spitfire: it was marginally faster when it came into service, and highly manoeuvrable, and it had the one thing the Spitfire had always lacked: long range. With drop tanks, the Mustang had a range of 1,000 miles, so would still be a formidable opponent against German fighters over their own

airspace, a rare combination. The Mustang became the high-altitude escort fighter for daylight USAAF raids over Germany, where it challenged the *Luftwaffe* for air superiority over Berlin—which came as a shock to Goering and Hitler.

Before the Mustang, the USAAF had only the two-engined Lockheed P-38 Lightning and the huge, single-engined Republic P-47 Thunderbolt, the largest single piston-engined aircraft ever built, both of which were huge by comparison. The Mustang eventually took over all escort duties from the P-38 and the P-47, and was widely used in the Pacific as well. It was the only fighter to challenge the Spitfire as the most successful of the war, which casts the historical achievement of the Spitfire in a very positive light given that the Mustang was developed several years later.

As the mood of the war changed, so the mood of the newsreels also changed. The year 1943 was still a year of transition, but the smell of victory was in the air. The RAF and USAAF bombing campaigns against Germany were building up. There was less of a feeling of backs against the wall and more of how and when are we going to get this war finished. In the middle of it all, the Spitfire still delivered the goods and acted as an ambassador for Britain's war effort, and the newsreels continued to reflect that. Newsreels such as *Spitfires in the Desert* and *Salvaging Spitfires* showed aircraftsmen picking aeroplanes up on flatbed trucks to repair after crash landings in the desert, but they were mixed with film that showed a new breed of Spitfire enthusiast—the people who wanted to endorse them and in so doing be seen with them, in the hope that a little of the Spitfire stardust would rub off on them.

227

228 SPITFIRE CELEBRATION: Maltese gather round a Spitfire Mk Vb of 185 Squadron on display in Castile Square, Valletta, close to the Church of Our Lady of the Victories (*right*) to mark the 25th anniversary of the RAF in April 1943. Air Vice Marshal Park climbs away in his personal Spitfire Mk V (*far right*), after his ceremonial take-off to mark the opening of Malta's new airfield at Safi built as part of the preparation for the invasion of Italy.

The Brazilian Ambassador was shown ceremonially presenting two Spitfires to the RAF to great applause, with handshakes in front of the named aircraft; there were similar films of the Cuban and Uruguayan ambassadors. General de Gaulle was also shown inspecting Free French Spitfire squadrons in the RAF. In April 1943, on the 25th anniversary of the RAF, Spitfires also played a prominent part.

In America, where 'Spitfire' was already well known as a name that stood for the values of freedom, it played a prominent part in 'The Battle of Britain', the fourth in a seven part, Oscar-winning documentary series called *Why We Fight*, produced and directed by Frank Capra for the US Information Office. The series was designed to brief US soldiers on why they should be in Europe, but it was also Capra's personal response to Leni Riefenstahl's *Triumph of the Will,* the classic Nazi propaganda film which expressed Hitler's values. The film received critical plaudits from the likes of *Variety*: 'It will emerge as one of the vital documents depicting a people's courage when the torch of freedom flickered at its lowest.' To reach his American audience, Capra placed the Spitfire firmly alongside the British people in a single narrative. The film was structured around the struggle

between democracy and totalitarianism, reminding Hitler that in democracies the people make war, not governments, and reminding his audience that a people's war was based on a huge, collective effort. He depicted the Battle of Britain as an inclusive national struggle rather than a battle between a small number of fighter pilots, intercutting sequences with people going about their daily lives: working to build armaments, serving in the voluntary services and in the armed forces, including anti-aircraft artillery, men and women on air bases — making them all part of the battle. Capra then skilfully used the Spitfire as a symbolic thread to bind the different groups of people in the film together, and in doing so he reinforced its iconic position within the British consciousness. The commentary summed up that inclusiveness in the line 'The RAF kept flying; the people kept working.'

Capra was drawn to the Spitfire as part of the story, but also as a weapon. It is the first and the last aircraft shown in the film, appearing just before the credits in a symbolic sequence with stirring music. In between, Spitfires dominate the flying sequences until the daylight phase of the battle is over, when the commentary sums up: 'the British Spitfire had proved to be one of the deadliest weapons ever put in the hands of Man.'

SPITFIRE COUSIN: the P-51D Mustang not only shares an engine with the Spitfire, it also shares its iconic status in America as a symbol of excellence in aviation. In one report comparing the P-51D with the Spitfire Mk XIV, any difference in performance was stated to be 'a matter of taste'. 15,875 Mustangs were built and, like its British cousin, it is still displayed at air shows and in air races today.

The skies of Europe, the Middle East and the Far East filled with aircraft as the tempo of the war changed. The arrival of the USAAF Eighth Air Force changed the face of the war too: it marked the beginning of the Combined Bomber Offensive on Germany: the RAF at night and the USAAF Eighth Air Force by day. Some senior British and American officers believed that Germany might still be brought to its knees without the need for a land invasion. However, part of the offensive was to neutralize the *Luftwaffe* prior to the Allied invasion of Europe when the time came on D-Day. It was the Allies' version of *Adlerangriff,* almost exactly three years after the day when Goering had promised Hitler to neutralize the RAF prior to invading Britain. The equivalent of *Adlertag* came in June 1943, with a directive called Pointblank. The two bomber fleets, together comprising approximately 4,000 heavy bombers, started the campaign against the *Luftwaffe*'s bases and the factories that produced its aircraft. But the Germans had dispersed production and kept the *Luftwaffe* flying.

In a twist of history, it was the long-range fighters which escorted the bombers, and fought *Luftwaffe* fighters for air superiority over Germany, that ultimately made it impossible for the *Luftwaffe* to defend its own skies, and by far the most effective fighter was the Spitfire's cousin, the USAAF P-51D Mustang. Robert Goebel flew Mustangs with the 31st Fighter Group, based at San Severo, Italy, in the Mediterranean Theatre of Operations (MTO).

230 SPITFIRE PORTRAIT: a study
of the low-level Mk XII
Spitfire by Charles E.
Brown, the photographer
who more than any other
captured its qualities and
personality and interpreted
it to public and enthusiasts
alike. Turning his back on
Fleet Street in the 1930s,
Brown specialized in air-
to-air photography for the
Air Ministry, the RAF and
the aircraft industry, and
his work is now part of the
RAF Museum collection.

Like Bud Anderson, he had flown P-38s earlier on
in the war. At San Severo in Spring 1944, he got his
first crack at the P-51:

*We soon found out that the P-51 Mustang was
indeed a different breed of airplane. It was fast,
for one thing … The P-51 was redlined at 505 and,
though it was no Spitfire, its turning ability wasn't
bad at all—especially if you sneaked down ten
degrees of flaps. It was pretty good in the climbing
department too, and accelerated very fast in a dive.
But the thing that really set the Mustang apart
from any other fighter, friend or foe, was its range.
With a 75-gallon tank slung under each wing,
it could perform the unheard-of: It could fly six-
hour missions.*

The Spitfire was once again called upon to move
with the times. While it would never match the
range of the Mustang, the Mk IX Spitfire was
a highly effective air-defence and air-superiority
fighter at altitude. However, in mid-1942, there
was a new threat at low level, from *Luftwaffe*
FW 190s making high-speed, low-level raids,
creating a need for a low-level fighter. Supermarine had another hybrid prototype, the Mk XII,
powered by a new engine, the Rolls-Royce
Griffon, which had been conceived as a replacement for the Merlin as early as 1940. The Griffon
was based on the Merlin, but with nearly forty per
cent greater capacity, at 36.7 litres, and a power
of 1,700 hp from its single-stage supercharger.
Its first flight was in a Spitfire Mk V airframe on
27 November 1941, in the care of Jeffrey Quill.
In August 1942, the first Griffon-powered Spitfire
arrived, confusingly designated both Mk XII and

Mk 20. It had a top speed of 355 mph at 2,000 feet. However, to meet the low-level threat, RAF planners had put great faith in the latest version of the Hawker Typhoon and as a start, a simple test was arranged at Farnborough in July 1942: three aircraft, the Typhoon, the captured FW 190, which was by then a year old, and a Spitfire Mk XII had a race at 2,000 feet. The Spitfire, flown by Jeffrey Quill, won and as a result entered its second, Griffon-powered generation, going into limited production to meet the immediate threat posed by the FW 190. It became operational in the spring of 1943, and was successful in several encounters with FW 190s from bases near Folkestone.

The technical battle to provide better performance at high altitude continued. Just as the Mk XII was becoming operational, the latest version of the Griffon 61 engine, with a two-stage supercharger and a five-blade propeller, was put in a prototype, the Mk XIV. It was tested at Boscombe Down by the Air Fighting Development Unit and swiftly found to be a significant improvement on the Mk IX, with a top speed of nearly 450 mph at 25,000 feet. In February 1944, they were flown in individual trials against a later development of the Typhoon, the Tempest, the Mustang III, the FW 190, and even against the captured Bf 109, a model which the *Luftwaffe* still flew in large numbers in its later variants. A long report showed that the Mk XIV's performance was best in top speed, climb, turn and roll, and while it was not quite the joy to fly that had endeared previous Spitfires to its pilots, taking more concentration, the report on the trials to the RAF planners concluded: 'The Spitfire XIV

is superior to the Mk IX in all respects. It has the best all-round performance of any present-day fighter apart from range.'

The Mk XIV was the last Spitfire to be produced in volume, but it was slow to reach front-line squadrons. By June 1943, Castle Bromwich was producing 320 Spitfires a month, ten times the rate achieved in 1940, and production peaked with 362 a month in September that year. By June 1944, however, there were still only three operational squadrons of Mk XIVs. With the Mustang and the FW 190, the propeller-driven fighter was reaching its zenith, and in 1944, the fruits of years of rapid technical development during the war were changing the face of aerial warfare. In great secret, the next big technical development was taking place in Britain and in Germany: jet fighters. Both countries' jets made their operational debuts in the summer of 1944. On 30 June, the first trials squadron of Germany's first jet fighter, the Me 262, was formed, and in July, the first two examples of Britain's first jet fighter, the Meteor F.1, were delivered to Fighter Command's 616 Squadron.

The same summer saw the Second World War move decisively towards Allied victory: on 4 June, Allied armies captured Rome; on 6 June, D-Day, they made the greatest amphibious landing in history in Normandy. There were also new threats: on 13 June, a second blitz began as London came under attack from Germany's robot weapon, the V-1 flying bomb. The Spitfire played a significant role in all three campaigns.

The advance through Italy to Rome had followed the British and American 'Torch' landings in North Africa, which culminated in the German

TOP COVER: Spitfire Mk Vs over Tunisia on 23 May 1943, ten days after the German surrender in North Africa. Seen by some historians as something of a sideshow, the Torch Landings and victory in the Western Desert were an important proving ground for combined operations between air, sea and ground forces, in which the Spitfire played its customary important part.

defeat in Tunis in May 1943. Between them, the RAF and USAAF had 267 squadrons based in the Mediterranean theatre: the Americans concentrated on bombers, the RAF, fighters—predominantly Spitfires. Malta had been transformed since the dark days a year previously, largely thanks to the energy of Air Marshal Sir Keith Park, and the island now acted as a base. As the date for the invasion of Sicily arrived, not only was there a war room and radar, there were forty squadrons of fighters, mostly Spitfires, including a Fighter Group and a Photographic Reconnaissance Wing commanded by Colonel Elliot Roosevelt, the President's son. The invasion fleet arrived off Sicily on the morning of 19 July 1943; the Spitfires had been tasked with maintaining air superiority throughout the sixteen hours of daylight, and patrolling the beaches. A total of 1,092 sorties were flown, leaving the *Luftwaffe* powerless to interfere with the landings, or to counter the bombers and fighter-bombers as they attacked supply lines, airfields and defensive positions. On the opening day, the Allies lost sixteen aircraft.

Within three days of the landings, the Allied air

forces were operating with air supremacy and the Spitfire squadrons moved with the armies, providing a mobile air-umbrella. Following the Italian surrender in September, the Germans continued to resist stubbornly, establishing a line across Italy south of Rome; the advance through Italy was no blitzkrieg, but the spring offensive that finally took Rome on 4 June 1944 would not have been possible without air superiority, in which the Spitfire played a crucial role.

Two days later, at the beginning of Operation Overlord, the D-Day landings, there were fifty-five squadrons of Spitfires assigned to make sure of air superiority over the landing beaches: around 650 fighters—about the same as the whole of Fighter Command in 1940. Other Spitfire reconnaissance aircraft had been playing a part in the deception for months beforehand, flying low and fast to take low-level photographs of every beach on the French Channel coast, to provide information about them for landings, but also to keep the Germans guessing where the attack would come. Where real precision attacks were needed, Spitfires and Typhoons kept up an almost

Close support: Spitfire Mark Vs (*left*) of 2 Squadron SAAF, based at Palata, Italy, flying in loose line astern formation over the Adriatic Sea on a mission to support Allied troops in the battle for Castelfrentano.

Wing Commander J.E. 'Johnnie' Johnson (*right*) , leader of 144 (Canadian) Wing RAF on the wing of his Spitfire Mark IX with his Labrador retriever Sally between sorties at B2/Bazenville in Normandy on 31 July 1944. By moving with the invasion forces using temporary airfields, his Spitfires were able to supply ground troops with swift protection against air attack.

daily series of attacks on German coastal radar stations which might give a warning of the attack and where it would come. Bomber Command and the US Eighth Air Force had been ordered off their strategic air-offensive against German towns and industry and oil depots to support Operation Overlord, and from April they had bombed *Luftwaffe* airfields in France as well as the Pas de Calais — to fool the Germans into believing that is where the landings would come. However, their biggest contribution was to wreck the French rail system to make it difficult for the Germans to mount a counter-attack. The tactical use of Bomber Command irritated the strategic bombing theorists, but Overload was made an absolute priority.

On D-Day itself, the Spitfire's task was air-superiority. In all, some 11,000 aircraft supported the landings, many of them highly vulnerable trans-ports and heavy bombers, but the Spitfire played a central role in making sure they could operate unmolested. Wing Commander Johnnie Johnson led three squad-rons of Spitfires as the Kenley Wing on D-Day, demonstrating the effec-tiveness of using over-whelming air power in support of land warfare. They made four trips over the Channel to patrol the beaches from RAF Ford near Chichester and did

not see a single *Luftwaffe* aircraft, much to their disappointment. As the Kenley Wing arrived back at dusk, night fighters were leaving to take over. Two days after the invasion, as the Allied armies moved inland from the beaches, special teams established forward airfields on the bridgehead, the first of which was at St Croix Sur Mer. On 8 June, Johnnie Johnson's wing moved there with thirty-six Spitfires. Seeing the Spitfires circle overhead and land, the French villagers turned out in force, with food and drink to welcome the pilots. From St Croix, Johnson led his wing daily to seek out the *Luftwaffe*, pushing the air-superiority umbrella well ahead of the advancing armies. The Spitfires were joined by other fighters, including ground-attack Typhoons, other heavy fighters and medium bombers, and before long, thousands

Fighting machine: Wing Commander A.G. Page of 125 Wing in the cockpit of his Spitfire Mk IXE (*above*), with a 500-lb bomb under the fuselage and two 250-lb bombs on wing racks, ready for take-off on 20 July 1944 at a temporary airfield in Normandy. Later that day, Page shot down his fourteenth enemy aircraft, a Bf 109, but returned to Longues wounded in the leg with his Spitfire damaged by anti-aircraft fire.

Strategic defence: a Spitfire Mk XII edging into position (*opposite*) in order to tip the wing of a V-1 flying bomb to destabilize its navigation system and send it on a harmless course; the two machines would have been flying at around 380 mph before the V-1's engine cut out.

of aircraft had been integrated into the huge, mechanized army that slowly ground its way across NorthWest Europe, shaping and preparing the battlefield for ground operations by attacking armour, supply lines, bridges and troop concentrations with bombs, rockets and cannon, often right in the front line.

While many Spitfires and others were supporting the army, many more were retained in their other, crucial role: the air-defence of Britain. Not only did the country and the population need to be protected, the southern ports and airfields were instrumental in keeping troops and equipment flowing to France as the campaign moved further into Europe. A week after D-Day, on 13 June, the Germans attacked London using V-1 flying bombs fired from mobile sites in France. It was another crisis, and the Spitfire rose to the occasion, as it always had in the past.

The defence against the V-1 was named Operation Crossbow, and brought together barrage balloons, anti-aircraft guns and a collection of the fastest fighters available: Spitfires, Mustangs, Mosquitos, Tempests and Britain's first jet fighters, the Meteor F.1s. The V-1 had a top speed just under 400 mph, making a straight-line tail-chase fairly pointless; the Spitfire pilot's best tactic was get above the rocket, then dive and open fire as it passed underneath. The squadrons assigned to the task were the Griffon-engined Spitfires, the Mk XII and Mk XIV. Given that the V-1 was a flying bomb, it was not possible to open fire closer than 100 yards or pilots would risk being engulfed in the explosion. Attacking them therefore called for high levels of marksmanship, and sometimes the pilots ran out of

ammunition in the attempt. When they did, some responded by flying alongside, getting the Spitfire's wingtip under the V-1's stubby little wings, then rolling it violently upwards, destabilizing the V-1's gyroscopic navigation system, sending it spiralling down to explode relatively harmlessly in the countryside south of London. The Germans fired around 10,000 V-1s at London, killing 6,184 Londoners and injuring 17,000. Only around twenty-five per cent of the flying bombs found their way through the defences, the majority falling to anti-aircraft artillery. The first fighter interception was on the night after the first launch, by a Mosquito night-fighter; the last was on 2 September, when Allied armies overran the launch sites in France. In between, fighters shot down 1,614 V-1s, most of them falling to the Tempest and the Mosquito. Spitfires destroyed 303, and three of those were the result of tipping them over; the same tactic was used by Flying Officer T.D. Dean of 616 Squadron, who intercepted a V-1 over the coast in Britain's first jet fighter, the Meteor, on 4 August 1944, when his guns jammed. The Meteor had a top speed of 495 mph, considerably higher than the Spitfire, but Meteors accounted for just thirteen victories over the V-1 in what was their first operational use.

The jet engine represented the fighters of the future, but in the last ten months of the war, both sides kept their jet fighters back from the front line for security reasons. The Meteor came into service at almost the same time as the German jet-fighter, the Me 262, which had a staggering 540 mph top speed, but in 1944, while they were conspicuously faster than their piston-engined

238 Ultimate spitfire: the PR Mk XIX ranks as one of the most functionally beautiful aircraft of the Second World War. With its high fuel capacity and the power of its Griffon engine, it represented the culmination of the technical development that had taken place during the war.

SPITFIRE VERSUS JET: an RAF intelligence officer examines the wreckage of a German Me 262 jet fighter/bomber flown by Hauptmann Hans-Christoff Buttman and shot down near Nijmegen, Holland, on 6 October 1944 by Spitfire Mark IXs of 401 Squadron RCAF.

predecessors, they were twin-engined, had only a short range, and lacked the manoeuvrability of the Spitfire. British and American fighter pilots developed tactics to cope with the speed advantage. One ruse was to scour the airspace around German airfields until an Me 262 was seen coming in, low and slow, then dive to maximum speed, firing as they were about to land. The Me 262 was deployed to protect German cities, particularly Berlin, from the bomber streams attacking the city, and their speed made them an effective opponent, but by that stage of the war, there were just too many Allied aircraft.

Under Hitler's direction, the Me 262 was developed as a high-speed offensive weapon, a fighter-bomber. On 5 October 1944, one such Me 262 fighter bomber was tasked with bombing a bridge at Nijmegen in Holland. Above the bridge, at 13,000 feet, were the Spitfires of 401 Squadron Royal Canadian Air Force, there to

protect the bridge from just such an attack. By the time the Me 262 pilot, Hauptman Hans-Cristof Buttman, realized he was under attack, it was too late: it took a total of three Spitfires almost queueing for a shot, but they out-manoeuvred him before he could use his excess speed to escape. Although it was born in the age of the biplane, the Spitfire had accounted for one of the first aerial victories over a jet fighter.

The Spitfire captured the spirit of the age in which it fought; it also determined that spirit more than any other fighter. The initial investment in engineering and design was repaid by its potential for development during the war: it was the only Allied aircraft to be operational, on the front line and in production throughout the war. In total, 22,758 were built in fifty-two different guises, including photo reconnaissance, fighter-bomber and the carrier-borne Seafire. An experimental Spitfire even flew close to the speed of sound. But its true forte was air defence and air superiority; it was a protector as well as an aggressive fighting machine. It fought over Britain, Malta, and North Africa, and made the major contribution over Italy and North West Europe, while the Mustang fought for air superiority over Germany. In an overwhelmingly technological war, in fact the high tide of mass, mechanized, industrialized warfare, the Spitfire ranks high among weapons such as radar, the Liberty Ship, the DC-3, the Jeep, the GMC 6-wheel truck, the M3 bulldozer and the atomic bomb—weapons of which it can be said that they made victory possible. They did the hard work, were in the right place at the decisive moments, shaped many

Second World War battlefields, and provided a psychological advantage to soldiers, sailors and civilians.

The Spitfire went to war in 1939 alongside the Gloster Gladiator, the RAF's last biplane fighter; in 1944, it fought alongside the RAF's first jet fighter; by 1945, Spitfire pilots were able to take on and shoot down the enemy's jet fighter, the Me 262. The last aircraft shot down in air-to-air combat in the war, a Japanese aircraft over Tokyo Bay on 15 August 1945, fell to a Seafire.

Few aircraft straddled the transition between the two ages of aviation so comprehensively, let alone so elegantly: the biplane and monoplane ages, the piston age and the jet age; the sub-sonic

SPITFIRE THEATRE: RAF personnel sit on a Spitfire, while others crowd around, to watch Carolyn Wright and Roberta Robertson tap-dance on a dismantled workbench during an ENSA show at a dispersal point on an airfield in Burma. The dancers and their accordion accompanist had just survived an attack by Japanese aircraft.

Spitfire Generation: fitters on Brown's West Island, Cocos Islands, in the Indian Ocean (*left*) fit a new mainplane to a Spitfire Mk VIII of 136 Squadron RAF.

Aircraftman Jim Birkett and Leading Aircraftman Wally Passmore work on the Merlin engine of a Spitfire Mk IX of 241 Squadron in southern Italy on a chilly day (*below left*).

and the supersonic age. In 1945, the Spitfire still looked modern, having absorbed the technical advances made during the war in its changing form: the Mk I, Mk V, Mk IX, Mk XIV and possibly the most elegant of all, the PR Mk XIX, were all unmistakably Spitfires, and they have carried that sense of their fighting heyday forward to today.

As the Second World War came to an end, the Spitfire had been honed into a remarkable fighting machine, part of the technological culture of the Second World War, part of creating the exhilaration and effort, the triumph and tragedy. As the sinews of war were cut, many love affairs came to an end, including that between the Spitfire and many of its pilots—for above all, it was the pilots who really loved the Spitfire. William R. Dunn, an American who flew Spitfires with 71 (Eagle) Squadron, RAF, puts it like this:

The Spitfire was a thing of beauty to behold, in the air or on the ground, with the graceful lines of its slim fuselage, its elliptical wing and tail plane. It looked like a fighter, and it certainly proved to be just that in the fullest meaning of the term. It was an aircraft with a personality all of its own—docile at times, swift and deadly at others—a fighting machine par excellence. *One must really have known the Spitfire in flight to fully understand and appreciate its thoroughbred flying characteristics. It was the finest and, in its days of glory, provided the answer to the fighter pilot's dream—a perfect combination of all the good qualities required in a truly outstanding fighter aircraft. Once you've flown a Spitfire, it spoils you for all other fighters. Every other aircraft seems imperfect in one way or another.*

PILOTS OF 611 SQUADRON: in Hornchurch, Essex, after a daylight sweep over France. Left to right: Flight Lieutenant E.S. Lock, Pilot Officer W.G.G. Duncan-Smith, Flying Officer P.G. Dexter and Sergeant W.M. Gilmour.

William Duncan Smith had told his flying instructor early on that he wanted to fly Spitfires, and did so for most of the war. As it drew to a close, and he was posted away from operational command; his last flight in a Spitfire made him emotional:

The next day I was to fly my Spitfire for the last time. I had flown her throughout my command of 324 Wing … a couple of slaps on my shoulder from the ground crew … The farewells were over … I opened up the power, and easing my Spitfire into the air … turned in a wide arc … I had time to reflect on my long partnership with this unique fighting lady … a joy to fly, a sureness of robust qualities, a challenge to risk all.

Johnnie Johnson, who finished the war having shot down more enemy fighters than any other Allied fighter pilot, all in a Spitfire, flew right through to

the end of the war. On his last operation, in May 1945, his squadron was patrolling near Kiel in Germany with orders to accept the surrender of enemy aircraft and escort them to a British airfield:

The Spitfire pilots spotted four Focke-Wulfs. The Huns waggled their wings, dropped their undercarriages and generally behaved in a nervous manner. The Spitfires flew on either side and eventually this strange little gaggle set course for our lines. My boys chatted about their prospects of acquiring Luger automatics and Lexica cameras. But the 190s landed at the first British airfield they saw and left the frustrated Spitfire pilots circling above.

The next morning we were not awakened by the powerful song of our Spitfires being run up on the pre-dawn checks. We realized then that the war was really over.

FLYING
LEGEND

The Allied victory in 1945 was a turning point in world affairs, the consequences of which remain with us today. It was a momentous shared experience for the generation that fought in that war, and for their great-grandchildren today, the sight and sound of the Spitfire is a poignant reminder of its past significance.

246 ANNIVERSARY FLYPAST
(*previous page*):
a formation of Spitfires
flying over Duxford in 1996
as part of the celebrations
to mark the 60th anniver-
sary of the first flight of the
prototype Spitfire in March
1936.

VICTORY FLYPAST 1945:
Douglas Bader swinging his
artificial leg into the cockpit of his Spitfire (*below*)
to lead some 300 Spitfires
and Hurricanes in the first
peacetime Battle of Britain
Day flypast over London
on 15 September.

THE ALLIED ARMIES halted on Luneburg Heath
on 8 May to take the German surrender. Three
months later, on 9 August, the second of two
atomic mushroom clouds brought the Japanese
surrender and the end of the war. The greatest
military machine in history started to wind down;
after six years of total commitment to war, Britain
relaxed, exhausted, and though the summer
and autumn of 1945 brought relief and rejoicing,
victory parades and street parties, it was also a
time to reflect on what had been achieved.

On VE Day, the government published a small
book to mark that achievement: *What Britain Has
Done*. It was based on statistics and started by
recording that Britain was the first country to go
to war with Hitler without being attacked first and
that it had been fighting Germany the longest. It

then moved to record that 'Britain in 1940 saved
the world from German domination by winning
the Battle of Britain all but single handed'. Two
days later, on 10 May, *Pathe Gazette* produced its
Victory Edition. The Battle of Britain was singled
out again, illustrated with pilots at readiness and
flying Spitfires, then German aircraft blowing up
and filling scrap yards.

Newspapers and radio followed suit: the
media marked the victory as a whole, ascribing it
to the collective effort rather than to individuals
and even less to particular weapons. Then, on
15 September 1945, the fifth anniversary of the
greatest day in the Battle of Britain, when the
country had been alone and vulnerable and
Fighter Command had turned the tide, the RAF
marked victory with a flypast of 300 fighters over
London. The occasion brought together the
survivors of The Few, including Air Chief Marshal
Sir Hugh Dowding, at North Weald fighter
station. The newsreels recorded Britain's most
widely known fighter pilot, the legless Group
Captain Douglas Bader, DSO and Bar, DFC, climbing into his personal Spitfire, his initials DB painted
on the side, to lead twenty-four squadrons roaring
over London. The streets were full of people
looking up, many of them in tears, as Fighter
Command's mighty armada flew through the rain
squalls, the sight of Spitfires and the sound of
Merlin engines evoking just a hint of the intensity
of fighting spirit they had experienced in the Battle
of Britain five years earlier when the country's
fate had depended on them.

Afterwards, when the pilots had climbed out of
their aircraft and the crowds had dispersed, many
of those present would have thought that the fly-

MEMORIAL FLYPAST: the RAF Battle of Britain Memorial Flight's Spitfire, Hurricane and Lancaster flying over Ripon Market Square, Yorkshire, on 12 May 2007. The BBMF makes over 700 individual aircraft appearances a year at over 500 events ranging from the Queen's Birthday Flypast over London to small village fêtes.

past marked the end of an era. Few of them would have believed that sixty years later, on 10 July 2005, a quarter of a million people would throng into central London to commemorate VE and VJ days, with millions more at home watching on television — most of them not even born in 1945. There were tears on upturned faces again as a Spitfire and a Hurricane escorted a Lancaster bomber of the RAF's Battle of Britain Memorial Flight (BBMF) as it showered a million poppy petals on central London. Five more Spitfires followed, and just as the Spitfire had been a symbol of victory in 1940, and in 1945, so in 2005 it had the power to draw people together through shared emotion, and a common sense of pride and Britishness.

Without the RAF's Spitfires, national events such as Remberance Day or the Queen's eightieth birthday in 2006 would not have been the same.

Following the great victory flypast in 1945, it became traditional for a Spitfire and a Hurricane to fly over London on Battle of Britain Day, but who would have believed that fifty-eight Spitfires, nearly five squadrons' worth, would still be flying more than sixty years later? And not just for official occasions: hundreds of air shows and even local fêtes around the country every summer would not be the events they are without a Spitfire paying a visit as a national symbol.

Even now there are flying Spitfires maintained by several air forces round the world, as well as many private individuals who are able to keep them flying and race them. The BBMF and the Imperial War Museum's hangars at Duxford have provided a seventy-year continuum since the Spitfire's first flight — a centre of excellence, skills and dedication to keep them part of the nation's great treasures, and play host to the Spitfire's seventieth birthday in 2006.

When the Second World War ended, the RAF had 5,864 Spitfires on its books — more than twenty-five per cent of the 22,789 that were produced. The only aircraft to remain in production throughout the war, the ultimate Spitfires, as the Griffon-engined variants became known, continued to come off the production line until 1948, even as Britain struggled to balance the economic burdens of building a welfare state, policing and restoring itself in its empire, and fighting the Cold War. The pace of re-equipping Fighter Command with jet fighters was sluggish, and the number of Spitfires was reduced dramatically, with many sold or given away, but the Spitfire was still an important fighter throughout the 1940s, and remained at the forefront of

photo reconnaissance well into the 1950s. The
Mk XIX — which had come into service in April
1944 and was for many admirers the most
beautiful and functional Spitfire ever built — still
had the range and the operational ceiling to be an
effective spy machine while it continued to evolve.

In May 1945, there were orders for 3,000 of the
latest fighting Spitfire, the Mk 21, which had been
designed to take over from the stalwart Mk XIV.
The Mk 21 could cruise at 450 mph at 25,000 feet
with its 2,000-plus horsepower Griffon 61 engine
and 11-foot propeller. However, when it had been
tested by pilots of the Air Fighting Development
Unit in December 1944, there were signs that
the great Spitfire tradition might be drawing to
an end. It was difficult to fly: take-off required full
port rudder and full port rudder trim to counter-
act the starboard yaw induced by the power of
the engine; once airborne, the pilot had to adjust
the rudder trim rapidly while also coping with
a highly sensitive elevator control and establish
a steady climb while adjusting trim and gathering
speed from below 180 mph, at low level, which
took very high levels of concentration. Even at
25,000 feet it was an uncomfortable aircraft to
fly: rudder movements created instability in the
horizontal plane which, if unchecked, developed
into a corkscrewing motion, making formation
flying and accurate gunnery difficult. The RAF
test pilots gave their view that technically there
was little to choose between the Mk 21 and the
Mk XIV it was intended to replace, and that in
combat, the Mk XIV was the better all-round
fighter. Their report ended ominously with the
comment: 'No further attempts should be made
to perpetuate the Spitfire family.'

The judgement was hasty. The problems were
solved by increasing the size of the tail and rudder
— but not before the first, unmodified, Mk 21s had
been delivered to the RAF in January 1945. Modified
aircraft were delivered to 91 Squadron in April 1945
and they flew armed reconnaissance missions from
Norfolk to northern Holland against the mobile
launching sites of Hitler's latest weapon, the
ballistic V-2 rockets being prepared to fire towards
London. Four squadrons of Mk 21s were part of
the occupation forces in Germany, the last and
most advanced Spitfires to take an active part in
the war. But the order for 3,000 Mk 21s was cut to
120 and longer-term developments of the Spitfire,
the Spiteful and the Seafang were abandoned.

There were two more developments of the
Spitfire after the war: the Mk 22 and the Mk 24.
The Mk 22 was delivered to one RAF squadron
before being handed over to the Auxiliary Air
Force. After that they were sold to Southern
Rhodesia where they formed the first two fighter
squadrons of the air force there until 1954.

The Mk 24 was the last of the line: just eighty-
one were produced, the last of which was the
very last Spitfire to come off the production
line in February 1948. They were delivered to
80 Squadron and served as part of RAF Germany
until July 1949, the last RAF Spitfires to serve in
Germany. The Squadron then moved to Hong
Kong, where it continued in RAF service until
January 1952 when their aircraft were handed
over to the Hong Kong Auxiliary Air Force.

The Auxiliary Air Force was given the prefix
Royal in 1947 in recognition of its part in the Battle
of Britain and the wider war, and when its twenty
squadrons were called up with the advent of the

250 L AST OF THE LINE: after
years of wartime
improvements, peace and
the advent of the jet fighter
brought cuts in Spitfire
development and produc-
tion. The most advanced
Spitfires, such as the Mk 22
(nearest camera) and the
Mk 21, continued with RAF
fighter squadrons in Britain
and Germany until 1948.
As jets arrived to replace
them, they were handed
over to the Royal Auxiliary
Air Force, where they
served on until 1951 before
again being replaced with
Vampires and Meteors.

Korean War in 1950, thirteen of those squadrons
were Spitfires — making up nearly a third of the
strength of Fighter Command as a whole. Spitfires
served in the RAuxAF until 1951, but they were
never called upon to fire their guns in Home
Defence after the war. In their lifetime, Spitfires
had equipped 116 RAF and RAuxAF squadrons.
From 1951 they were replaced with Meteor and
Vampire jet fighters.

With their higher speed, Meteors and Vampires
had taken over the role of interception and air
defence as early as November 1945. The RAF High
Speed Flight had been re-constituted with the sole
purpose of using jets to establish the first post-war
official speed record. On 7 November 1945, Group
Captain H.J. Wilson established a new record
of 606 mph and on 7 September 1946, Group
Captain E.M. Donaldson raised it to 616 mph.

Britain had finished the war with one of the
most technically advanced aircraft industries in
the world, and one of only two to develop jet
fighters. The German industry had been more
advanced in 1945, but it was virtually destroyed
and the secrets of its wartime research into jet
engines, rocket engines, ballistic weapons, anti-
aircraft missiles, and, crucially, high-speed design
all passed to the Allies. One of the most significant
advances in design made by German scientists
was to sweep back the wings. Britain's Meteor
and Vampire were wartime designs with first-
generation jet engines and straight, rather than
swept-back, wings, and by 1946, they already
looked dated.

Swept wings would change the shape of the
fighter forever. They were the key to higher
speeds, and both Britain and America, whose

industries had research aircraft and jet fighter designs with straight wings, either abandoned or modified them as a result of the captured German data. Speed was the objective again, and the new Holy Grail was supersonic flight: flying past the 'sound barrier' which had been encountered close to Mach 1 by high-speed fighter pilots in Spitfires, Mustangs and Meteors during the war.

Britain abandoned plans for the straight-winged, 1,000 mph Miles M.52 jet-powered research aircraft. Instead, in the struggle to be first, de Havilland put swept wings on a Vampire fuselage and named it the DH 108 — but it broke up in mid air, killing the test pilot, Geoffrey de Havilland. In America, the National Advisory Committee for Aeronautics (NACA) and the newly independent USAF persisted with their straight-winged design, the Bell X-1, a rocket-powered research aircraft which had to be dropped from the bomb bay of a B-36 bomber. On 14 October 1947, Captain Charles 'Chuck' Yeager flew faster than sound for the first time. This achievement was kept secret at the time, to give NACA time to absorb what it had learnt. America's first jet fighter, the P-80 Shooting Star, was straight-winged, as was its replacement, the F-86 Sabre, but the F-86 was re-designed with swept wings and flew for the first time on 1 October 1947. With the data from Yeager's X-1 flights, it flew supersonically on 26 April 1948, making it the first operational supersonic fighter.

Meanwhile, the Soviet Union, which had been supplied with Spitfires by Britain during the war, made huge efforts to bring its own technology up to date, and its equivalent to the F-86, the MiG-15, flew for the first time on 30 December 1948. The

F-86 and the MiG-15 both entered service in 1949 and the Soviet Union sold its Spitfires to the People's Republic of China. Meanwhile the RAF and the Royal Navy turned to the two Battle of Britain suppliers, Hawker and Supermarine, to produce prototypes of new jet fighters. Hawker worked on Specification E38/46, which became the swept-wing Hunter, while Supermarine, who had already produced a straight-winged naval jet fighter, the Attacker, in 1946, redesigned their aircraft to incorporate the faster swept wings. The new Supermarine fighter became the Swift, and it flew for the first time just a day before the MiG-15, on 29 December 1948. But in those post-war years, Britain could not afford the development costs for the next generation of fighters; by 1950, it was a poor third in the league of aeronautical nations. America and the Soviet Union had moved decisively ahead.

The Second World War had changed more than just the shape of fighters, it had changed the world: socially culturally, geopolitically and militarily. Barely two years after it was over, the world was divided by Cold War ideologies centred on the United States and the Soviet Union. Aircraft, and hence aircraft industries, would play a central role in the Cold War from the start, with the result that the world's aircraft industry went through a technical revolution even bigger than that of the mid-1930s. However, even after all its work on the jet engine and the other development work which had taken place during the war, Britain fell behind. The Labour government was preoccupied with turning the wartime economy into a peacetime economy, and new jet fighters did not take priority over building the

End of an era: a photograph showing the Supermarine Swift as the natural successor to the Spitfire in the RAF's all-jet future. It was not to be: as the Spitfire grew into a flying legend, the Swift became a sad footnote in the RAF's history; shortly after it was abandoned, the name Supermarine disappeared too, in the rationalization of Britain's aircraft industry.

welfare state. Meanwhile, overseas, Britain was either seeking to re-establish the Empire, or withdraw from it. The effect was to extend the life of the Spitfire as new and existing air forces looked for fighters.

The list of nations that could not aspire to jet fighters in the 1940s and early 1950s, and for which the Spitfire provided a stop-gap, was a long one. Most West European countries that had been occupied by Germany during the war, and whose air forces had disappeared, acquired Spitfires, among them France, Belgium, Holland, Norway, Denmark, Yugoslavia, Greece and the former enemy Italy. It was the same with countries that had been occupied by the Japanese — such as the Philippines, Thailand and Burma, which bought Seafires direct from Britain, then bought Spitfires from the Israelis when they moved on to Meteors. In the Middle East, Israel, Egypt, Syria and Turkey flew Spitfires, as did neutral countries such as Portugal, the Republic of Ireland and Sweden, which bought fifty PR Mk XIXs to keep watch on

the Soviet Union in the Baltic region, and the People's Republic of China had bought some from the Soviet Union. In all, over thirty air forces from superpowers to newly independent nations operated Spitfires, giving a second generation of fighter pilots worldwide a chance to experience its special qualities, spreading the legend and establishing it once again as an expression of modernity and national aspiration. Britain had surplus Spitfires and they were both a practical and, to an extent, inspirational way of creating the nucleus of a fighter force in the immediate post-war period, especially in those countries whose pilots had flown Spitfires with the RAF during the war — such as Australia, Canada, New Zealand, India, South Africa, Rhodesia, Poland and Czechoslovakia.

The Royal Canadian Air Force, Royal Australian Air Force, and Royal New Zealand Air Force all had their own Spitfire squadrons within the RAF; No 457 Squadron moved to RAAF Livingstone at Darwin where it fought against the Japanese navy and air force.

254 EXPORT: after service in the Battle of Britain and the wider war, pilots of 310 (Czechoslovak) Squadron RAF, led by their Commanding Officer, Squadron Leader J. Hartman, flew their Spitfire Mark IXs to Prague, where they paraded on 13 August 1945. With the communist coup in 1948, the Czechoslovak airmen were regarded as suspect or traitors and dismissed; some of their Spitfires were sold to Israel.

The Spitfire was familiar throughout the British Empire. The Indian Air Force had received its first Spitfires in October 1944 and during the war it fought alongside the RAF against the Japanese in Burma; in recognition of its contribution was given the prefix 'Royal' in 1945. Between 1945 and 1946, the RIAF took over fourteen squadrons of Spitfires, mainly Mk VIIIs and Mk XIVs, but including two squadrons of photo reconnaissance Spitfires. When India became independent and was partitioned into India and Pakistan in July 1947, two air forces were created and the Spitfires were incorporated into the RIAF. In the Kashmir War that followed, from October 1947 to the peace agreement in January 1949, No. 1 PR Flight RIAF was used in the Kashmir Valley, particularly at the battles of Badgam and Shelatang. And today, the IAF has maintained a Mk VIII in flying condition which appears at IAF Day displays.

In 1945 there were three Czechoslovak Spitfire squadrons in the RAF, Nos. 310, 312 and 313, all of which had served with distinction since the Battle of Britain. With the liberation of Czechoslovakia, the squadrons returned home complete with around fifty-five Mk IX Spitfires, where they were

rebranded as S-89s and formed the backbone of the re-constituted Czechoslovak air force. Throughout the period up to the Communist coup in February 1948, the Spitfires were a frequent sight at air displays and developed a wide public profile.

Just as Czechoslovakia was becoming part of the Soviet empire, Israel, formerly part of Palestine, was moving to independence. The new state was formed on 14 May 1948 and was almost immediately embroiled in a war with its Arab neighbours. The tiny Israeli air force had managed to build two Spitfires out of parts found at recently vacated ex-RAF stations, and despite a ban on arms sales to Israel by Britain, it had bought around twenty Avia S.199s — Czechoslovak copies of the Bf 109G. On the other hand, Britain had supplied Spitfires to both the Egyptian and Syrian air forces, and as soon as the British left Israel in July 1948, the Arab air forces joined their armies in a war against the new state. Israel then negotiated to buy around fifty Spitfires from Czechoslovakia. Not all were delivered in time, but with hair-raising flights across Europe in the autumn of 1948 they eventually became the backbone of the Israeli air force's 101st fighter squadron.

In its War of Independence, Israel defended its airspace vigorously and in doing so, shot down fifteen Spitfires, ten of the Egyptian air force and six RAF Spitfires operating from Egypt — the only example of Spitfires engaged in combat with other Spitfires. It was a sad chapter in the history of the Spitfire when at dawn on 7 January 1949 four RAF Spitfires flew over an Israeli roadblock on Egyptian territory prior to an armistice that had been arranged for 2 p.m. that day. Israeli anti-

IMPORT: Ezer Weizman's personal Spitfire is kept in flying condition by the Israeli air force; he served in the RAF before founding the IAF, and his aircraft is flown at national ceremonies, including here at his own state funeral as the former President of Israel in 2005.

255

aircraft fire shot down one of the RAF Spitfires and the other three circled overhead as the pilot bailed out and landed. Claiming later that they did not recognize the RAF markings, two Israeli air force volunteer pilots attacked and shot down the other three, killing one of the pilots. Three RAF Spitfires sent to investigate the disappearance of the first flight were shot down later in the day. It was in that inglorious attack that the last Spitfire was destroyed in aerial combat.

The Israeli air force continued to buy Spitfires, including thirty from Italy, and they remained in service until 1955 when the last eighteen were sold to Burma. Many of the Israeli pilots had learned to fly and served with the RAF during the Second World War, including Ezer Weizman, who both commanded the Israeli air force and later became President of Israel. In recognition of the part played by Weizman, one of the Spitfires

which the Israelis had rebuilt from an Egyptian they had shot down became his personal machine, and was restored to immaculate condition. In honour of the part played by both pilots and Spitfires in the birth of the nation, the Israeli air force still maintains it. Sixty years later, in 2005, that Spitfire flew a mournful farewell over Ezer Weizman's state funeral.

As Britain struggled to afford an all jet-powered fighter force at home, and sought to re-establish its Empire, Spitfires were stationed at bases along its old trade routes in places such as Malta, Cyprus, the Suez Canal Zone and in the Persian Gulf, and particularly at the great entrepôt cities such as Singapore and Hong Kong. They were active in three roles against the communist threat in the Far East: in Malaya, Korea and Hong Kong. During the Malayan Emergency, a twelve-year counter-insurgency war that started in 1948, Spitfires flew hundreds of ground attack missions with bombs and cannon fire against guerrilla camps; the last such sortie was led by Wing Commander Wilfrid Duncan-Smith, who had first flown Spitfires in 1940. On 3 July 1950, in the early stages of the Korean War, Seafires from HMS *Illustrious* attacked Haeju airfield in Korea and were subsequently involved in attacking railway lines and other targets in North Korea, but their limited range was a handicap and the air war in Korea soon became a war between jets.

China supported North Korea in that war, and although full-scale military operations were confined to the Korean peninsula, the RAF carried out discreet photographic reconnaissance from Hong Kong using PR Mk XIX Spitfires along the Chinese coast and in some sorties over the

256 SPITFIRE RENAISSANCE: there are some fifty Spitfires still flying in 2008, more than for most of the previous half-century. Built in 1945, this Mk XVI was sold by the RAF in 1954 and has since been lovingly restored and flown by a number of owners in Britain, America and Canada.

258

SPITFIRE RECORD-HOLDER: Flight Lieutenant Ted Powles, who, on 5 February 1952, while serving with the Meteorological Flight in Hong Kong, set an altitude record for the Spitfire of 51,550 feet and a speed record of 690 mph (0.94 Mach) in a dive. The speed record, which is unofficial, remains the highest speed ever achieved by a propeller-driven aircraft.

Chinese mainland. In 1951, Flight Lieutenant Ted Powles flew 107 sorties to take photographs of Chinese airfields, particularly on the island of Hainan, at the extreme limit of the Spitfire's range; on one occasion he flew a sortie lasting three and a half hours, and ran out of fuel just before touching down at Kai Tak. Powles clearly enjoyed taking the Spitfire to its limits: on 5 February 1952 he reached 51,550 feet in a PR Mk XIX, then dived earthwards again, the aircraft vibrating as it reached transonic speeds, the controls almost rigid. Later analysis of the data showed that he had reached 690 mph (0.94 Mach), very close to the speed of sound; in one flight he had set two records for the Spitfire that still stand today, though the speed record was open to some doubt. No. 80 Squadron's Spitfires were steadily replaced by twin engine Hornets, but some remained on charge.

On the Queen's Birthday, 21 April 1955, Spitfires carried out a celebratory flypast at Kai Tak: the aircraft's last official duty. It had been nineteen years since its first flight and seventeen since it had

first entered operational RAF service at Duxford.

The delays in producing home-grown swept-wing jet fighters had been such that in 1953 the RAF had bought 428 Canadair-built F-86 Sabres to equip thirteen Fighter Command squadrons for Home Defence while they waited for the Hawker Hunter and the Supermarine Swift. The change-over process began as the last Spitfires left Hong Kong to be replaced by first generation, straight-winged Vampires and Venoms, issued by Fighter Command just as the Swift and Hunter were due to arrive, around five years after the United States and the Soviet Union. The first Swifts had flown in 1947 but were not introduced until February 1954, with 56 Squadron. They handled poorly and were grounded in August that year after a series of accidents, some of them fatal. The problems were largely solved with the Mk 4, but the Swift never entered service as an RAF fighter.

The Hawker Hunter, which had first flown on 19 June 1950, was introduced into RAF service in July 1956. Like the Swift it had been rushed into service and it suffered from a series of teething problems, but it was clearly a capable fighter, and it became highly regarded by pilots in spite of its very short range. Supermarine and Hawker had built aircraft that had fought alongside each other in 1940, but they were not destined to do so again. This time, the competition was settled in Hawker's favour. However, Supermarine did supply the Royal Navy with an expensive jet fighter, the Scimitar, which flew for the first time in January 1956 and entered service in January 1957.

Just as the new British jet fighters were coming into service, the British government carried out a far-reaching Defence Review which had a

LONG SERVICE: this Spitfire PR Mk XIX (PM631), delivered to the RAF just after the end of the Second World War, was one of the original aircraft around which the RAF Historic Aircraft Flight was formed in 1957—and it is still flying over half a century later (*above*), making it the BBMF's longest-serving aircraft.

DEFENDING THE COLONIES: Spitfire Mk XIVs of 132 Squadron lined up on the flight deck of the escort carrier *HMS Smiter* (*opposite below*) as she enters Hong Kong harbour on 22 September 1945. The squadron took over responsibility for the colony's air defence, and Spitfires played a key role there for a decade before beig replaced with jets.

profound effect of the RAF. It was influenced by many considerations, but foremost amongst them was a growing recognition that Britain was a declining world power and could no longer afford an air force on the scale of the RAF at the time. When the 1957 Defence White Paper was published, it represented a triumph for the theory that the days of the manned fighter, even the manned aircraft itself, were drawing to a close and that fighters in particular would be replaced by surface-to-air guided missiles. The Bloodhound missile, it argued, was the best way to deal with the threat of the strategic bombers which Russia was now building, and which were equipped with H-bombs. Britain's next generation of research aircraft aimed at supersonic fighters; the single-seat Saunders Roe SR.53 and SR.177 and the two-seat Fairey F.155, which were either in prototype form or advanced stages of development, were scrapped. The one survivor was the English Electric P.1, which became the last British fighter in the form of the double sonic Lightning.

The White Paper, known as the 'Sandys Storm' after Duncan Sandys, the minister responsible,

had implications that went much further than just scrapping new front-line fighters. It was explicit that future contracts for aircraft would be given only to companies that could demonstrate that they had rationalized from several separate contractors, many of them based on companies founded before and during the Great War, into larger, well-capitalized businesses. By the early 1960s, Britain's aircraft industry was unrecognizable—down to two large corporations, BAC and Hawker Siddeley, which, by 1977, had become one: British Aerospace. In 1966 Rolls-Royce became the single aero engine supplier. After nearly half a century of making bespoke aeroplanes, Supermarine disappeared, just the kind of artisan producer which did not suit the brave new world. Meanwhile the Spitfire, its greatest product, had passed into history as an operational aircraft. There were still quite a number of Spitfires flying, including three PR Mk XIXs operated by a private company to make daily high-altitude flights to collect weather data for the RAF, which they continued to do until 1958, but the Spitfire was about to enter a completely new lease of life.

PUBLIC RELATIONS:
'Thanksgiving Week'
in October 1945. The RAF
contributed a Spitfire for
public display in North-
ampton Market Square
(*left*), getting it close to
the people. The RAF
formation teams which
had been such a feature
of the interwar years
were revived in 1956
with the Black Arrows
aerobatic team of Hawker
Hunters (*above*); however,
the Spitfire remained a
great attraction.

While Spitfires had been in service, it had been relatively easy to arrange the Battle of Britain flypast each year, but as the last RAF operational Spitfires disappeared, they seemed destined to become earthbound, mere 'gate guards', parked at RAF station guardrooms to welcome visitors.

However, there were some who were not ready to see the Spitfire pass out of the RAF flying inventory completely. They had grown up with it, and for them it had become part of the image of the RAF, a symbol of its purpose. The British love of air displays was undiminished, and in a future in which the RAF would shrink, change, and steadily withdraw from the Empire, and where the National Service it had relied on for its recruits would end, the idea that the Spitfire might become both a recruiting sergeant for the RAF and a way of remembering the nation's finest hour took hold. It was as if there was an instinct for history within the RAF, a feeling they needed to retain a flying

connection with the Battle of Britain. So in the same year that an axe was being taken to oper-ational fighter squadrons, and that the Soviet Union put the first satellite into orbit, in July 1957, the RAF Historic Aircraft Flight was born at the Battle of Britain fighter station at Biggin Hill. It had three Spitfires and one Hurricane.

Two of those Spitfires were PR Mk XIXs of 1945 vintage; one of them, a PR Mk XIX, PS915, is flying in the RAF today, well over sixty years after it was delivered. Ironically, it was by preserving Spitfires as antiques that the Spitfire was available to perform one last operational duty in the RAF: in 1963, at a time when the double-sonic Lightning was possibly going to be deployed in support of British troops facing counter insurgency from Indonesia in Brunei, a PR Mk XIX was flown in combat simulations to develop tactics for the jet fighter pilots to use against the Mustangs which were still flown by the Indonesian air force.

The Spitfire was a reminder of a deeper truth about military operations: that the need to fight for control of airspace in war cannot be wished away. The 1957 White Paper, with its recycled theory that the single-seater fighter was obsolete, turned out to be just as misguided the second time around. The Lightning became the Spitfire of the Cold War for Britain. Every day for three decades, it was at readiness to intercept Soviet reconnaissance bombers as they probed the effectiveness of the defensive radar screen that had protected Britain since 1940. They never shot any down, but flew alongside them over the North Sea and the Mediterranean, their air-to-air missiles highly visible, escorting them peacefully out of British airspace, not a job that could have been entrusted to a Bloodhound missile. In hot wars, the experience was the same: that manned fighters were an essential part of any serious air force — as the Vietnam War, the two Indo-Pakistan wars, the

Falklands Conflict, and the seven Middle Eastern wars between 1967 and 2004 showed. Successful air operations today still depend on skilled pilots in technically advanced, fast, manned aircraft, who are able to dominate an area where ground or sea operations are contemplated, and, once that superiority is won, to be integrated into ground and sea operations at all levels.

The Spitfire outlived Fighter Command. In 1968 it was merged with Bomber Command to create Strike Command, a single entity for all the RAF's jet aircraft. With the passing of Fighter Command, and of Supermarine a decade earlier, and the steady disappearance from the RAF's ranks of the generation of airmen with little tufts of coloured silk above their uniform breast pockets to remind others of what had been achieved, the links to the Second World War slowly dwindled. At the same time, the social, cultural and economic upheaval of the late 1950s and early 1960s saw the passing of relationships, sights, sounds, certainties and priorities that had been familiar to the generation who had fought the war. As they did, that wartime experience suddenly re-appeared in books and in films in which the story of the Spitfire emerged as part of the RAF's and the nation's narrative.

The Historic Aircraft Flight articulated that new enthusiasm. As it developed, slowly at first, it had to scrounge other Spitfires, either to fly them or cannibalize them for parts. And so a renaissance of the Spitfire as a popular national icon began. A curious industry developed, part RAF, part private entrepreneurship, based on enthusiasm for the Spitfire as *the* historic flying aircraft. It was led by an informal network of people not unlike those who had been involved with the Schneider Cup, who had believed in R.J. Mitchell's genius, who had based a battle of national survival on the Spitfire's prowess, and who had coaxed ever more out of it during the war. Their common goal was to keep Spitfires flying.

Today, the Spitfire is the ultimate rich boys' toy. In America, highly-polished Spitfires are raced against other Second World War fighters, especially Mustangs. A Spitfire costs well over £1m to buy, depending on its state of preservation, and thousands of pounds an hour to fly. Clive du Cross built an exact replica of the prototype Spitfire, K5054, the original having crashed and been destroyed on 2 September 1939, killing the RAF test pilot. Wealthy pilots — and a few of those prepared to pay thousands of pounds for the privilege of being a passenger in one of the few two-seater versions — can still experience the unique thrill of flying a Spitfire the way they were made to fly: twisting and turning in a blue sky one minute, pulling up into a loop at over 300 mph from near ground level the next.

More Spitfires are flying now than at any time since the early 1950s. A small but highly skilled industry has grown up around restoring Spitfires, centred in Britain at Duxford, where a private company at the Imperial War Museum's Flying museum has its workshops, and with the BBMF. In fact, the industry could now, apart from some engine parts, build a new Spitfire from scratch. Many restorations are getting towards that point anyway, and need to be to meet the demands of the Civil Aviation Authority safety standards. They may be rather mix-and-match aircraft and as such not conform precisely to any particular wartime specification, but in many respects, that reflects the position during the war, when early Marks were re-engined and battle damage repaired with what was available.

Spitfires are still the prize exhibits in many of the world's aircraft museums, but it is in flight that they still make their greatest impact. In addition to the privately-owned restorations flown at air shows and for filming, many Spitfires are preserved in flying condition as symbols of many air forces' history. The RAF still has five Spitfires and they are flown on occasions of national importance in Britain, America, Canada, Australia, New Zealand, India and Israel. On the weekend of 2 and 3 September 2006, to mark seventy years since the first flight, the Spitfire had a birthday celebration at Duxford, attended by enthusiasts, owners and pilots with their Spitfires, and a great many modern military and civil aircraft too — flying tributes from around the world to an aircraft that is truly a flying legend itself.

STAR AND CELEBRITY

True icons are timeless. The powerful historical context of the Battle of Britain—the courage of the pilots, the singularity of the aircraft, the narrow margin of victory and its strategic importance—is well known, but the Spitfire has transcended that context. Since last firing its guns in anger, it has slipped effortlessly into popular culture, where its place is assured.

266

ALL-STAR CAST (*previous page*): Michael Caine simulating flying a Spitfire in his role as the rather aloof Squadron Leader Canfield in the 1969 epic feature film *The Battle of Britain*.

RE-ENACTMENT (*below*): in 1946 the RAF cooperated with the BBC to make a television broadcast with pilots who had flown in the Battle of Britain; from relaxing on the ground, they scrambled and flew for the cameras. In 1954, the BBC then made a major television documentary series, *War in the Air*, the first of scores of programmes to use Spitfires.

FREED FROM THE CONSTRAINTS of censorship, the mass media of the late 1940s continued to live with the physical constraints of the wartime economy. Publishing still had to work with paper rationing; the apparatus of mass communications in radio and film, which had been harnessed as part of the national effort during the war, took time to adapt to peace. However, freed from the immediacy and tensions of war, the BBC, newspapers and newsreels changed their tone to a much more positive, even light-hearted approach based on victory, even if the reality was that the country was in a climate of economic struggle.

In September 1945, a Movietone newsreel, *Britain Can Make It*, echoed the classic wartime documentary, *Britain Can Take It*; it showed a broken-up Spitfire being made into toys, furniture and kitchen units as part of the promise of a return to the consumerism of the late 1930s. Newsreels created many variations on the theme of swords being turned into ploughshares. Pathe Gazette showed an Oxford factory producing cars in November 1945 and according to the commentary

it was using parts intended for Spitfires; to make the point, a Spitfire flew overhead.

The French newsreels were less inhibited in their appreciation of the Spitfire. On 19 November 1945 Pathe Gazette showed *Here is Michelle de Lys*, a three-minute movie which celebrated the Free French contribution to the air war. In it the French star plays the girlfriend of a French Spitfire pilot: she waits in a restaurant for him to arrive, keeps a place for him at the table, spurns the advances of other men until he arrives, when his presence is overpowering to her. She sings and dances can-can for him, then at dawn, he takes her to see his Spitfire and takes off, the message so clear as to be almost painful: if you want the girl, fly a Spitfire.

In 1947, defence was once again a prominent theme as the Cold War preoccupied the nation. A whole week was set aside to mark victory in the Battle of Britain, a week in which Spitfires were very much in evidence, both in the air and on newsreels. The commentary for the major film on the battle evoked the Few, but was aimed too at all the people who had made sacrifices during the war, recalling their fortitude in difficult economic times, associating the population at large with victory, including Churchill's words: 'This is no war of chieftains or of princes, of dynasties or national ambitions; it is a war of peoples and causes, a war of unknown warriors.'

Newsreels changed with the mood of the nation as a semblance of domestic normality began to return. The British social scene also spluttered back into life, slowly returning to the days of the great air pageants that had been a feature of the 1920s and 1930s. On 2 September 1948, Pathe showed the air races at Lympne as a

Defining moment: a Spitfire roars above a suburban London street, part of depicting the experience of Bill Rohan, a young boy growing up in the chaos of wartime London, in the 1987 feature film *Hope and Glory*.

great social and celebrity occasion under the title *Spitfire Beats Jet*. There was a huge crowd, and the VIPs included Noel Coward, Douglas Fairbanks Jnr and his wife; it also included Lettice Curtis, taking off to break the women's speed record in a civil registered Spitfire. The finale showed Group Captain John Cunningham racing a Vampire against a Spitfire at low level; the Spitfire won by yards.

Another newsreel showed Queen Elizabeth inspecting No. 600 (City of London) Squadron RAuxAF at Biggin Hill on the occasion of her becoming the Honorary Air Commodore. She gave a speech about the people who had won the war and the contribution made by the RAuxAF, then the engines of nine rather muscular-looking Spitfire Mk 22s burst into life in clouds of smoke; they taxied out majestically and took off for a

flypast. By associating herself with the Spitfire and acknowledging its place in the Battle of Britain, to which she made several references in her speech, the Queen mirrored the attitude of Britain at large: invoking a symbol of victory at a time when the memory of war and its uncertainties had not yet faded. Britain, like the rest of the world, still hovered between peace and war. In the west, the Berlin Airlift was in full swing; in the Far East, the newsreels showed Spitfires beefing up the garrison at Hong Kong as the Communists triumphed in the civil war, and from 1950, Britain was engaged on the ground in the Korean War.

But as the RAF operational squadrons slowly swapped their Spitfires for jet fighters in the 1940s and 1950s, the fate of many was to be scrapped, or to finish up as proud gate-guards or in museums.

268

OFFICIAL ICON: Spitfires have appeared on many stamps over the years. When Mauritius commemorated the island's 'efforts in the fight for freedom' in 1991, it chose to depict one of two Spitfires the island bought through the Spitfire Fund (*above*). A British commemorative set to mark the 25th anniversary of the Battle of Britain in 1965 included a stamp dedicated to the Spitfire (*centre*) and a 1997 set, on British Aircraft Designers, showed the RAF's Mk II against a cloud sculpture evoking the designer R.J. Mitchell (*below*).

A tiny number eventually found a new lease of life flying with the Battle of Britain Memorial Flight, but in the same period, Spitfires found a new career moonlighting outside the RAF, where the British film industry was responding to a popular demand for real stories about what had actually happened in the war — those stories which had not been told during the war for security reasons. There was a steady flow of films, from newsreels to features, that were not only entertaining, they enhanced the sense that the Spitfire had performed even more than many people had known, enhancing its aura of quiet invincibility.

As the 1950s dawned, there was a change of mood. Feature films and books about the Second World War were enormously popular, but unlike the books, newsreels and movies that had been published during and immediately after the war, these were a mixture of fact and fiction. The quintessential fighter pilot in fiction was Biggles, whose adventures had continued throughout the war. From 1945 to 1970, when W.E. Johns died, at least one, and often two Biggles books were published in every year. In 1953, the first Biggles Omnibus was published, and on the cover, the hero appeared with a Spitfire. The stories were very much based on the individual, rather than the collective effort, fitting in with the new spirit of the age.

Among the first post-war factual books to chronicle the story of fighting in a Spitfire came, in 1951, from France: *The Big Show* was by Pierre Closterman, an aeronautical engineer and Free French pilot who served in the RAF. He had flown 420 operational sorties and had been elected as a member of the French parliament after the war, a man unafraid of emotional directness and with a gift for words. He had also developed a profound relationship with the Spitfire which he wished to express in print:

All my life I shall remember my first contact with a Spitfire … at last I had flown a Spitfire. How beautiful the machine seemed to me … a masterpiece of harmony and power, even when I saw her now, motionless. Softly, as one might caress a women's cheeks, I ran my hand over the aluminium of her wings, cold and smooth like a mirror, the wings which had borne me. I would have a Spitfire of my own, which would hold my life in the narrow confines of its cockpit, and which I would love like a faithful friend.

flattening the grass under his wings; then he pulled up in a zoom that made the engine howl like a giant in agony, a zoom that brought a cry of delight to Bertie's lips. As straight as an arrow sped the Spitfire, straight towards the Junkers.

The German pilot saw it coming, and swung round to bring his guns to bear. But he was too late. Much too late. Indeed, it is doubtful whether, at the finish, he knew where the Spitfire was. The desperate manner in which he banked suggested this.

Tug, travelling vertically upwards, fired only a short burst from underneath. Then he was past. But the instant he was above his quarry he flattened out, turned like a flash of light, and, at point-blank range, brought his nose, streaming fire, slowly across the Junkers from prop.-boss to tail-skid. The effect was as though a band-saw was passing through it. It broke in halves. One wing went up and tore off at the roots. The fuselage began to fall, slowly at first, but with swiftly increasing speed.

On the ground nobody spoke.

The Junkers's fuselage, minus wings, went into the ground just beyond the boundary hedge like a torpedo. There was a roar like a clap of thunder as its bombs exploded.

Tug cut his engine, side-slipped steeply to within a hundred feet of the ground, levelled out, turned into wind, and dropped the Spitfire

As straight as an arrow sped the Spitfire, straight towards the Junkers

269

POPULAR ICON: Biggles' relationship with the Spitfire started with the publication of *Spitfire Parade: Biggles Goes to War* in 1941; W.E. Johns worked with the Air Training Corps to encourage boys to apply for pilot training, and his books were so effective that the Air Ministry asked him to create a female character, Worrals, to encourage girls to join up.

Pierre Closterman wrote a second book, *Flames in the Sky*, in 1952, broadening his theme of the humanity behind the statistics of the air war, and once again picking out the Spitfire as not only British but special:

The Spitfire, for instance, is typically British. Temperate, a perfect compromise of all of the qualities of a fighter ideally suited to its task of defence. An essentially reasonable piece of machinery conceived by cool, precise brains and built by conscientious hands. The Spitfire left such an imprint on those who flew it that when they changed to other types they found it very hard to get acclimatized.

That same year, 1952, saw the release of the first feature film about the Battle of Britain, *Angels One Five*, based on a fighter station during the battle. It included pilots, but also all the other ranks, trades and specialists from the control room to the fitters and riggers, and reflected the wartime tradition of the RAF as a collective enterprise, without singling out individuals. It was shot with the cooperation of the Air Ministry, which allowed the producers, John Gossage and Derek Twist, both ex-RAF officers, to use the Kenley fighter station. Hawker lent them its last flyable Hurricane and the Portuguese air force, which was just disposing of its last Hurricanes, lent them five more to use as props. It was what today would be called a drama documentary, about people not action, in the tradition of *The First of the Few* and the 1945 feature film *The Way to the Stars*, both of which were made with the support of the RAF and USAAF and which reflected the wartime reality and spirit. *Angels One Five* clearly showed the need for people-based stories of the war, with plots and characters with whom the cinema audience could identify. It was a huge commercial success.

In *Angels One Five* there was a lone Spitfire parked on the airfield, but Britain's favourite aircraft featured much more strongly in *Malta Story*, which followed in 1953. This film focused more on the individual pilot and had a star-studded cast, including Jack Hawkins and with Alec Guinness as the photo-reconnaissance pilot who discovers the Italian plan to invade Malta.

The interest in the air war in film soon transferred to television and in November 1954 a series of fifteen half-hour programmes was broadcast, *War in the Air*. It covered in detail the period from 1935 to 1950, which was almost exactly the period when the Spitfire was the RAF's dominant fighter and a symbol of victory. It was highly acclaimed and reached an audience of sixty per cent of those who had television sets — which amounted to about seventeen per cent of the adult population of Britain — and for twenty years it was required viewing for all new RAF recruits. Another television production, which did not include a Spitfire but in which its presence was acutely felt, was Peter Graham Scott's live and highly acclaimed production of Richard Hillary's Second World War classic book, *The Last Enemy*. It was produced for Battle of Britain Week 1956.

The same year, *Reach For The Sky*, the story of Douglas Bader, emerged; written by Paul Brickhill, himself a wartime Spitfire pilot. It was to become a classic of the 1950s air war genre. Bader had been one of the few names the public recognized throughout the war: despite losing both his legs in an air crash, he had gone on to great success. An ace with twenty-two enemy aircraft to his credit and a leader of exceptional talent in the air and on the ground, he escaped three times from German captivity and led the victory flypast over London in 1945 in a Spitfire with his initials on the side. Bader was the nearest thing the RAF had to a living celebrity, and the book was a huge success: over 100,000 copies were printed initially, but these and subsequent print runs sold out within weeks. The book was a biography, covering Bader's whole life, but it included more than a passing reference to the Big Wing controversy of the Battle of Britain. The film rights were quickly sold, Kenneth Moore was signed up to play Bader; the Air Ministry once again lent the producers RAF Kenley as well as four Spitfires for the flying sequences, and *Reach For The Sky* was released in 1956.

Bader had flown Hurricanes in the Battle of Britain, but he had shot down his first German aircraft in a Spitfire over Dunkirk; in the film, when he is seeking to rejoin the RAF in 1939 after losing his legs eight years earlier, and is telling a particularly sceptical clerical Warrant Officer that he has been successful, he says: 'Mr Blake, where can I buy a Spitfire?' And when he is released from Colditz by the American army, his first question to the Colonel is: 'Any Spitfires round here?' Although some critics did not like it and it won only one of its four BAFTA nominations, Best British Picture, it was a huge box-office success and made Bader even more a symbol of triumph over adversity. And the Spitfire was there, almost a technological equivalent of the man, instrumental in securing victory.

THE RANK ORGANISATION PRESENTS

KENNETH MORE

REACH FOR THE SKY

U

BASED ON THE BOOK BY PAUL BRICKHILL

THE STORY OF DOUGLAS BADER

ALSO STARRING

MURIEL PAVLOW · LYNDON BROOK · LEE PATTERSON · ALEXANDER KNOX

SCREENPLAY BY LEWIS GILBERT · PRODUCED BY DANIEL M. ANGEL · DIRECTED BY LEWIS GILBERT

THE BOOK AND THE FILM: Douglas Bader's autobiography set a new standard in iconic impact in the 1950s, reaching huge audiences eager to read and see the compelling story of personal, human, and national struggle for survival, and the endorsement of the Spitfire which it implied.

The commercial success of both book and film was already being emulated by other Battle of Britain pilots. Again in 1956, the story of Wing Commander Stanford Tuck was told by Larry Forrester in *Fly For Your Life*, and Johnnie Johnson, still in the RAF at the time and the highest-scoring ace against German fighters, all of them taken from Spitfires, wrote *Wing Leader*. Even those who were not well known during the war found a public eager to hear their personal stories: *The Quick and the Dead*, by Squadron Leader Warburton, who had flown Spitfires against Allied and captured German fighters with the Air Fighting Development Unit, and with the RAF High Speed Flight in 1946, wrote an account of his experiences — which also excoriated the government and the aircraft industry for their poor post-war performance.

The following year, another double-amputee Spitfire pilot, Colin Hodgkinson, who described himself as 'a poor man's Bader', wrote an amusing account of his fighting career, which had included shooting down two Focke-Wulf 190s. And then in 1959, the incomparable fighter pilot, survivor and leader, Al Deere, who was also still serving in the RAF, wrote *Nine Lives*. The flurry of books inevitably raised the issue of the clash of policies between 11 and 12 Groups during the Battle of Britain. Deere's book argued, as a personal opinion, that 11 Group's Park had been right to operate the more flexible squadrons rather than the more cumbersome wings. He argued his case coolly and eloquently, pointing to Park's policy of using the Spitfires to draw the enemy fighters away from their task of protecting the bombers as a winning tactic:

… the enemy bombers, shorn of the majority of their escort, were set upon by the defending Hurricanes which, excellent as they were, could not have coped so effectively without the intervention of the Spitfires.

In the world of aircraft design the name of Mitchell is synonymous with that of the Spitfire, the outstanding fighter of the war. In my written report on the combat I stated that in my opinion the Spitfire was superior overall to the Me 109, except in the initial climb and dive; however, this was an opinion contrary to the belief of the so-called experts. The Spitfire, with a better rate of turn than the 109, had the edge overall in combat. There may have been scepticism about my claim for the Spitfire, but I had no doubts on the score, nor did my fellow pilots in 54 Squadron. Later events, in the Battle of Britain, were to prove me right.

Another personal story had been published in 1957: *Leader of the Few, The Dowding Story*, by Basil Collier. It was, again, a full biography of Air Chief Marshal Lord Dowding. His vision was evident in another book published in 1958 which covered the role of the Spitfire in its other great function, photographic reconnaissance. It was not exclusively about the Spitfire, but Constance Babbington-Smith, Britain's pioneer photographic interpreter, wrote *Evidence in Camera, the Story of Photographic Intelligence in World War Two*. It recorded how Dowding had a meeting with Wing Commander Cotton who asked him for two Spitfire Mk Is to experiment with in January 1940, and how Dowding had seen the point immediately, giving him two Spitfires, even though they were in such short supply.

The Spitfire played a part in nearly every book about the air war that was published in the late 1950s. Its history emerged from those accounts in a piecemeal fashion, but almost always positively. Ironically, the publishing boom had coincided with yet another landmark in the story. PS915, the last PR Mk XIX, retired from the civilian Meteorological Flight on 9 July 1957, the same month that the RAF Historic Aircraft Flight was formed.

In 1961, a new type of history appeared, a day-by-day account of the battle with a foreword by Lord Dowding, the result of a huge amount of research: *The Narrow Margin, The Definitive Story of the Battle of Britain*, by Derek Wood with Derek Dempster. It covered the whole battle, and for the first time was not seen through the prism of a particular personality or unit.

The following year, an epic film was released, *The Longest Day*, telling the story of the D-Day landings in a similarly comprehensive format involving thousands of men, tanks, trucks, landing craft, ships and aircraft re-enacting a range of incidents and stories. It was a huge commercial success, and three years later it was to become the inspiration for another epic film, this time about the air war. On 13 September 1965, just before Battle of Britain Week 1965 celebrated the 25th anniversary of the battle, a Spitfire and a Hurricane of the RAF Historic Aircraft Flight were flying over Hyde Park in rehearsals for the flypast. Seeing them gave the film producer S. Benjamin Fisz the idea of making an epic film about the Battle of Britain, doing what *The Longest Day* had done for D-Day in 1962. It would be a film on a scale that covered the whole of the battle, from many viewpoints, and do so with a star-studded

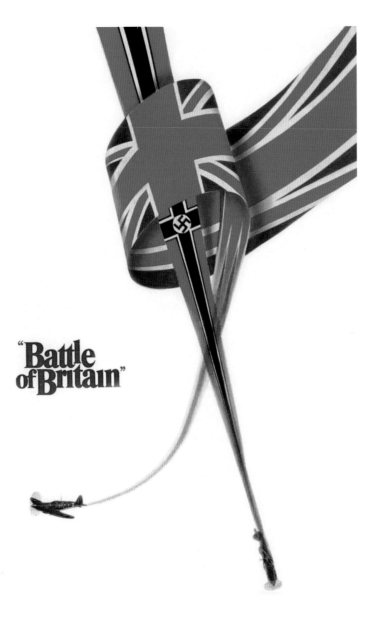

"Battle
of Britain"

Mahaddie, a wartime bomber pilot, was hired to source the aircraft and put together the team of pilots to fly them. For the *Luftwaffe*, Mahaddie managed to borrow fifty operational Heinkel 111 bombers from the Spanish air force, which still operated them, and buy the parts to build twenty-eight Messerschmitt 109s, which the Spanish were selling as scrap; he also found a team of largely Spanish and American pilots to fly them. In an ironic twist, by the 1960s, both German aircraft were powered by Rolls-Royce Merlin engines. The filming of the '*Luftwaffe*' took place in Seville, where flying sequences of massed bombers were shot from a specially converted B-25 Mitchell bomber. The ground sequences showing Goering reviewing his men and machines were also shot in the clear blue skies of southern Spain; after that, the production moved to Britain.

Mahaddie had managed to find twenty flyable Spitfires, some of which were still owned by the RAF, others in private hands, but by 1968 when the filming took place, there was only one flyable Hurricane. As well as the aircraft, and technicians with the expertise to make them flyable, the RAF agreed to provide the production with pilots, and the Air Ministry also lent Duxford, North Weald and Debden airfields, which were largely unchanged since the war, to recreate Fighter Command. The flying sequences were coordinated from Duxford, where the Spitfires mingled with the Heinkels and Messerschmitts as they arrived in force from Spain. On occasions, it was something of a reunion — with some of the stars of the Battle: Douglas Bader, Robert Stanford Tuck, Al Deere, Ginger Lacey and Lord Dowding (who by this time was aged 86) rubbing shoulders

RENAISSANCE: the poster for *The Battle of Britain* in 1969 brought a sense of the national struggle to a new generation, and provided the injection of money, enthusiasm and expertise that led to the rebuilding of the Spitfires that form the backbone of today's airworthy family.

cast. And unlike *The Longest Day*, it would be shot in colour. The big difference was that whereas *The Longest Day* had had a completely justifiable American dimension, *The Battle of Britain* would be about Britain alone. It took Fisz several years to put together what at the time was the huge budget of around £8.5m and find the cast, production team, technical crew and, above all, the aircraft to make it.

A company called Spitfire Productions was created to make the film. Adolph Galland, who had written his account of the battle in 1953, *The First and the Last, The Rise and Fall of the Luftwaffe*, was hired as a consultant; Group Captain Hamish

with the stars of the film: Robert Shaw, Michael Caine, Trevor Howard, Kenneth More, Christopher Plummer, Nigel Patrick, Ian McShane and Edward Fox.

In characteristic style, the Spitfire played a central, but understated, role in the film. It was in the flying and aerial fighting sequences that it excelled, a highly recognizable shape and sound that provided the link to 1940 and the battle itself. The film script was a vindication, if one was still needed, of the way Dowding and Park had fought the battle, showing the value of his quick and flexible responses to changing German tactics, and the unwieldiness of the Big Wings; in fact, Leigh-Mallory, who had been killed in an air crash in 1944, is made to look rather foolish. It was also a vindication of the Spitfire itself, though curiously all the best lines about the British aircraft are written for the German actors, emphasizing the respect they had for their nemesis. One *Luftwaffe* pilot, without a shred of irony, says: 'When I get to England, I'm going to try out a Spitfire …'; an intelligence officer, on being told that the RAF is running out of Spitfires while still getting reports of them attacking from Scotland down to the Channel, dismisses a pilot's testimony with scorn: '… not even a Spitfire can be in two places at once …'; and in the famous encounter between Reichsmarschall Goering and Galland, the best one-liner in the whole film: 'Give me a squadron of Spitfires.'

The Battle of Britain was a compromise between history on an epic scale and the kind of close-up, intimate human drama at which cinema excels. Given the number of experts and veterans who advised on the production, including

Dowding himself, whose portrayal by Laurence Olivier was a high point in the film, it was well received by an air-minded audience at its premier on Battle of Britain Day 1969. However, with a final cost of more than $13m, *The Battle of Britain* did not make money. The critics were mixed in their response: there was admiration for the flying sequences, though some purists considered the use of late-model Spitfires to be taking too much licence with history — even though there was no viable alternative. Other critics, while admiring the flying sequences as a landmark in film production, believed that the scale of the flying prevented the development of the characters.

It was a film based on the action and not the emotion of the key characters, and in that it did represent a particular perspective: of the fighter pilot as hero, locked in a battle for control of his emotions. The mix of characters was, however, not representative of the social background of those who took part in the battle and the film perpetuated certain myths, giving the impression that the Battle of Britain was won by Dowding and Park with some rather well-bred RAF officers with public-school accents, chiselled good looks and loud voices flying Spitfires; in addition, there was only one Sergeant Pilot in the central cast, while the reality was that they had been the core of the Few. The other loser historically was the Hurricane — but that, sadly, was unavoidable: there were simply not enough of them left to take part.

The winner in that context was the Spitfire, which found itself at the heart of the flying sequences, the most memorable parts of the film.

DEFINING IMAGES: despite its all-star cast, which included the cream of British actors, *The Battle of Britain*, more than any other film, became famous for the epic scale of its flying sequences, which set new standards of authenticity and attention to detail. They also drew on the status and good looks of the Spitfire.

Unlike in *Angels One Five* or even *Reach for the Sky*, the flying in *The Battle of Britain* was central to the film. Those sequences show off the Spitfire not only in the context of fierce aerial combat but also against a calmer backdrop of blue skies, fluffy white clouds and beautiful English countryside, where its sheer beauty shines through to great effect. But battle is what the Spitfire was built for, and what it does best. In the moments when the action focuses on Spitfires shooting down Bf 109s, and they twist in the upper air, suddenly revealing the shape of those elliptical wings, even the most amateur aviation enthusiast is in no doubt that he is looking at a Spitfire.

After the filming had been completed, the producers donated a Spitfire Mk IIa of 1940 vintage to the RAF Historic Aircraft Flight. The number of flyable Spitfires had grown and there were certainly more Spitfires flying at the end of the filming than there were at the beginning.

The Battle of Britain was released in 1969, and it represented a milestone in the Spitfire narrative. It came nearly thirty years after the battle it depicted, and at a time when the RAF was changing and shrinking: Fighter Command had disappeared in 1968, at the height of Britain's withdrawal from the Empire. Unlike *The Longest Day* seven years earlier, *The Battle of Britain* was released into what was very much a post-war climate. The post-war generation had grown up without the experience of battles of national survival, and no longer served *en masse* in the armed forces following the end of National Service. It was an anti-war decade, in which attitudes were shaped by the threat of nuclear war over Cuba, the quagmire of Vietnam, civil

CROWD PULLER: a famous Spitfire Mk IX takes a bow in front of the grandstand at Goodwood before a flying display. Delivered to the RAF in 1943, it served with the Netherlands air force, including on counter-insurgency operations in Indonesia, and with the Belgian air force before returning to take part in *The Battle of Britain*. It was owned and flown by Ray Hannah, former leader of the Red Arrows and founder of the Old Flying Machine Company, who also took part in *Piece of Cake*, *Empire of the Sun*, *Memphis Belle*, *Saving Private Ryan* and *Tomorrow Never Dies*; he died in 2005.

rights, marijuana and the Prague Spring. While the 1950s had been a high tide of success for war films, that tide had ebbed, to be replaced in the cinemas of the 1960s by James Bond, the Beatles and even Thomas More (*A Man for All Seasons*). The newsreels disappeared too, as people turned to television. By the time of the first moon landing in 1969 — not to mention the inauguration of Concorde, the Jumbo Jet, and the Harrier 'Jump Jet' — television was firmly established in British homes.

At this time, the Spitfire might have faded gracefully into the history of the Second World War. That it did not was in part due to its continued presence in the air, but also thanks to its enduring presence, and that of the Battle of Britain, in the popular imagination. If the 1960s were about anything at all, they were about the end of deference and the beginning of a new British popular culture based on merit and on talent. Celebrity status was no longer accorded to distant icons simply on the basis of visibility:

in this new, interactive society, admiration was more often bestowed on those people, and things, with which the public felt personally involved. In this climate, the Spitfire, having been a formidable weapon and a symbol of military prowess during the war, adjusted to peace by turning to the other side of its character and personality — which had been there from the beginning, but which had lain dormant while the more serious business of war was dealt with: its talent as a crowd-pleaser.

As a performer, the Spitfire was a star that could hold a crowd's attention by making people feel part of the performance: spellbound and involved at the same time. For the wartime generation, many of whom already had some kind of connection to the Spitfire, having built them, serviced them, armed them, repaired them and flown them, it had never been remote, never aloof. It had worked hard and given all that it could during the war, and more. And for the post-war generations, it was elegant, authentic, entertaining and media-friendly.

In the 1970s and 1980s, the Spitfire made a transition from the exclusivity and secrecy of war to the inclusivity required by the growing power and pervasiveness of the mass media. It was a transition that drew in a very British kind of interest, from technicians, historians, writers and just plain enthusiasts as well as from the rich men and women who wanted to keep Spitfires airworthy for the sheer thrill and enjoyment of flying them. Small groups and networks of people formed, not unlike those who had gathered around R. J. Mitchell during the Schneider Cup period and at the conception and birth of the Spitfire in the mid-1930s.

Meanwhile, the flow of books continued. One such was *Fighter* by Len Deighton, which was published in 1977 with a foreword by A.J.P. Taylor. Deighton was a man of the 1960s — he had written spy thrillers, such as *The Ipcress File*, cookbooks, and the screenplay for *Oh What a Lovely War* before turning his hand to this latest book. What he produced was an analytical history, shorn of personal heroics, concentrating instead on technology; it pointed up the huge discrepancies

between the RAF's claims during the Battle of Britain and the reality. But despite its dispassionate style, it could only endorse the general view of the Spitfire's qualities: 'The Spitfire had proved itself an excellent all-round weapon, with faults but no inherent weaknesses.'

At the same time, books about the experiences of wartime fighter pilots continued to stir the public imagination, and many of them had the Spitfire woven into their story. *Sky Tiger, The Story of Sailor Malan* was one, written by Norman Franks in 1980. There was also a second book on Douglas Bader, *Flying Colours, The Epic Story of Douglas Bader*, by Laddie Lucas, published in 1981 — the same year that Group Captain W.G.G. Duncan Smith brought out his *Spitfire into Battle*. On top of the biographical accounts, books purely about the Spitfire began to emerge almost as a sub-genre: in 1975, the RAF Museum had published the *Manual of the Spitfire Mk V* in facsimile, aimed very clearly at the enthusiast market; in 1982, Alfred Price wrote *The Spitfire Story*, a book about the development of the aircraft. Price went on to write around twenty-five books about the Spitfire, including *Spitfire Mk V Aces* and *Spitfire: A Complete Fighting History*, reversing the trend by focusing the stories of the pilots' exploits through the aircraft. Jeffrey Quill wrote the Foreword to *The Spitfire Story*, and the following year, in 1983, Quill also committed to

ORIGINAL MODEL: the first Airfix kit, released in 1952, was of Sir Francis Drake's *Golden Hind*, but at 6/- it was deemed too expensive. The following year, a 1:24 scale model of the Mk I Spitfire was an instant success at 2/-. The first airfix models came in a plastic bag — the box (*right*) wasn't introduced until the 1970s.

SUPERMARINE SPITFIRE Mk I

280 PIECE OF CAKE (*previous pages*): five Spitfires fly in loose formation during the filming of ITV's 1988 television drama. The iconic beauty of the Spitfire has always attracted film-makers, but in this case there was controversy over the historical accuracy of the series.

LONDON TRIBUTE: a replica Spitfire was displayed in Trafalgar Square in March 2008 (*right*) as part of the campaign to have a statue of Air Vice-Marshal Sir Keith Park erected there to mark his contribution to the defence of the capital.

paper his own account of the Spitfire during the war: *Spitfire, A Test Pilot's Story*.

With four years to go until the fortieth anniversary of the Spitfire's first flight, in March 1984, The Spitfire Society was formed by a former Spitfire pilot, Group Captain David Green. Its aim was to link people throughout the world whose lives had in some way been involved with or touched by the Spitfire. The Society, which published a regular magazine dedicated to the aircraft — called, inevitably, *Spitfire* — quickly evolved into a clearing house for aviation enthusiasts of many different kinds who wished to research, study and assess the educational and historical value of the information relating to the Spitfire, its design, development and operations.

Where the feature film and the newsreel had left off, television had taken over as a medium, and the stories of the Second World War

continued to exert a powerful hold on audiences. In 1973, a major television series, *The World At War*, looked at the whole war in twenty-six parts. It was a resounding success, both with critics and with audiences. There was no programme on the Battle of Britain, but it featured in Episode 4, 'Alone'. The intimacy of television brought the human experience of war into the nation's sitting rooms, and the Spitfire featured extensively in documentary series such as the BBC's *Reaching For the Skies*, screened in 1988, both through archive film intercut with specially shot sequences with flyable Spitfires and interviews with veterans, a technique that was both historical and modern.

The individual experience of the air war was also featured in television drama. The author Derek Robinson, who had served his National Service in the RAF at a time when Spitfires were still flying, wrote *Piece of Cake*, published in 1983, which follows a fictional fighter squadron from service in France before the Dunkirk evacuation to the height of the Battle of Britain. Based on the growing factual knowledge about the RAF in 1940, the mistakes, the muddles and the dysfunctional relationships within its ranks, it challenged many of the heroic perceptions of the Battle of Britain. Although his previous novel, *Goshawk Squadron*, had been shortlisted for the Booker

Downed all over Kent, just like the Luftwaffe.

www.shepherdneame.co.uk

The BOTTLE of BRITAIN

SPITFIRE COMMERCIAL: an advertisement for Spitfire Ale, whose advertising campaign is based on creating light-hearted associations with the historical role played by the Spitfire in the nation's defence.

Prize in 1971, *Piece of Cake* did not do particularly well as a book. However, it was just the kind of story that could work for television, and was commissioned at the comparatively high cost of around £5m for six one-hour episodes.

The television producers of *Piece of Cake* had one of the same problems that the film producers had faced with *The Battle of Britain* — a lack of the right kind of aircraft. Only Hurricanes had been stationed in France, not Spitfires, but, while there were plenty of flyable Spitfires in 1988, and enough Bf 109s, many of them having been restored to flying condition for *The Battle of Britain* in 1968, Hurricanes were in very short supply. The Battle of Britain Memorial Flight, as it was known by the mid 1980s, had two airworthy Hurricanes, but the producers did not have the support of the RAF, and turned to private owners — who could only supply Spitfires. For a production based on a novel that had set out specifically to give an accurate portrayal of the reality of 1939 and 1940, it was a mistake. By using Spitfires, the series started out on the wrong historical foot — and stirred up old arguments over whether Spitfires should have been sent to France.

The flying sequences were superbly shot, making the best use of the skills and enthusiasm of the pilots, who after all were being paid to do what they loved doing, flying their Spitfires in mock combat. But in spite of that *A Piece of Cake*, while it was not a flop, fell below expectations.

The audiences gradually declined and though it still attracted high viewing figures for the final episode, it really only succeeded in stirring up a hornet's nest among the surviving RAF pilots. It challenged the historical record and the mythology of a heroic episode in British history, and in doing so it challenged the memories of many of those who had been involved — who were of course unimpressed by the argument that it was, after all, good television.

Three years after *A Piece of Cake* was broadcast, in 1991, ITV produced a second drama set among the Few of 1940: *A Perfect Hero*, also based on a novel from the early 1980s. It reverted to the more conventional historical view, with Nigel Havers playing a flawed hero who gets badly burned in his Spitfire, with strong echoes of Richard Hillary and *The Last Enemy*, and was a success for ITV. A decade later, two foreign producers made films that dealt with the American and Czech participation in the Battle of Britain: *Pearl Harbour* and *Dark Blue*, both of which also used restored Spitfires for filming.

There is no doubt that without the film industry there would be fewer Spitfires flying today. As the cycles of anniversaries come and go, there seem to be more Spitfires flying and more media available through which their sheer presence can be seen and appreciated. Just as the Spitfire has graced newspapers, magazines, newsreels, films and television over the years,

Loving restoration: sixty years after being delivered to the Royal Navy, Seafire SX336 flew for the first time in decades on 3 May 2006. It had been restored following its recovery from a scrap yard in 1973, but had not flown in the intervening thirty-three years.

it has also adapted its star qualities to the new media age. Type 'Spitfire' into Google and you get tens of millions of responses, directing you to everything from the detail of drawings, test pilots' reports, fighter pilots' logbooks, combat reports, countless photographs, paintings, clubs, societies and online modelling clubs. The Spitfire could have been made for the age of the internet: individuals find and chat to each other online, join clubs, swap stories, view outtakes from *The Battle of Britain*, and get involved in countless other activities based around their shared love of the Spitfire. Its place in British culture is reinforced daily through dialogue between the small and large communities that have developed around particular aspects of the Spitfire story.

For the 60th anniversary of the Battle of Britain in 2000, many past and existing books on or of the Spitfire were re-published. Many of them were the personal stories of pilots who flew these aircraft in combat: *Fighter Pilot's Summer*, by Paul Richie with Norman Franks, published in 1993, followed on from his classic *Fighter Pilot*, written during the war; *Spitfire Offensive*, by Wing Commander R.W.F. Sampson, also with Norman Franks in 1994; *True Stories of the Battle of Britain, as told by the People who were there* in 2000 and two new books, *First Light*, by Geoffrey Wellum in 2002 and *Fighter Boys, Saving Britain 1940*, by Patrick Bishop in 2003 — national bestsellers that regularly featured in the book charts. *Spitfire Pilot*,

first published in 1942, was re-published after sixty-four years and in 2006 *Spitfire, The Biography* by Jonathan Glancey also appeared.

The Spitfire's seventieth birthday party was held in July 2006 at Duxford, where it had entered RAF service in 1938. Now home to the Imperial War Museum, and full of vintage machines, both airworthy and static, Duxford is the closest the Spitfire has to an ancestral home. The guest list was a long one, though some did not make it because of bad weather: heavy rain and strong winds. The modern jet trainers, operational fighters and bombers turned out in strength, including the RAF's Shorts Tocano and Hawk training aircraft, the USAF's F-15E Strike Eagle and the RAF's Tornado GR4 bomber. But the comparative youngsters were greatly outnumbered by aircraft of the Second World War generation, including one of the few airworthy DC-3s, whose first flight was before that of the Spitfire; two Hurricanes; a Harvard, on which many wartime Spitfire pilots had been trained; a P-51D Mustang; an F-86A; and the RAF's last Canberra, an aircraft that had enjoyed an even longer operational career than the Spitfire.

Above all, it was the Spitfire's day. The Battle of Britain Memorial Flight was unable to attend because of the weather, and not all the flyable Spitfires were there because many had been committed to other air shows. But the weather cleared on the Sunday afternoon just enough to

FULL CIRCLE: members of the RAF Living History Group walk along a line of Spitfires at Duxford (*below*) on 16 Oct 2005 to add a period feel to the idea of the air display. Enthusiasm for the Spitfire and its achievements continues sixty-seven years after the first Spitfires arrived at Duxford in late 1938.

allow a display, and as soon as that was forecast the crowds turned out, blocking the approach roads to Duxford. There were some fifteen Spitfires, including four two-seaters and a Seafire, all in peak condition. Their pilots flew formations of five and seven aircraft at a time before breaking up into individual displays of aerobatics. Despite the weather, it was a great day.

The air show remains the best way to see and to appreciate the Spitfire. For all the films, videos, books and television programmes, there is nothing to compare with the sight and sound of a Spitfire flying overhead, where its star qualities are at their most tangible. After aerial combat, the Spitfire's natural home is the air show, the spectacle that is nearly as old as aviation itself, for that is where people come face-to-face with the icon, feeling its presence and its impact on them and on others. Since 1945, no victory flypast has been complete without a Spitfire to lead it; today, no air show is over until the Merlin engine has

sung its final song. In seventy years, Spitfires have given tens of thousands of flying displays, and thrilled millions of people. The Battle of Britain Memorial Flight alone attends some 700 air shows and other events every year.

283

Spitfires don't just belong to the big summer air shows: in September 2007, at the 56th Alfrick and Lulsley Show in Worcestershire, the fine weather drew 3,000 people to the cake stalls, the tug o' war, and the 'dog that looks most like its owner' competition, all to raise money for local charities. The highlight, though, was a Spitfire which arrived overhead and tumbled through a spectacular routine of aerobatics reminiscent of the idyllic film footage shot during the war. As it left for another appointment, the show's chairman, Bridget Lewis, could have been speaking for the whole country when she told the Worcester News: 'The Spitfire was absolutely spectacular— everyone stopped dead when it arrived and started clapping and cheering.'

BIBLIOGRAPHY

284

A Fighter Pilot; *Tattered Battlements, A Malta Diary*; Peter Davis 1943.

Aeronautical Chamber of Commerce of America; *The Aircraft Yearbook for 1935*; ACCA, 1935.

Babington Smith, Constance; *Evidence in Camera, The Story of Photographic Intelligence in World War II*; Chatto & Windus, 1958.

Beckles, Gordon; *Birth of a Spitfire*; Collins, 1941.

Benton, Charlotte, Benton, Tim, and Wood, Ghislane; *Art Deco 1910-1939*; V&A Publications, 2003.

Bingham, Victor; *Merlin Power*; Airlife 1998.

Bishop, Patrick; *Fighter Boys, Saving Britain 1940*; Harper Collins 2003.

Boot, Henry and Sturtivant, Ray; *Gifts of War, Spitfires and other Presentation Aircraft in Two World Wars*; Air-Britain, 2005.

Bowyer, Chaz; *1936-68 Fighter Command, The Story of Britain's Crack Fighter Squadrons*; Sphere Books, 1981.

Brickhill, Paul; *Reach for the Sky, Douglas Bader, His Life Story*; Collins 1954.

Bungay, Stephen; *The Most Dangerous Enemy, A History of the Battle of Britain*; Aurum Press, 2000.

Capra, Frank; *Why We Fight, Episode 4, The Battle of Britain*; War Activities Committee of the Motion Picture Industry, 1943.

Clostermann, Pierre, DFC; *Flames in the Sky*; Penguin, 1957.

Clostermann, Pierre, DFC; *The Big Show*; Chatto & Windus, 1972.

Collier, Basil; *The Leader of the Few, The Dowding Story*; Jarolds Publishers (London), 1957.

Crook, David, Flight Lieutenant, DFC; *Spitfire pilot, A Personal Account of the Battle of Britain*; Greenhill Books, 2006.

Deere, Air Commodore Alan, DSO, OBE, DFC and Bar; *Nine Lives*; Crecy Publishing, 2005.

Deighton, Len; *Fighter, The True Story of the Battle of Britain*; Pimlico, 1977.

Duncan Smith, Group Captain W.G.G., DSO, DFC; *Spitfire Into Battle*; John Murray, 2002.

Fielder, Arkady; *Squadron 303*; Peter Davies, 1942.

Flying Officer X; *How Sleep the Brave*; Jonathan Cape, 1943.

Forbes, Athol, Wing Commander, DFC and Allen, Hubert, Squadron Leader, DFC; *Ten Fighter Boys*; Collins, 1942.

Forrester, Larry; *Fly For Your Life, The Story of R.R. Stanford Tuck, DSO, DFC and Two Bars*; Granada, 1979.

Franks, Norman; *Sky Tiger, The Story of Sailor Malan*; Crecy Books, 1994.

Galland, Adolf; *The First and the Last*; Methuen, 1955.

Glancey, Jonathan; *Spitfire, The Biography*; Atlantic Books, 2007.

Gleed, Wing Commander Ian, DFC; *Arise to Conquer*; Victor Gollancz, 1942.

Graves, Charles; The Thin Blue Line; Hutchinson, undated.

Griffiths, Harry; *Testing Times, Memoirs of a Spitfire Boffin*; United Writers, Cornwall, 1992.

Hamilton, Nicola, Ed; *From Spitfire to Microchip*; The Design Council, 1985.

Hillary, Richard; *The Last Enemy*; MacMillan, 1943.

Holmes, Richard Ed; *Oxford Companion to Military History*; OUP, 2001.

Holthusen, Peter J.R.; *The Land Speed Record*; Foulis/ Haynes Publishing Group, 1986.

James, Derek N.; *Schneider Trophy Aircraft 1913-1931*; Putnam, London, 1981.

James, Henry C. and Strueby, Kay; *The First of the Few*; British Aviation Pictures, 1942/ Slam Dunk Media.

Jennings, Humphrey; *Listen to Britain*; 1942.

Johnson, 'Johnnie'; *Wing Leader*; The Reprint Society, 1946.

Liddell Hart, B.H.; *The Tanks, Vols I & II*; Cassell, 1959.

Lloyd, Sir Ian & Pugh, Peter; *Hives & The Merlin*; Icon Books, 2004.

Loftin, Laurence K. Jnr.; *The Quest for Performance*; National Aeronautics and Space Administration, 1985.

Lucas, Laddie; *Flying Colours, The Epic Story of Douglas Bader*; Hutchinson, 1981.

Mackenzie, S.P.; *The Battle of Britain on Screen, 'The Few' in British Film and Television Drama*; Edinburgh University Press, 2007.

March, Peter R.; *The Spitfire Story*; Sutton Publishing, 2006.

Ministry of Information, issued by, 1945; *What Britain Has Done 1939 – 1945*; Atlantic Books, 2007.

Ministry of Information, issued by; *The Battle of Britain, August – October 1940*; HMSO, 1941.

Ministry of Information; *What Britain Has Done 1939-1945*; MoI, 1945, re-published Atlantic Books, 2007.

Mitchell, Gordon; *Schooldays to Spitfire*; Tempus, 2006.

Mosely, Leonard; *Battle of Britain*; George Weidenfeld and Nicolson, 1969.

Nayler, J.L. / Ower, E.; *Aviation: its technical development*; Peter Owen and Vision Press, 1965.

Pindar, Ian, Editor; *The Folio Book of Historic Speeches*; The Folio Society, 2007.

Price, Alfred; *The Spitfire Story*; Silverdale Books, 2002.

Price, Dr Alfred and Blackah, Paul; *Supermarine Spitfire, Owners Workshop Manual*; Haynes, 2007.

Price, Dr Alfred; *Spitfire Mark I/II Aces 1939-41*; Osprey, 1996.

Quill, Jeffrey; *Spitfire, A Test Pilot's Story*; Crecy Publishing, 1996.

Richards, Denis and Saunders, Hilary St. G.; *Royal Air Force 1939-1945 Volume II The Fight Avails*; HMSO 1954.

Richey, Paul, Wg Cmr, with Norman Franks; *Fighter Pilot's Summer*; Grub Street, 2004.

Richey, Paul; *Fighter Pilot*; Cassell, 2001.

Rouse, Wally; *'Born Again' Spitfire PS915*; Midland Counties Publications (Aerophile), 1989.

Sampson, Wing Commander RWF, OBE, DFC & Bar, with Norman Franks; *Spitfire Offensive*; Grub Street, 2002.

Smith, J.R. & Kay, Anthony; *German Aircraft of the Second World War*; Putnam, 1972.

Steinhilper, Ulrich & Osborne, Peter; *Spitfire on My Tail, A View from the Other Side*; Independent Books, 2006.

Tanner, John, Ed.; *The Spitfire Manual*; Arms and Armour Press, Crown Copyright, 1976.

Townsend, Peter; *Duel of Eagles*; Weidenfeld and Nicolson, 1970.

Wellum, Geoffrey; *First Light*; Penguin, 2003.

Whittell, Giles; *Spitfire Women of World War II*; Harper Press, 2007.

Wing, Sandra Koa; *Mass Observation, Britain in the Second World War*; The Folio Society, 2007.

Winterbotham, F.W.; *The Nazi Connection, The personal story of a top-level British agent in pre-war Germany*; Weidenfeld & Nicolson, 1978.

Wood, Derek, with Dempster, Derek; *The Narrow Margin, The Definitive Story of the Battle of Britain*; Arrow Books, 1969.

NEWSPAPERS, PERIODICALS, NEWSREELS & WEBSITES:

Cambridge Daily News; Movietone News; Pathe News; Southampton Evening Echo; Variety; Worcester Evening News; www.battleofbritain.net/bobhsoc/ ; www.raf.mod.uk/bobhome.html ; http://museum.woolworths.co.uk

INDEX

ACKNOWLEDGEMENTS

288   Weidenfeld & Nicolson would like to thank all copyright holders who have kindly supplied photographs or quotations for use in this book. We have made every effort to acknowledge the correct copyright holder but will, if notified, correct any errors or omissions in future editions.

Advertising Archives: 281; Aeroplane Magazine/www.aeroplanemonthly.com 34b; AKG Images: 108, 226r; Andrew Linscott / Alamy: 247; Anthony Gross CBE RA, Imperial War Museum: 209; AP/AP/PA Photos: 222; Arno Burgi/DPA/PA Photos: 75bc; Arthur Gibson: 11, 219; Aviation Pictures: 31, 36l, 39, 73, 75bl, 75br, 82, 107tr; Aviation Pictures/Austin J. Brown LBIPP: 115, 245; /Boulton Paul Aircraft Limited: 125b; /Crown Copyright: 35; /Hawker Aircraft Limited: 57, 76; /Imperial Airways: 107cr, 85; /Morane Saulnier: 75tl; /Rinaldo Piaggio SPA: 43tr; /Savoia-Marchetti SPA: 43l; /Science Museum: 48; /Vickers Ltd: 37; /Vickers-Armstrong Limited: 68, 69t, 69b; /Vickers-Supermarine Limited: 33, 78b, 83; Bettmann/Corbis: 17tl, 75cr, 92, 107tl; Reproduced with the permission of Birmingham Libraries and Archives: 195; Bob Thomas/Popperfoto/Getty Images: 72, 98; Bridgeman Art Library: 56r, 62; Central Press/Getty: 27; Charles Brown/RAF Museum: 86-87, 200-201; Charles Cundall RA/Imperial War Museum: 130b; Courtesy Gordon Mitchell and Solent Sky Museum: 30, 34, 45br, 78t; Courtesy Hornby Hobbies Ltd: 277; Cuthbert Orde/Imperial War Museum: 129l; David Savill/Topical Press Agency/Getty Images: 187; Denis A. Barnham/Imperial War Museum: 207t; Eddie Worth/AP/PA Photos: 130t; Eric Dumigan: 153; Eric Long / National Air and Space Museum, Smithsonian Institution: 91; Eric Ravilious, Imperial War Museum: 167; Everett Collection/Rex Features: 8; Fox Photos/Getty Images: 44, 113, 145; Frances Macdonald/Imperial War Museum: 168; George Konig/Keystone Features/Getty Images: 266; George Rodger/Magnum Photos: 137t, 146; Gloster Aircraft Co./Aviation Pictures: 36r; Herbie Knott/Rex Features: 262, 278-279; Hipix/Alamy: 268t; Hugh W. Cowin/Rex Features: 3 & 15, 138-139, 218, 230-231, 250-251; Hulton Archive/Getty Images: 24, 117, 121b; Illustrated London News: 99; Used with the Permission of The Trustees of the Imperial War Museum, London: 56l, 58, 88, 100, 100b, 101, 102, 120, 121t, 122, 123, 124, 125t, 126t, 126b, 133, 136t, 136b, 141l, 141r, 142, 143, 147t, 157, 158, 169l, 169r, 170t, 170b, 171, 173, 174, 175, 176, 178tl, 179l, 179r, 180, 180-181, 183, 184, 189, 191, 193, 194t, 198, 198b, 199l, 199r, 204, 205t, 205b, 207b, 208, 211-212, 217, 221, 224t, 224b, 225, 228l, 228r, 233, 234, 235, 236, 237, 240, 241, 242t, 242b, 243, 254, 258b; /The Art Archive: 63, 178tr; J Dibbs/Aviation Images: 154, 156, 159-160, 210, 214, 215, 229; J. A. Hampton/Topical Press Agency/Getty Images: 71, 89, 111; J. Dibbs/Aviation Images: 13; John Mansbridge/Imperial War Museum: 129r; John Stroud Collection/Aviation Pictures: 220; Jonathan Hordle/Rex Features: 55; Keystone/Getty Images: 93, 139, 163, 178b, 246; Kobal Archive: 273; Lordprice Collection / Alamy: 94; Loretta Askill/Alamy: 276; Martin Stott: 4-5, 7, 282; Mary Evans Picture Library: 19tr, 59; Max Schirner/Topical Press Agency/Getty Images: 96; MEIR AZULAI/AFP/Getty Images: 255; Kind permission of Dr Gordon Mitchell: 6; Kind Permission of Jim Mitchell/Solent Sky Museum: 79; Moviestore Collection: 226l; Musee De L'Air et de L'espace: 23; museum.woolworths.co.uk: 162; National Air and Space Museum, Smithsonian Institution: 19br, 20; National Motor Museum/Heritage Image Partnership: 95t, 95b; National Railway Museum/Science Museum: 107b; Norman Wilkinson CBE/Imperial War Museum: 194; Used with the kind permission of Old Forge Publishing: 105; P Jarrett/Aviation Images: 165; P Wallick/Aviation Images: 256-257; PA Photos: 50-51; Paul Nash/Imperial War Museum: 147b; Peter Harholdt/Corbis: 107tc; Picture Post/Hulton Archive/Getty Images: 197; Popperfoto/Getty Images: 17tr, 17br, 74, 127, 137b, 182, 182b, 253, 260; RAF Museum: 40-41, 47, 65t, 118-119, 203, 261; Reproduced with the permission of Royal Mail: 268c, 268b; Rex Features: 1, 196, 283; Richard Eurich RA/Imperial War Museum: 150, 166; Richard Paver Photography: 103-104, 134, 148-149; Richard Winslade/Aviation Images: 155, 177, 238-239, 248, 259; ROLAND MAGUNIA/AFP/Getty Images: 10; Rolls-Royce Heritage Trust: 43br; Ronald Grant Archive: 265, 267, 271; Royal Aeronautical Society/Aviation Images: 157b; Science Museum: 19l, 21l, 21r, 22, 26, 42l, 42r, 45, 46, 52; Sid Bradd Collection: 105b; Solent Sky Museum: 53, 64, 67; Stefan Rousseau/PA Wire/PA Photos: 280; Stephane Beilliard/AirTeamImages: 75tr; The Art Archive/Alfredo Dagli Orti: 109; The Art Archive/RAF Museum Hendon/Eileen Tweedy: 57b; The Flight Collection: 80-81; Topham Picturepoint/PA Photos: 61; Topical Press Agency/Getty Images: 18, 25, 28, 29, 49; U.S. National Archives: 32; Ulrich Grueschow, MilitaryAircraft.de: 72t; Underwood & Underwood/Corbis: 16; United Artists/Kobal Collection: 275; William A. Atkins/Getty: 38; WRVS: 135; www.biggles.com: 269.

First published in Great Britain in 2008
by Weidenfeld & Nicolson
10 9 8 7 6 5 4 3 2 1

Text © Ivan Rendall 2008
Design and layout © Weidenfeld
& Nicolson 2008

A CIP catalogue record for this book is available from the British Library.

ISBN: 978 0 297 85511 8

Design by Ken Wilson
Editorial by Debbie Woska
Picture research by Heather Vickers

Colour reproduction by DL Interactive UK
Printed and bound in Italy

Weidenfeld & Nicolson
The Orion Publishing Group Ltd
Orion House
5 Upper St Martin's Lane
London WC2H 9EA

An Hachette Livre UK Company

The Orion Publishing Group's policy is to use papers that are natural, renewable and recyclable products and made from wood grown in sustainable forests. The logging and manufacturing processes are expected to conform to the environmental regulations of the country of origin.

SCALE IN FEET

DETAIL ONLY SHOWN WHERE DIFFERENT FROM F.XIX

F.XII

ICE GUARD SOMETIMES FITTED

NON RETRACTING TAILWHEEL EARLY AIRCRAFT ONLY

I.F.F. AERIAL

UNDERSIDE OF PORT WING AND TAILPLANE

EARLY TYPE UNDERCARRIAGE FAIRING

UPPER WING BULGE

OIL COOLER

WHEEL WELL INTERIOR

THIS SIDE OF £ SHOWS F.XIVc

INTERCOOLER RADIATOR IN FRONT COOLANT RADIATOR BEHIND

UPLOCK LUG

UNDERCARRIAGE RETRACTION MECHANISM EARLY LEG SHOWN

TWO PANELS STARBOARD ONLY

HINGE

I.F.F. AERIAL

HINGE

DROP TANK HOOK BOTH SIDES

30 GALLON DROP TANK

HOOK TO SWING TANK CLEAR ON RELEASE